Cultural Diversity and Global Media

Cultural Diversity and Global Media

The Mediation of Difference

Eugenia Siapera

✸WILEY-BLACKWELL

A John Wiley & Sons, Ltd., Publication

Library of Congress Cataloging-in-Publication Data

Siapera, Eugenia.
    Cultural diversity and global media : the mediation of difference / Eugenia Siapera.
        p.   cm.
    Includes bibliographical references and index.
    ISBN 978-1-4051-8047-4 (alk. paper)–ISBN 978-1-4051-8046-7 (pbk. : alk. paper)   1. Mass media and minorities.   2. Mass media and globalization.   3. Mass media and culture.   4. Mass media and ethnic relations.   5. Mass media–Social aspects.   6. Transnationalism.   I. Title.
    P94.5.M55S53 2010
    302.23089–dc22

                                                        2009045862

A catalogue record for this book is available from the British Library.

Set in 10/12.5 pt Galliard by SPi Publisher Services, Pondicherry, India
Printed and bound in Malaysia by Vivar Printing Sdn Bhd

1   2010

Contents

1

(Re)thinking Cultural Diversity and the Media

1.1 The Crises of Multiculturalism

When, in January 2009, Barack Obama was inaugurated as the forty-fourth President of the United States, the first mixed-race person to hold such a post, an infectious jubilation spread across the world. Surely now, people thought, everything is possible. If in the USA, where slavery and discrimination are still part of living memory, a non-white man can be elected president, then justice and equality for all is within our grasp. Others still might raise a question: surely now, they might say, what is the point of any talk of discrimination and racism? The very election of an African-American president shows that racism and discrimination, if they even exist, play only a small part in the success of an individual. Surely now, some people might argue, the case is won: all ethno-cultural groups are equal, and success or failure is a matter of individual ability. Whatever the wider significance of this historic victory, the vocal comments on Barack Obama's ethnic background are a testament to the continued importance and special status of ethno-cultural diversity.

While Obama's electoral victory represents for some a significant victory for cultural diversity, other recent events have triggered a more polarized and spiteful reaction. Specifically, the post-9/11 world saw attacks on multiculturalism unprecedented both in numbers and ferocity, with the world's media providing social analysis and comment, a platform for politicians attacks, as well as behaving as political actors in their own right. "The veil of multiculturalism has been lifted, revealing parallel societies where the law of the state does not apply," argued the German magazine *Der Spiegel* following the Madrid 2004 bombings. "Adopt our Values or Stay Away, says Blair," read a *Daily Telegraph* headline at the end of 2006. In 2005, the decision of the Danish newspaper *Jyllands-Posten* to publish cartoons depicting the Prophet Mohammed provoked a major crisis with wide ramifications, including the loss of life. In March 2008, the BBC's "White Season" promised to look into the ways in which immigration is marginalizing the British white working class; although more nuanced than it sounds, "White Season" ended up framing immigration as responsible for the increasing marginalization of whites. A documentary called *The Poles Are Coming* (BBC, 2008) succeeded in "racializing" Polish workers, presenting Eastern European immigration in terms of an invasion. In the meantime, heated debates, civil and uncivil exchanges, and occasionally even ferocious attacks are encountered in various online environments, including discussion fora, listservs and blogs.

Only a few years ago, at the peak of identity politics in the 1980s and 1990s, difference was celebrated, with people claiming special status as members of distinct cultural groups, with states drafting policy that protected diversity, respected cultural difference, and created a space in which minority cultural and religious practices could be practiced alongside the dominant ones. So what happened? How did these celebrations of diversity turn sour? Georgiou and Siapera (2006) attributed this backlash against multiculturalism to three sets of reasons: firstly, to the failures of existing policies to deliver equality and justice for all social groups; secondly, to the pressures of neoliberal globalization, which push nations to an ever-increasing competition with other nations for scant resources and vanishing wealth; thirdly, to the post-9/11 geopolitical situation, which prioritized questions of security over all other issues, including those of equality and justice. Whatever the root causes of the backlash against multiculturalism, one thing is certain: that diversity and difference are once more becoming signifiers of problems, tensions, conflict, and friction.

In a surprising, and worrying, agreement across the political spectrum, both conservative and liberal/left-wing commentators have attacked multiculturalism, effectively blaming cultural diversity for current social ills. Segregation, inter-community violence, alienation, as well as high unemployment, strain on welfare services, and insecurity have all been blamed on cultural diversity, and on the increasing flows of immigration. The left critique of multiculturalism accuses it of focusing on cultural difference at the expense of continued material inequality that corresponds to class rather than cultural divisions (Malik, 2005; see Siapera, 2006b). This has the effect of eroding the basis for social solidarity and leading to (ethnic) group enclaves, which are segregated from the rest of society, and which, furthermore, are undemocratically ruled by unelected community leaders (Alibhai-Brown, 2000; Malik, 2005). In these terms, multiculturalism is problematic, according to its left critics, because it shifts the focus from demands for equality for all and places it on particularistic demands for special treatment. Moreover, in its politically correct extreme, multiculturalism is responsible for censorship and the destruction of free speech. In the end, these particularistic demands, if met, destroy democracy as we know it, since democracy can no longer be about equality before the law, free speech, state neutrality, and so on. Rather, multicultural democracy appears a contradiction in terms, since it is premised on the creation of separate rules for separate groups that ultimately create inequality and oppose the rule of the many.

The left-wing theorist Slavoj Žižek (1997a) argues that multiculturalism must be seen as the "cultural logic" of multinational capitalism. This is because multinational capitalism relies on a superficial acceptance of difference in order to be able to expand across the world. But for Žižek, multiculturalism is a kind of racism, because it is premised on a distant respect for other cultures, understood as enclosed, "authentic" communities, thereby rejecting all those who question and criticize other cultures as intolerant, creating thus a vantage point from which to claim superiority. It is, in other words, a privileged and patronizing position that on the one hand empties cultures of all their contents and on the other barely disguises its support for globalized capitalism. For Žižek (1997a: 45), the problem is that multiculturalism does the ultimate service for capitalism by rendering invisible and normal the economic backdrop against which all struggles take place, globalized capitalism:

> [t]he problematic of multiculturalism – the hybrid coexistence of diverse cultural life-worlds – which imposes itself today is the form of appearance of its opposite, of the massive presence of capitalism as universal world system: it bears witness to the unprecedented homogenization of the contemporary world.

In these terms, Žižek's point is that multiculturalism, and its intellectual supporters, hide the true nature of globalized capitalism and deflect any struggles against it. The proper left response, therefore, is to move away from a celebratory acceptance of all cultures and to take sides against capitalism and its homogenizing forces. This ultimately involves a rejection or perhaps more accurately a politicization of difference. This means that difference is not to be neutralized through a superficial acceptance, but it must fight against all those who seek to control and subjugate it, as well to detract from the goal of "universal emancipation," which involves actual resistance both against global capitalism and fundamentalisms of all sorts.

"When I hear the word 'culture' I reach for my gun" is an infamous statement by Josef Goebbels, the Nazi Minister for Propaganda. Indeed, this statement, also quoted by Žižek in the above article, is an eloquent summary of the right-wing critique of multiculturalism. Conservative critics of multiculturalism find in it the basis for discrimination against "whites" or the majority culture, which leads some to assume a defensive ethnocentric position, fighting against all other identities. Shohat and Stam (2007: 124) summarize the right-wing critique in seven points: (1) multiculturalism is seen as benefiting minorities against the general interest; (2) multiculturalism is a recent phenomenon; (3) multiculturalism is anti-Western; (4) multiculturalism is a separatist movement; (5) multiculturalism is "therapy for minorities" or "underdog history," therefore not relevant for all society; (6) multiculturalism anachronistically imposes politically correct ideas and concepts on educational curricula; (7) multiculturalists are either puritanical "party poopers," who seek to impose a politically correct version of events on everybody, or irresponsible hedonists, ready to accept and try everything. From a conservative perspective, therefore, multiculturalism ends up victimizing the silent majority, the "white man," who becomes marginalized and whose needs are considered no longer relevant. Indeed, to some extent the BBC "White Season" repeats this notion of disregard of the needs of the white majorities.

Right-wing politicians and commentators repeat and amplify these points. Some see in multiculturalism the seeds of the destruction of society, continued violence, and loss of unity. The British Conservative politician Enoch Powell delivered his infamous "Rivers of Blood" speech in 1968, in which he claimed, quoting one of his constituents, that "in fifteen to twenty years the black man will have the whip hand over the white man." And in the best-known passage, he argued that the Race Relations Bill passed at the time meant that "immigrant communities can organize to consolidate their members, to agitate and campaign against their fellow citizens, and to overawe and dominate the rest with the legal weapons which the ignorant and the ill-informed have provided. As I look ahead, I am filled with foreboding; like the Roman, I seem to see 'the River Tiber foaming with much blood.'" More recently a number of right-wing parties have arisen on a xenophobic platform in several countries, such as Jean-Marie Le Pen's Front National in France, Jorg Haider's Austrian Freedom Party, the Vlaams Blok/Vlaams Belang in Belgium, the Australian One Nation Party, and the Italian Lega Nord, to name but a few. All these political parties assume a critical stance against multiculturalism considering that it disadvantages the locals and promotes division and unfairness. The political position of such parties is a defensive, protectionist one, with policy proposals including curbs on immigration, repatriation of immigrants, and an end to all policies favoring culturally diverse groups. Their ultimate solution to the "problems of multiculturalism" is therefore to get rid of diversity and return to the (imaginary and illusionary) unity of the past.

Attacked by both right- and left-wing theorists and commentators, multicultural-ism's days seem numbered. But, perhaps, to paraphrase Mark Twain, rumors of multi-culturalism's death have been greatly exaggerated. Most of these critiques hinge on the precise definition of multiculturalism. For many of its critics, multiculturalism is turned into a straw man, accused of all sorts of issues, often quite contradictory: for instance, how can multiculturalism be blamed both for privileging minorities and for minority violence against majorities? Presumably, if minorities were favored they would not harbor any resentment leading to riots and similar violence. How can it be blamed for the erosion of social solidarity in favor of particularistic cultural identities, when any society that hears and meets groups' demands is by definition solidaristic, in the sense of understanding and supporting such claims? It seems that multiculturalism is all things to all people, lacking a precise definition, which leads to constant misun-derstandings and critiques. Shohat and Stam (2007) argue that multiculturalism's right-wing critics purposely distort and misrepresent multiculturalism in their attempt to return to some kind of imaginary unity and harmony. But equally, left-wing cri-tiques betray a similar mourning over lost utopias, which are linked to the inability of the left to form a convincing and mobilizing critique against global capitalism. But, argue Shohat and Stam, scapegoating multiculturalism and denouncing difference will not strengthen the left; nor will it lead to the demise of global capitalism.

In his impassioned defense of multiculturalism Paul Gilroy (2006) argues that the permanent crisis of multiculturalism shows a kind of post-imperial melancholia. Rather than acknowledging the violence and injustices involved in colonialism, post-imperial countries such as Britain are in denial. The gap that was left when empires dissolved, along with the pressures of globalization, has led to a loss of identity, which in turn has been associated to anxiety and feelings of loss. Post-imperial identity is, for Gilroy, constructed on the basis of guilt and denial, but also "in opposition to the intrusive presence of the incoming strangers who, trapped inside our perverse local logic of race, nation, and ethnic absolutism, not only *represent* the vanished empire but also refer consciousness to the unacknowledged pain of its loss and the unsettling shame of its bloody management" (p. 101). Attacks on multiculturalism therefore reveal this underlying logic: it is "them," the strangers, the foreigners, those different from "us" who are responsible for "our" loss of identity, harmony, and unity. Notwithstanding this melancholic post-colonial identity, Gilroy points to examples of "multiculture in action," of ordinary multiculturalism as the lived experiences and everyday encounters between identities in urban multicultural centers. This everyday conviviality of multi-culture is the antidote to post-colonial melancholia, argues Gilroy, and it shows that beyond policy, beyond official, intellectual, or party-political responses to the so-called crisis of multiculturalism, in the end lived experiences and encounters between different people set the agenda. And this agenda is not necessarily a negative one, but rather one marked by ambiguity, uncertainty, and unpredictability. Multiculture is the term adopted by Gilroy to refer not to the regulation of difference through policy and its ideological underpinnings, as in multicultural*ism*, but to the sum of the various cultural differences in all their unruly complexity, their antagonisms, and their conviviality. In the context of this book we shall adopt the term cultural diversity to refer to this, since "multiculture" might appear to be a neologism that mystifies further rather than allowing for a careful examination of the relevant issues.

Who is right? Should we adopt Gilroy's optimism, or Žižek's critical stance? Should we follow calls for renewal, or dismiss multiculturalism as passé? Perhaps more than anything, the ongoing debate shows the continued relevance of multiculturalism. The continued "crisis" of multiculturalism represents the need to keep on thinking and reformulating our ideas of cultural diversity, togetherness, identity, and difference. And in these terms, this book constitutes another moment in the continuing debate on the relevance of difference. Its main contribution is located in the following two arguments. Firstly, that cultural diversity, which includes identities, and experiences of, and encounters with, difference, is always-already *mediated*, that is, constructed, (re)-presented, and experienced through the media of communication. Secondly, this mediation points to a double bind in cultural diversity: on the one hand, the mediation of cultural diversity is involved in efforts to produce and subsequently control a certain version of it; on the other hand, this very mediation undermines such efforts by inserting a degree of instability, thereby keeping open the processes of mediation. The second argument in the heart of this book is that this play between control and instability is a necessary, but not sufficient, condition for the debate on multiculturalism to remain open and vibrant. The following section will explain and elaborate further on these arguments, while the final section will explain the structure of the book.

1.2 The Mediation of Cultural Diversity

To understand the relevance of the media, we have to turn to socio-historical theories that looked into the characteristics and specificity of contemporary societies. Social theorists from Max Weber to Anthony Giddens understand and define the current historical phase in which the world finds itself as modernity. Modernity is often seen as the historical period starting as early as the fifteenth century, which is characterized by processes of increasing rationalization, secularization, and individualization. In short, modernity is the phase in which humanity entered when it began criticizing and seeking to shape the world based on reason and rationality rather than on tradition and spiritual belief. The German sociologist Max Weber understood modernity as the "disenchantment of the world," that is, as the shift from a world ruled by superstition, dogmatic religious beliefs, and "magic" towards a rational society, ruled by reason alone.

But modernity is itself evolving. Thus, the British theorist Anthony Giddens defines late modernity as a dynamic process, no longer exclusively relying on the means-ends instrumental rationality described by Weber, but rather on reflexivity, or the "regularized use of knowledge about circumstances of social life" (Giddens, 1991: 20). In other words, contemporary societies are characterized by their attempts to steer and guide themselves through producing and applying new knowledge. This reliance on knowledge and information is also highlighted by Ulrich Beck (1992), who argues that modernity has entered a phase of reflexive modernization: contemporary societies, argues Beck, rely on knowledge and information, on the basis of which they subsequently evolve. The same emphasis on knowledge, information and communication is found in Manuel Castells' work (1996) on the network society. According to Castells, we are witnessing a new shift within modernity precipitated by the new information technologies; the network society can only function on the basis of information and communication that is produced and disseminated by new, digital, technologies. If, therefore, we accept the main premises of these theoretical perspectives, the role of the media is a fundamental one: as disseminators of information, as platforms for communication and to an extent even as producers of new knowledge. In these terms, current societies rely heavily on the media.

But here we want to take this argument further. The media's role is not merely as transparent tools of information and communication. Much more crucially, they form an integral part of modernity, present from its very start, and developing alongside it, and giving it its current shape and form. This argument draws on John Thompson's work on media and modernity.

For Thompson (1995) the media, mainly in their widely disseminated print or electronic form, are involved in the transformation and reordering of social relations, especially those regarding publicness and visibility, as well as self-understandings and identities. For Thompson, the media have fundamentally transformed social interaction through creating a new type, that of mediated interaction. Specifically, mediated quasi-interaction, as Thompson calls it, has certain defining characteristics: rather than being dialogical, it becomes monological; and rather than addressing one person, it addresses infinite others; in addition, this type of interaction extends in time and space, in contrast to face-to-face oral interaction, which disappears the moment it is uttered. The rise of this type of (mass-) mediated social interaction, and the relative power it offers to communicators, can be linked to the rise of powerful and globalized media corporations. The production and distribution of symbolic goods by such corporations enters and therefore alters communication flows in society.

In these terms, following Thompson, nothing can any longer be the same since it is (also) mediated, that is subjected to the processes and specificities of the media. Visibility, or publicness, the ways in which things, people, and issues become visible to others, goes through the media: these can only be visible from the angles or perspectives selected by the media; they can be visible to millions of people or conversely become invisible; and their publicness is monological or uni-directional, in the sense that the spectators and their reactions are themselves not immediately visible. Tradition, or the ways in which we relate to our past, is also transformed or "remoored," as Thompson puts it: it is not destroyed by the ultra-modern media, but rather moved from its original contexts, reinvented with some parts of it acquiring more importance than others, and used for different purposes. The self, finally, which Thompson, following Giddens, understands as a reflexive construction, is constructed on the basis of symbols, and new knowledge encountered in the media. The broader point that Thompson makes is that these transformations have fundamental and radical implications on how lives are lived, selves are formed, and politics is conducted in contemporary societies.

It follows, therefore, that cultural diversity is also mediated. By the term cultural diversity we understand the sum of the various kinds of difference – ethnic, "racial," or cultural, including their intersections or co-articulations with gender and sexuality, and also the debates, controversies, and conflicts, as well as the conviviality, warmth, and solidarity, associated with these. We understand, and interact with, cultural diversity, and we construct our cultural identities (also) in and through the media. This is not to say that face-to-face or personal encounters with others play no part in such interactions and constructions. However, we want to insist that these encounters do not take place in a vacuum; rather, in a media-saturated world, all these encounters are more or less mediated – that is, not determined, but interactively (or for some dialectically) influenced by the dynamic associated with the media. In these terms, we cannot apprehend diversity in a direct manner – if this was ever possible – but rather only through the ways in which it is mediated.

But what does this mediation precisely entail? Very schematically, the mediation of cultural diversity accepts that cultural diversity necessarily traverses the processes associated with the media. And these include processes of production and circulation, construction and representation, as well as reception and use. In other words, cultural diversity is (re)produced and distributed through the media, which construct and represent it in certain ways, and which are in turn received and put to use by audiences. This, we should clarify, does not mean that cultural diversity only exists because of the media. Rather, following Thompson, we want to suggest that, while cultural diversity is historically and politically produced, the media reappropriate it, dislodge it from its original contexts, and transform or "remoor" it. In other words, the media resignify and attach certain meanings and significance to cultural diversity which then become entrenched and widely used. Subsequent encounters and interactions with cultural diversity may then mobilize such mediated meanings, or at least use them for orientation. However, this emphasis is somewhat one-sided in that it attributes all the power to the production part of mediated communication, overlooking the dynamism of the contexts of its reception and use. We need therefore an understanding of mediation that allows for its dynamism, or, as Roger Silverstone (2005) put it, for its dialectic character to emerge.

More specifically, it is clear that the mediation of cultural diversity is involved in attempts to contain it and control its meaning and significance. And to an extent such efforts are successful. This is because, in contexts of mediated communication, the relationship between communicators, producers, and receivers is uneven and asymmetrical, with producers having more power than receivers. However, and this is a crucial point, this power is not absolute, and control of mediated cultural diversity is not total. In contrast, receivers or audiences of mediated cultural diversity can and do openly contest its representations. Or, they also misinterpret them or appropriate them in unexpected and unpredictable ways. Such unpredictable interpretations and uses end up influencing subsequent reproductions of mediated cultural diversity. Moreover, the boundaries between producers and consumers of mediated cultural diversity are not always as clear cut: consumers can also become producers themselves, while producers are always also consumers of mediated cultural diversity. At the same time, the processes of mediation take place in a certain historical, socio-cultural, economic, and political context, which in turn feeds into them, and contributes to the mediation of cultural diversity. All these become sources of instability and introduce disruptions and tensions in the mediation of cultural diversity, which then must be understood as dynamic and unpredictable. Perhaps the best way to understand this mediation is to think that it involves, on the one hand, attempts to control and contain cultural diversity. These may influence the debate, shape policy decisions, and affect self-identities and understandings: they may, in other words, change and mould cultural diversity in certain ways. On the other hand, such efforts are variously met with resistance, acceptance, differential appropriation, unpredictable use, and so on, all of which feed into subsequent mediations and reproductions of cultural diversity: these end up shaping and influencing cultural diversity as well, even if their relationship is asymmetrical. In short, mediation involves a constant tension between control and/ or containment of cultural diversity and defiance, opposition to, but also negotiated acceptance of, such efforts.

Understanding the ways in which cultural diversity is mediated, therefore, is necessary for understanding its centrality, significance, and importance for contemporary societies. At the same time, however, mediated cultural diversity is always in a tension both between control and its opposition, as we argued above, but also within its constituent components, that is, between different identities and ideas, practices and beliefs, as we saw in the previous section. There is no easy way, no straightforward criteria by which to determine what is more just, fairer, better for all involved. In these terms, it is crucial to allow for these tensions, disagreements, and conflicts to take place; it is crucial, in other words, for the debate on cultural diversity (or multiculturalism) to remain open to new challenges and ideas, as any closure would end up imposing unnecessary and problematic limits. From this point of view, the constitutive tension in processes of mediation is a necessary condition for this debate to remain open, since it is a dynamic process that cannot be controlled by any of those involved. Does it suffice, however? Since mediation forms the structural backdrop of this debate, its actual substance or contents cannot be determined by such structural processes. Thus, much more is needed for the debate to take place in ways commensurable with the democratic principles of inclusion, equality, and freedom. In particular, each of the constitutive processes of mediation, which include production, representation, and reception, have to be examined in detail and assessed on the extent to which they operate on the basis of democratic principles. Such an assessment must pose questions such as: to what extent are production processes inclusive of cultural diversity? Or, which kinds of representations of cultural diversity are more conducive to thinking and questioning alterity and sameness, identity and difference? Or, finally, to what extent do audiences' interpretations of mediated cultural diversity contribute to the continuation of the debate? These are some of the questions that we will approach in this book. However, before approaching such questions we need to understand and contextualize cultural diversity in historical, empirical, and theoretical and normative terms. The next section will detail the structure of the book and explain the role and arguments of each chapter.

1.3 The Structure of the Book

Understanding multiculturalism as the effect of the processes that constitute difference points to the need to examine how difference is constituted. As a second step, we need to examine the variations in the constitution and management of difference across the world: what types of multiculturalism do we encounter in different countries? How do different countries across the world deal with difference? How do the various nations that comprise the world treat different communities and groups found in their territories? What are the factors that can explain the variation in this treatment? More importantly, how should we address the questions raised by cultural diversity? What kind of policy is the fairer for both majority and minority cultures? Chapters 2, 3 and 4 will address some of these questions, by looking first at the way in which cultural diversity has been historically produced by the rise of the nation state and nationalism (Chapter 2). Thus, the rise and rise of the nation-state (Mann, 1997) is a contentious issue, which has led to a heated debate on the origins, nature, present, and future of this form of socio-political organization. Chapter 2 will therefore discuss the various theories of the nation and nationalism, questioning them as to their implicit position on the role of the media, and assessing them on the basis of how much room they leave for cultural diversity to flourish. Chapter 3 will then map the specific multicultural trajectory that different countries have followed. We will look at the specific policies developed and applied in different countries in their quest to deal with difference. The main premise and argument here is that different historical, political, and socio-cultural contexts produce different ways of dealing with difference, both informal, which we can refer to as "practices," and formal, institutionalized ones, which we can refer to as "policies." This variation in policies and practices reflects ongoing tensions both within nations as well as between nations and the pressures of globalization. While Chapter 3 describes the different existing approaches to multiculturalism and cultural diversity, Chapter 4 focuses on theoretical and normative approaches: it asks: how ought we to treat cultural diversity? What kinds of approaches offer both theoretical clarity and political solutions to these issues?

More specifically, to understand the production of multicultural practices and policies, as well as theories and politics, we need first to trace the production of the nation itself. Why? Because, to speak of multiculturalism – critically or not – presumes the existence of its converse: mono-culturalism, or in other words, the existence of nations understood as homogenous cultural and political entities. It is clear that, if we speak of difference, we presume sameness and identity – one cannot exist without the other. At least since the days of Hegel and his master and slave dialectic, we know that identity presumes, and is reflected in, difference, and vice versa. In producing identity, in thinking about who *we are*, we must engage with the question of who *we are not*, and with the boundaries set around our selves and our group. In tracing therefore the history and practices of multiculturalism across the globe, we have to begin with the nation.

While in theoretical, abstract, terms the nation is an empty form, its actual history betrays its rootedness in European modernity. It is within European modernity that the nation state found its most explicit articulation as well as its political application. From there – and then – onwards, the history of the nation is in many ways the history of the expansion of Europe, or more broadly the "West." In these terms, the history of multiculturalism entails the beginnings of Europe as a pastiche of nation-states, their expansion, colonization, and conquest of overseas territories, and the rise of globalization. The practices of accommodating difference, of thinking about difference per se and its role within a nation, reflect these historical contexts, as well as the historical, political, and socio-cultural particularities of specific territories.

Taking these into account, Chapter 3 will discuss the concrete multicultural practices encountered across the world. Beginning with Europe, it looks into the various ways in which different European nations have dealt with difference. The specific nations we will treat here in more detail include the UK, France, and Germany; the former two represent former colonial powers, while Germany's specificity is located both in its historical past, its involvement in the two world wars, and its reliance on immigrant labor to accomplish its industrial "miracle." We will subsequently discuss the ways in which "immigration countries" have developed in accommodating differ-ence – the specific countries discussed include Canada and the US. Thirdly, a discus-sion of multicultural practices needs to look at those countries that are "constitutionally different," that is countries in which difference has been there explicitly since their very foundation. The focus here will be on two countries, India and Nigeria.

What conclusions might we draw from this discussion? Firstly, that the question of accommodating – or repressing – difference is as complex and vexed as the question of difference itself. History, politics, culture, and for some even biology emerge as explanatory factors of the many routes followed by people and nation-states in their quest to deflect tensions, and to provide solutions to perceived or actual problems brought about by the existence of difference. It follows, secondly, that it is very dif-ficult to produce a simple model of an ideal multicultural policy to be adopted by all. The problems, tensions, and accommodations of difference are specific to specific contexts, and to the extent that this variation exists, it requires different and specific ad hoc solutions. This, however, must not be taken to mean that "anything goes" as far as multicultural policies are concerned, or that different policies and practices are of equal value. Indeed, the question of how to assess these policies looms large over this discussion.

This issue will be dealt with in Chapter 4, which will discuss the different theoretical and normative models that developed in order to justify and explain multiculturalism. Must we always accept difference, even to the detriment of our identity? Should we privilege differential treatment over equality? How can we retain unity faced with a variety of incompatible practices, ethics, and customs? In the end, how can we resolve these dilemmas? This chapter will critically review the different answers offered by different theoretical and political perspectives. The main argument in this chapter is that the dilemmas of multiculturalism call not for a permanent resolution, but for a constant reflection on the problems faced, along with a realization that there are no "final solutions." At the same time, none of these theories actually considers the mediation of cultural diversity and its role in the multicultural dilemmas. Overlooking the mediation of cultural diversity results in oversimplified positions and to an overall inability to deal with the complexity of contemporary multiculturalism.

The task of theorizing the relationship between the media and cultural diversity is undertaken in Chapter 5. Specifically, this chapter discusses the various ways in which the relationship between the media and society has been conceptualized, and, within these, the room and role allocated to cultural diversity. The critical review of various positions concludes with a discussion of a theory of the mediation of cultural diversity. Theoretically, this involves an understanding of the role of the media as directly, and dialectically or at least reciprocally, involved in all aspects of contemporary socio-cultural, political, and economic life. Following upon and developing further argu-ments by Jesus Martin-Barbero (1993) and Roger Silverstone (2005), this chapter argues that the media influence and shape institutions, structures, ideas, beliefs, and so on, and are in turn influenced by these. The exact forms that this mutual and reciprocal influence takes are always unstable and unpredictable. As we argued in the previous section, when it comes to the mediation of cultural diversity, the media (re) produce, distribute, and represent cultural diversity, thereby to an extent controlling the ways in which it is understood, and shaping its significance and role in society. At the same time, however, audiences can and do respond to such attempts in ways that feed back into the mediated reproduction and representation of cultural diversity. In empirical terms, a theory of mediated cultural diversity means that we need to study all kinds of processes involved in this mediation. This includes production, representation, and reception. The remaining chapters of the book attempt to do just that.

Chapter 6 discusses the production of cultural diversity, beginning with the ways in which it is theorized, and discussing various studies and findings as well as various practices and policies adopted by media organizations. The conclusion here is that the production of cultural diversity is differentially shaped by political economic and organizational factors as well as by conscious and reflexive efforts to remove barriers for participation of cultural minorities in media production. An implicit argument involved here is that, if there were more minority media professionals, then mediated cultural diversity would end up being fairer and more accurate. Chapter 7 examines this argument by looking at minority or diasporic media, and their role and specificity. Not surprisingly, minority media are controversial: do they make a positive contribution to multicultural democracies, or do they actually contribute to the fragmentation of the public sphere, resulting in further ghettoization and the break-up of society? Chapter 7 discusses the various arguments and positions, concluding that from a mediation point of view, these media must also be seen as dialectically involved in socio-political processes. This further implies that their contributions cannot be a priori determined, but rather examined on a case by case basis.

The question of representation is found at the heart of any discussion on the media. But what is precisely its role and significance? What exactly, to quote Stuart Hall (1997), is the work of representation? Chapter 8 looks at the various theoretical propositions that sought to explain the role and function of representation. It argues that, within a theory of mediation, the work of representation must be seen as dynamically involved in the control of cultural diversity, but also in opposition to this control. Representation must therefore be understood as involved in the containment, control, and domination of cultural difference; but it also actively involved in the subversion, questioning, and rejection of such efforts. In these terms, an account of representation needs to show how it works, how it can be effective both in containing cultural difference and in subverting such efforts. This tension in the work of representation is captured by a performative approach, which shows that language and representation must rely on the one hand on the repetition and reproduction of the same meanings, images, and symbols, but in different contexts. These contexts, in turn, disrupt and destabilize these meanings, attaching new ones in ambiguous and unpredictable ways. In this manner we can explain the dynamism of representations, the ways in which they are replicated and persist over the years, but also their shifts and changes.

Chapters 9 and 10 describe the various representations, adopting the term "regimes of representation," to denote the structural similarities and force of the various representational systems. Chapter 9 discusses the racist, domesticated, and commodified regimes of representation of cultural diversity, showing the ways in which they seek to

> **Box 1.1**   Some definitions
>
> **Cultural diversity**: the existence of groups with their own unique, culturally (as opposed to individually or biologically) derived characteristics (see Parekh, 2002). Such groups may share some commonalities of origins, histories, and traditions, and systems of beliefs and practices. In this case we can speak of "ethno-cultural groups," to point to the specificity of this kind of difference. Parekh (2002) refers to this ethnically mapped difference as communal diversity. This is the kind of diversity that will be at the centre of this book.
>
> **Multiculturalism**: refers to the acceptance of this kind of plurality in society and to the need to rethink the ways in which societies function in order to accommodate and serve difference.
>
> **Media and mediation**: these point to the centrality of the media in late (or for some post-) modernity, and to the necessity of understanding the ways in which cultural diversity is co-constituted in and through the media.

dominate, contain, and exploit cultural diversity. Typically, these regimes are seen as emerging out of majority or mainstream media. Chapter 10, in contrast, discusses two regimes that emerge out of cultural diversity itself, the essentialist and alternative regimes. Both are seen as contributing to the destabilization and disruption of the previous regimes, but both are encountering conceptual and political problems. However, the work of representation is incomplete until it is pinned down in its contexts of reception.

Chapter 11 spells out the various ways in which people receive, consume and use mediated cultural diversity. It traces the ways in which people's background, conceptualized in terms of Pierre Bourdieu's social capital, leads to different interpretations of the same representations. It further follows the productive ways in which encounters with the media construct identities, while finally, it discusses the active interventions by which audiences have sought to hold the media accountable for their actions. The chapter concludes with an argument in favor of keeping open existing, and creating new, channels for communication between media and their audiences.

While Chapter 11 concludes the cycle of mediation, which includes production, representation, and reception, the advent of the new media introduces new elements and perhaps shifts in the mediation of cultural diversity. Chapter 12, the final chapter in this book, examines the relationship between the internet and cultural diversity. This chapter argues that, while the internet blurs the lines between production, representation, and consumption of cultural diversity, it is still useful to retain these terms for analytical purposes. Examining then online production, representation, and use, it concludes that the key process for the online mediation of cultural diversity is use: both private and personal, public and political it allows for the continued contestation of identities and claims, as well as for the creation of new commonalities and a new commons. On the other hand, caution should be exercised here, as the possibilities offered by the internet are not necessarily always actualized.

In all these chapters, the tension between control/containment of cultural diversity and responses to these remains central. This, we argue is the main tension of mediated

cultural diversity, which acts like a motor, taking cultural diversity to new and unpredictable places. Because of this tension mediated cultural diversity remains dynamic,
and any resolutions to its dilemmas remain temporary. Equally, however, all these
chapters pay full attention to the institutional, structural, and historical factors that
affect cultural diversity and its mediation. Mediation does not take place in a vacuum
and neither does it uni-directionally determine the world around it; rather, it, too, is
reciprocally (or dialectically) influenced by the historical, socio-cultural, political, and
economic context. Studying mediated cultural diversity entails a study of this, the
broader context within which mediation takes place. Just as Karl Marx argued that
men make history in circumstances they have inherited from the past, mediated cultural diversity produces and is produced in a context shaped, but ultimately undeter-
mined, by history, politics, economics, and socio-cultural factors.

2
Theorizing the Nation

This chapter is concerned with the specificity of the nation-state as a form of organization and its involvement in the production of ethno-cultural diversity. A central assumption of this chapter, and much of the book, is that ethno-cultural diversity acquires meaning only in a broader context that revolves around ideas of homogeneity, similarity, and sharedness of identity. One of the first questions posed by cultural diversity is: diverse in relation to whom? Different from what? To understand cultural diversity, therefore, we must understand the context that produced it. This context is the context of the nation-state, which, we will argue here, is a modern form of organization, meaning that it is part and parcel of modernity, and accompanies the historical, political, and social transformations associated with this epoch. This, however, is already a contentious argument, since there are those who claim that nations have existed since time immemorial. But what role does the history of the nation play in understanding multiculturalism? What difference does it make to claim that the nation is modern or primordial? And if we accept that it is indeed a modern form of organization, why or how did it come about? And what is the role of the media in all this? These are some of the questions and debates that this chapter will address. It will begin with a discussion of the various theories of the nation, following Anthony Smith's well-known classification of primordial versus modernist theories, and it will conclude with a short discussion of globalization.

2.1 Theories of the Nation

The importance of theories of the nation is (at least) twofold. Firstly, in theorizing the nation, such perspectives produce explanations that may ultimately acquire political significance. Certain conceptions of the nation – which might stem from or precede theoretical approaches – become widely diffused, forming part of commonsense understandings and eventually influencing policy decisions. We will see more specifically in Chapter 3 how different countries have enshrined their commonsense understandings – often backed up by academic research – into law and policy. Secondly, theories of the nation contain implied theories of difference. This, in turn, is crucial

> ## Box 2.1   Nations and nationalism: some working definitions
>
> **Ethnie**: the "ethnic" basis of the nation (historical, cultural, linguistic) (Smith, 1986).
> **Nation-state**: the political community.
> **State**: a human community that (successfully) claims the monopoly of the legitimate use of physical force within a given territory (Weber, 1919/2004).
> **Nationalism**: the ideological proposition that the ethnic and political community should always coincide (Gellner, 1983).
> **National identity**: the (self-)ascriptions that form the substantive part of the nation. The answers to the question: What is it to be Chinese/Indian/English/British, etc.?

for understanding how different groups of people are received in certain contexts. Indeed, theories of the nation have put forward several propositions regarding the nation's origins, evolution, and destiny, some of which have clearly influenced policy decisions and everyday practices towards difference. We can classify these theories under two broad categories: those advocating the primordial and perennial character of the nation, and those viewing it as a construct. Anthony Smith (1998) refers to the former as the primordial paradigm and to the latter as the modernist one.

2.1.1 Primordialism and perennialism

According to Anthony Smith (1998, 2000) the main argument underpinning this approach is that nations exist because they reflect primordial attachments. They are present as the earliest possible form of community, reflecting ties that are based for some on biology, while for others on culture and association. Smith cites Pierre van den Berghe as an exponent of the former position and Clifford Geertz as an exponent of the latter. Van den Berghe (1967) is a socio-biologist who sought to explain nations and nationalism by means of biology. He views nations as extended kin groups, and argues that people's practices seek to maximize the socio-biological advantages they enjoy, including ensuring their (genetic) survival and well being – this is referred to as "inclusive fitness." According to this perspective, people tend towards "nepotistic" behavior: they look to their kin for protection, support, cooperation, attachment, etc. Large groupings are no more than superfamilies, reflecting in large scale what goes on in family circles. And in order to determine who is a family member, people look for similarity markers, including those of race, culture, and language. This is how this view explains the homogeneity found within nations, as well as the violent passions they sometimes generate.

While a socio-biological primordial approach considers commonalities of culture, language, and so on, as indicating an underlying biological or genetic commonality, the culturalist primordial approach focuses on cultural commonalities as such, and considers them as the essence or core of the nation. For this approach, which Smith associates with the work of the anthropologist Clifford Geertz, the primordiality of the nation lies precisely in these commonalities of customs, traditions, language, religious practices, and so forth. Looking at the new states created after colonialism on the basis of often ancient societies or nations, Geertz (1973) argues that these are brought together because of cultural similarities and attachments rather than because of the rational decision of people to commit themselves to their new state. For Geertz, it is this kind of primordial attachment that sustains the nation as a distinct grouping – and this primordial attachment is seen as stemming from a series of cultural (rather than biological) "givens", such as "being born into a particular religious community, speaking a particular language, or even a dialect of a language, and following particular social practices" (Geertz, 1973: 259). In this view the homogeneity of the nation both pre-exists its organization into a political community or a state and also sustains the nation as such, through generating strong feelings towards it.

Both the biological and the culturalist variants of primordialism attribute a certain naturalness to the nation. For both, it is natural to form ties of "blood, speech [and] custom," to quote Geertz (1973: 259) once more, and it is natural therefore to seek to protect those attached to you, even at the expense of those who are not part of your group, and even if it sometimes leads to violence and exclusion. Smith locates the difference between primordialists and perennialists precisely at the level of this naturalness. Perennialists (e.g. Hastings, 1997) hold that nations have existed since time immemorial, but they do not necessarily think that they are natural. Conversely, for primordialists, the nation exists precisely because it is a "natural" form of organization, i.e. it has socio-biological origins. For perennialists the nation is fundamental as a form of organization: particular nations may come and go, but the form of association is perennial: continuous, and immemorial. This is why, as Smith (1998) argues, the perennialist will not make a distinction between ethnic or national attachments, as these are considered to be merely different manifestations of the same thing, the same type of socio-political organization. Of course, primordialism and perennialism are not mutually exclusive, so that one may believe that nations as a form of organization have existed since time immemorial because they reflect a natural need for association between people sharing important commonalities.

What is the role of the media within this perspective? Given that the national community is seen as primordial or perennial, the media can only function as a platform for this perennial community to express its (singular) will. From this point of view, the role of the media is a limited and transparent one: since the community is a natural or at least ever-present one, the media can only serve the community through providing it with the means by which to communicate and transmit its will. Clearly, the role of the media as transparent vehicles for communication is one hotly contested by media theorists. As we shall see other positions allocate a more involved role to the media in the creation and maintenance of the nation-state.

Although primordialism and perennialism have gone a long way towards explaining some of the issues involved in understanding the nations and nationalism, they suffer from a number of problems. Firstly, the insistence of both approaches on the fundamental and unique position of the nation as a form of organization overlooks its historical evolution and specificity. Neither position can explain the particular manifestation of nations, and their organization into political communities, and neither position can account for the dynamic nature of nations, the changes across time, the shifts in loyalty and allegiances, the variation in the intensity of feeling they generate.

On the other hand, as Smith points out, these positions rightly highlight the passions that national attachments give rise to, and their often violent nature, often at odds with economic explanations. Nevertheless, the socio-biological position is reductionist, as the explanations for the nation are reduced to a single biological position that "we" need this type of community for "inclusive fitness." The culturalist explanation, on the other hand, appears deterministic in that it overlooks national dynamism – the clear observation that nations evolve and change over time. Both approaches ignore the role of history and the contingent nature of nations.

In more political terms one could criticize these positions because of their implications for understanding difference. Ethno-cultural difference, following the logic of these two positions, is the product of very deeply seated socio-biological and cultural factors. If these explanations were taken seriously, what options would be open to policy makers when dealing with difference? These would look more or less like this: because we form strong bonds and attachments to our own communities, outsiders will naturally be excluded or cast aside or even exploited for the benefit of "our own" community. And since this is only natural, we might as well come to terms with it, accept it as fact, and save our energies for the creation of a world in which each community will be homogenous enough to avoid (internal) conflict. Policy makers cannot write policies that oppose the natural order of things.

It is difficult to accept the political implications of this paradigm, even if it is relatively widespread and convincing, and the theorists are well intentioned. As Smith points out, there are similarities between this paradigm and versions of "organic nationalism" according to which nations form organic communities with certain innate and essential characteristics, which have existed throughout history, and form its main actors. This version, associated with the German Romantics, might be seen as underlying the types of policy and practices towards ethno-cultural difference encountered in Nazi Germany. While primordialists and perennialists refute this "organic" connection, focusing instead on the role played by nations and nationalism in sustaining communities, it is easy to see their similarities. Generally speaking, however, the relatively long history of a world divided into nations, of national sentiments, myths, and traditions, make this position a popular one. Similar explanations are offered by some media in accounts of wars and ethnic conflict: it is only natural, they argue, that we will always favor our own ethno-cultural group, so ethnic conflict will always arise. Such inevitability is certainly absent from the constructionist accounts to be discussed next.

2.1.2 The modernist paradigm

Smith (1998) classifies economic, political, sociocultural, and constructionist approaches to the nation, which, he argues, all share certain common arguments. The central tenet of such approaches is the thoroughly modern character of the nation and nationalism, which emerged at the same time as modernity, capitalism, and the industrial revolution. From this point of view, the nation, as well as nationalism, must be thought of as a distinct form of organization and not merely the same as other types of communities. There is nothing "primordial," therefore, about the nation, as it is modern through and through. Thus, developments such as the rise of the media, industrialism, bureaucracy, urbanization, and so on enabled the development of an unprecedented form of organization, that of the nation-state. Smith names the well-known theorist Ernest

Gellner as one of the main exponents of the modernist paradigm. While other theorists highlight economics as the main explanatory variable for the rise of the nation and nationalism (e.g. Nairn, 1977), we will rather eclectically focus here on the work of Ernest Gellner, Eric Hobsbawm, and Benedict Anderson, as they insisted on the importance of socio-cultural factors, alongside economic and political ones.

Specifically, Gellner (1983) argued that in pre-modern, agricultural societies, there was little need for an educated and technically able workforce. The feudal social organization was based on a large number of people working as peasants in land belonging to the aristocracy. Their knowledge, skills, and abilities were enough for cultivating the land, and there was no need for anything else. At the same time, the clergy and the aristocracy, who were the spiritual and political leaders respectively, effectively controlled the peasantry through the provision and control of a set of beliefs and through the application of rewards and punishments for loyalty and its lack. People mostly lived in relatively small, internally homogenous communities, with little prospect for movement beyond the confines of their own community. With the rise of industrialism, however, came the need for a technically able workforce, for larger communities, and for different sources of organization, social bonds, loyalty, and control. These developments were, in turn, associated to standardized education, the rise of cities, and the eventual appearance of the nation and nationalism.

Firstly, standardized education was necessary, as people needed to be able to do the same things in the same manner, and also to communicate effectively in a single language. Localized dialects, folk traditions, and customs, stories and practices become equally standardized, more widespread, and formal. Gellner refers to this as passing from a "low" to a "high" culture. Secondly, as more and more factories were built, requiring more and more workers, people abandoned their villages and concentrated in sprawling urban centres, which subsequently became cities. Urbanization involved the displacement of a population, thereby removing the special bond they had with their own little communities, territories, and villages. Thirdly, while in small communities people knew each other, and knew who belonged there and who didn't, in the emerging big cities they lacked this type of bond. The nation then developed as a new form of community, binding people together through cultivating the belief that they belonged together, that they had a common way of doing things, that they had a certain homeland, and that they should be ruled by people from within their community. Hence, the nation depends on the rise of nationalism, or the ideology that the ethnic basis of the nation should always be the same as that of the political elite that governs the nation.

For Gellner, nationalism precedes the formation of the nation-state, because the latter requires a sort of conceptual basis, found in nationalism. Of course nationalism may build upon existing traditions and beliefs. As Gellner (1983: 54) put it: "It is nationalism that engenders nations and not the other way round. Admittedly, nationalism uses the pre-existing, historically inherited proliferation of cultures or cultural wealth but it uses them very selectively and it most often transforms them radically." In addition, while nationalism claims to represent the people, their own and true culture, it is in fact a deception, as it represents the imposition and dominance of a high culture that replaces the local folk cultures previously in place. And it does so by means of mass and standardized schooling, which serves the needs of a bureaucratic state organization and an industrial and capitalistic economy. Within this perspective, the role of the media is one of supporting this standardization that supported the building of the nation-state. The adoption of a standard language and style of speaking by the media helped, alongside a standardized education, to homogenize the nation. From this point of view, it was not the media contents or messages that bound the nation together; rather, the media contribution to the creation and maintenance of the nation can be located in its ability to address the nation in a standard, common language and style.

Notwithstanding its concocted nature, nationalism can give rise to very strong passions and loyalties, mobilized in the service of industrial capitalism, and the military and political establishment, as well as the world order that sustains it. On the other hand, however, it might run out of control, particularly given the uneven spread of capitalism and development across the world. This uneven spread meant that, as Gellner put it (p. 57), "the course of true nationalism never did run smooth." What Gellner wants to show here is that, despite its movement towards standardization, homogenization, and the kind of equality these are linked to, nationalism often failed in its quest, resulting in conflict and fission. Gellner refers to two principles of fission, which are also seen as giving rise to "new units," i.e. new "nations" or communities: the principle of barriers to communication and the principle of inhibitors of social entropy. Firstly, members of a nation-state need to be able to speak the same language in order to communicate and for their bureaucracy to run efficiently: failure to adopt the standardized language and culture then results in problems in communication which must be eradicated. On the other hand, those who do not speak the same, standardized language and who fail to adopt the same cultural practices are seen as hostile to a newly formed community that has to preserve and transmit its distinctiveness. The second source of conflict and division is that of the so-called inhibitors of social entropy. Gellner thought that these "inhibitors" were those who possessed certain kinds of traits that could not be assimilated even after several generations. Typical "inhibitor" traits are skin pigmentation and religion. People whose skin pigment is different to that of the majority of the nation, or whose religion is different to that of the nation, are then threatening the social entropy, remaining a thorn in the nation's side and a source of permanent potential or actual tension.

Difference here is seen not as a natural barrier to harmony but rather as the outcome of nationalism. As such, someone like Gellner would argue that, if we want to get rid of prejudice, discrimination, and other attempts to control difference, then we must get rid of nationalism. And since nationalism "creates" nations, in getting rid of it we are also destroying nations. It seems, therefore, that, although this position in political terms is the exact converse to the primordial/perennial one, it ultimately ends up juxtaposing the nation and difference in a very similar way: they are just not compatible. Although this lack of compatibility is not attributed to natural or biological factors, the upshot of Gellner's modernism is that either the nation goes or difference goes. This is because nations must strive towards homogeneity and standardization while difference moves the opposite way towards fission and heterogeneity, ultimately leading to conflict. Thus, despite the very useful introduction of historicity in accounting for the creation of nations, nationalism, and cultural difference, this account does not lend itself to the creation of policies that may support the existence of multiple cultures in the same territorial and political context. It implies that, for this to happen, we cannot have nation-states, but an altogether different form of organization. For Gellner this form would be a supranational one, which would accept a canton-like existence of different cultures. But the one culture-one state principle of nationalism cannot accept the existence of difference within the confines of the nation. However, if we observe the world around us we can see that this is clearly not the case. Although in many ways things are far from ideal, no wholesale destruction of difference has taken place in nation-states as one would expect – although perhaps Gellner is right in pointing to various "ethnic-cleansing" strategies during phases of nation-building.

In addition, there are some important theoretical problems with Gellner's account. Most notably, these include the functionalism of this approach. What Gellner has done, argue his critics, is to see the outcome (industrial society) and guess how this was achieved (through nationalism), positing a necessary relationship between these two. Thus, looking at the existence of nation-states, he extrapolated that it was necessary for these to exist in order to give rise to industrial capitalism. But of course this may not be the case at all, as it may be that they are both outcomes of another factor, not found yet, or it may be that their relationship is the other way round: that nationalism is the outcome of a striving towards industrialization. In addition, this link cannot explain the existence of nationalistic movements in non-industrialized countries – for example Greece in the 1800s, and the more recent nationalistic movements of former colonial territories in Asia. From our point of view, it is clear that Gellner's modernism cannot serve multiculturalism either politically or theoretically. We can retain, however, his emphasis on the historical contingency of the nation-state, and the central role of culture and language in its creation.

Building on such insights, we can discuss another modernist position insisting on the centrality of history and culture, proposed by the historian Eric Hobsbawm. For Hobsbawm and his collaborators (1983), the cultural homogenization of the nation-state is due to practices that impose certain traditions as central for the nation. Such traditions, e.g. the public ceremonies of the British monarchy, the July 4 and Thanksgiving celebrations in the US, the Gandhi Jayanti national holiday in India (2 October) and other similar festivities and celebrations across the world, are, for Hobsbawm, invented, top-down traditions that posit a continuity between past and present, which in turn serves to hold the nation together. "'Invented traditions,'" argues Hobsbawm (Hobsbawm and Ranger, 1983: 1), "is taken to mean a set of practices, normally governed by overtly or tacitly accepted rules and of a ritual or symbolic nature, which seek to inculcate certain values and norms of behaviour by repetition, which automatically implies continuity with the past." As invented communities, nations had to form some sort of common bond that would hold the community together and which would also help replace past bonds and ties. While Gellner noted that this common bond is a "high culture" that presents itself as the singular national culture, Hobsbawm focuses on the invented nature of this culture and tradition, and the importance of forging links with the past. Such claims of the historical continuity of the nation are crucial both for bonding and solidarity, but also to legitimate the very existence of the nation and its authorities, and to demand the loyalty and allegiance of those living in it.

Within this perspective, the role of the media is crucial. Invented traditions must be replayed and disseminated regularly across the nation if they are to take hold. The media can become an important means by which such invented traditions are disseminated and replayed, eventually forming part of the nation's consciousness. Indeed, the ritualistic reproduction of national narratives, such as for instance the Queen's Christmas message in the UK and other televised ceremonies, contribute to the maintenance of the nation through upholding its (invented) traditions. Indeed, this type of theorization is given credence by media theorists, who highlight the media references to the everyday, banal symbols of the nation as pivotal in the creation and maintenance of the nation-state. For example, Mick Billig (1995) spoke of the banal references to symbols such as the flag or the national anthem in the context of everyday life as crucial for the reproduction of the nation and nationalism. On the other end, media events, such as the Olympic Games, the Eurovision Song Contest, the FA Cup final, or other similar televised events, help create and celebrate a common culture, which functions in ways similar to an invented tradition (Scannel, 1989; Dayan and Katz, 1992).

Perhaps the most distinctive contribution of Hobsbawm's concept is the emphasis on the behavioral and normative demands made by the nation; it is through such ritual practices that one comes to identify oneself with the nation, that one acquires a national identity and a bond with people who may otherwise be complete strangers. It is through such habitual practices that nations acquire social cohesion and socialize their members, who then come to share the same beliefs, values, and practices. And the strength of invented traditions is such that people may die in defence of what they see as their homeland, their values, and their beliefs. Additionally, the focus on the invented nature of such practices and beliefs highlights the functional aspect of nationalism, which is then mobilized to legitimate and support the nation-state and to create emotional ties between its members. Finally, the continuity with the past helps establish a historical claim on the territory, language, customs, and beliefs, which is then used to include or exclude various others. With this is mind, we may ask: what room does Hobsbawm's position leave for difference?

Clearly, although difference is in the first instance ignored – or perhaps actively suppressed – in favor of similarity and commonality, the invented tradition allows, and even invites, others to join in. Because of the need to ritually re-enact parts of the invented tradition, through reading history textbooks at school, through national ceremonies and celebrations, through parades, songs, flags, etc., others may join in even if they have no links or shared history. They become members of the same national community by virtue of endorsing this invented tradition. But this, of course, comes at a cost: that of ultimately overlooking difference in favor of commonality. Thus, people with different cultures are allowed to become members, but only insofar as they are willing to adopt the invented tradition as their tradition, or in other words only insofar as they are able and willing *to assimilate*. Needless to say, Hobsbawm himself was very critical of such invented traditions, which he saw as representing top-down efforts to control consciousness and prevent the establishment of other forms of community, based on common interests (such as class for instance).

However, the power that invented traditions hold over people is beyond any dispute. At the same time, the need for social cohesion, brought about by sharing values, beliefs, and traditions, is evident in societies that suffer from the anxiety of modernity (Giddens, 1991): on the one hand they are faced with the loss of traditional systems of belief and custom, while on the other new ideas and ideologies have failed (or refused) to fill in the vacuum created by this loss. The result is an often half-baked resurrection or attempt to rebuild such (invented) traditions and claim continuity between past and present. For instance in public rhetoric in the UK there are a lot of public calls for a return to "British values," which, however, remain vague, ill defined, and far too general to be associated with a single nation-state. But the call is ultimately a call for assimilation: let's all be the same, let's all endorse the same values, let's all celebrate the same holidays, rituals, and so on. From this point of view, we see that the fate of difference is ultimately to be destroyed, sacrificed at the altar of social cohesion and homogeneity.

Although useful in highlighting the artificial nature of history, Hobsbawm's approach is often criticized because of its assumption of a top-down perspective in which people are seen as dupes, manipulated and used as pawns in the hands of powerful interests. If we accept that nationalism is a top-down ideology in the hands of the elites, then it follows that it is mostly the working classes that fall for it. Yet there is no evidence that this is the case (O'Leary, 1998). Nationalism seems to affect people across the class spectrum. At the same time, there is no reason to assume that people are easy to manipulate through the direct imposition of ritualistic practices. Throughout history we have seen variations in traditions (imposed and inherited), appropriations of top-down, high-cultural practices by marginal groups, rejection of certain practices, in short all sorts of negotiations of top-down narratives of belongingness. In the end, however, we must agree with Hobsbawm that part of the hold of the nations and nationalism is explained through the repeated rituals and stories, ceremonies and celebrations that form the glue that keeps nations together. But the artifice that Hobsbawn rightly highlights poses a question: how is it that such invented traditions become the norm and appear natural and widely accepted?

The answer is perhaps to be found in the work of Benedict Anderson. Cultural homogenization and standardization is also found at the heart of Benedict Anderson's *Imagined Communities* (1983). In this important book, Anderson offers a comprehensive explanation and theory of nationalism that unfolds through a definition of the nation. This, argues Anderson in his famous formulation, "is an imagined political community – and it is imagined as both inherently limited and sovereign" (1983/1991: 3). The element of imagination is crucial for Anderson because it highlights the fact that people imagine or think themselves as part of a larger community even if they will never meet all of the other community members. Moreover, and here lies an important difference between Gellner and Anderson, imagination emphasizes the creative and generative aspect of the nation: it is not its falsity/genuineness that characterizes a nation, but rather the style in which the nation is imagined. The nation is characterized as inherently limited because there are always boundaries around it, even if they are flexible, there are always those belonging to the nation and those who don't. And it is imagined as sovereign, argues Anderson, because it came to being at the time of the Enlightenment, the American and French Revolutions, which demolished the *ancient régime* of dynastic, divinely ordained monarchies. Finally, it is imagined as a community because, notwithstanding the actual divisions and inequalities within the nation, it is premised on a spirit of "deep horizontal camaraderie" (p. 7).

Anderson then moves on to establish the cultural beginnings of the nation as an imagined community. These he traces back to the rise of what he calls print capitalism. Print capitalism contributed to "nation-building," or perhaps "nation- imagining," in several ways. First, print capitalism worked through standardizing and spreading vernacular languages, replacing the formal languages spoken earlier. In addition, print capitalism, particularly through printing novels and newspapers, helped to create a common time frame, in which the nation and its society (or the people who comprise it) move together, sharing time. They have a past, present, and future that are common. Finally, print capitalism helped through spreading narratives and imaginings of the nation as a united community. Anderson discusses works such as the Filipino novel *Noli Me Tangere* (José Rizal, 1887), in which the Filipino nation (which at the time was under colonial occupation) is imagined as such through a common address (the author addresses directly his Filipino readers), and through a common time frame – the time in which the events of the novel unfold is also the real time experienced by the readers. These imaginings, argues Anderson, subsequently enabled the formation of nations as imagined communities which were subsequently mobilized to form their own political communities, often through revolutions and nationalistic movements.

An important part of Anderson's argument is that nationalism must be seen as interacting with the type of political community that pre-existed it. We can recognize, therefore, various types of nationalism, which have emerged as a response to their historical predecessors. He then makes a distinction between "creole" and "official" nationalisms, corresponding to those emerging in colonized territories and in former empires respectively. "Creole nationalism" emerged in areas that had no homogenous cultures, histories, etc., but which then created themselves as distinct nations. His primary example is America, in which the United States established itself as a nation separate from its metropolitan nation, England, and the nations of South America declared their own independence from their colonial masters and established themselves as nations of both settlers and indigenous people, having distinct identities and cultures. Official nationalism, in contrast, emerged in territories that formed core part of empires. Anderson cites the examples of Imperial Russia, the so-called Celestial Empire in China, and the Ottoman Empire to show the type of nationalism that emerged when former empires sought to imagine themselves as nations (see also Anderson, 2001).

Among theorists of nationalism, Anderson is one of the first to emphasize the constructive role of the media in bringing about the nation-state. As part of a convergence between the technology of printing and capitalism, the rise of print media is seen as the catalyst for the creation of the nation-state as we know it today. One the one hand, print technology and capitalist expansion allowed for the wide dissemination of novels and newspapers, which in turn supported the construction and propagation of myths and narratives of common origin, belongingness, and common destiny. At the same time, print media allowed readers to imagine themselves as part of the same community with others, whom they would never see and who lived miles away. They, furthermore, allowed for the wide dissemination of a standardized language, which would be adopted as the nation's official language. In terms of both technologies and contents the media were pivotal in the creation or imagining of the nation-state.

It is this emphasis on ideas and cultures, and on print capitalism and media – the combination of historical, cultural, and material elements – that is especially useful for our purposes. Firstly, Anderson's insistence on the creative aspects of nationalism is crucial: if we can imagine the nation as a united political community, then we can imagine it as capable of including various others, even if these do not necessarily belong to the "historical" narrative of the nation. In other words, imagination is the key to the development of a new kind of community that can accommodate difference. Nothing is a priori excluded, nothing is given. Indeed, creole nationalism is the very example of this kind of extended and inclusive imagining of the nation.

Secondly, however, the limitations of the nation are present: the community must be limited – otherwise we would lose it altogether, it would merge with other communities. And that means that there must be boundaries of belongingness. Thirdly, if the nation is to be sovereign, to govern itself, then it must come up with rules as to who belongs and how. Thus, although this account creates ample room for difference, it stresses also the inherently limited character of the nation, and consequently its limited acceptance of difference.

Moreover, Anderson recognizes the importance of historical and material factors. In his 1992 lecture at the University of Amsterdam, and in various interviews since then, Anderson discussed the importance of the rise of global media, such as satellite television and the internet, in the development of long-distance nationalism. Through these media, as Anderson puts it, some of the most ardent nationalists live in countries other than their own: Sikh nationalists in the USA and Canada, Jewish nationalists in the USA, Turkish nationalists in Germany, and so on. From our point of view, and notwithstanding some of the criticisms levelled against Anderson, his perspective opens up important avenues to understand not only nationalism, but also the development of multiculturalism in nation-states previously imagined as stable, homogenous communities. Moreover, Anderson's perspective allows an exploration of the different ways in which multiculturalism has been conceived and applied across the world. Following Anderson, just as the nation has been imagined in different styles, and also in response to what was there before it, various approaches to multiculturalism have emerged as a function of the way in which the nation has been imagined in the first place. But more importantly, out of the "canon" of thinkers of nationalism, Anderson emerges as the one who appears to allow for the simultaneous existence of nationalism and the nation-state and difference, precisely because of the nature of the nation as an imagined community.

2.1.3 The curious case of ethnosymbolism

Finally, a discussion of approaches to nationalism wouldn't be complete without a reference to the perspective known as ethnosymbolism. One of the most well-known scholars of nationalism, whose work has been pivotal in understanding nationalism and the nation, is Anthony Smith (see 1986, 1998). His perspective, known as ethnosymbolism, forms a unique contribution to theories of nationalism in that he attempts to provide a bridge between modernism and primordialism. Smith discusses the nation as a modern form of organization, highlighting the relationship between the nation and modernity, but he also focuses on the importance of ancient myths and symbols in bringing and holding the nation together. In this respect, he accounts for the persistence of the nation, but disagrees with views of an entirely modern nation.

Ethnosymbolism posits a continuity between pre-modern and modern forms of belongingness, arguing that the nation is characterized by some persistent features that follow it across time. These are its myths, especially myths of ethnic similarity and proximity, and the myth of a "golden age." Smith's argument is that nations rely on a set of myths about themselves, about belongingness and glorious histories, which hold them together and sustain and justify their existence, while also mobilizing them if necessary. These myths, in this sense, are perennial: they follow the nation across time. Pivotal in the sustenance and communication of these myths are the nation's intellectuals – the poets, authors, and academics, especially historians. They are responsible for the continuity of the nation's myths, for providing bridges between past and present and for disseminating these to the nation's members (Conversi, 2006). It doesn't, therefore, take a huge leap of imagination to infer the crucial role that media can play in this theory. However, and here is where things get complicated, the assumption is that people passively and uncritically receive and reproduce what they see in the media – an unwarranted assumption as media scholars have insisted (see Chapter 5). However, Smith remains convinced that the continuity of the symbols of the nations cannot be attributed to industrialism (Gellner), print capitalism (Anderson), or manipulation (Hobsbawm). For Smith the persistence of such myths implies that they are somehow linked to historical reality, at least in the sense that they have been continuously transmitted in the historical record (Smith, 1986: 15). The creation of a nation therefore cannot be *ex nihilo*; rather it has to follow and rely upon already established myths and symbols that have prefigured and structured an ethnic community. From this point of view, Smith does not accept the constructedness of the nation, but rather sees in it continuity and historical circumstance.

Although this position clearly deserves a more detailed treatment, we must insist here on the constructedness of the nation in terms more or less similar to those of Anderson because it provides the broader framework within which multiculturalism can exist and be supported. Conceding the existence of symbols and myths as ancient or primordial evidence of the ethnie that subsequently formed the nation may be seen as precluding the development of a multiculturalism that is premised on the equality of all citizens. As long as the nation is linked to an ethnie with ancient origins, anyone who does not have the same genealogy will be seen as separate, at best tolerated and at worst excluded by the nation. Perhaps there is still room for the imagining of ways in which both the ethnie and the "newcomers" can exist as equals – but this is precisely a way of imagining the existence of a nation beyond its ancient roots, myths and symbols towards its future, which, and here we must all agree, is a matter of common construction.

2.2 A Word on Globalization

The common element of the above approaches is that nations constitute a form of organization that is likely to persist over time. However, the rise of globalization has led many to question the continued viability of the nation-state. Globalization, defined as the intensification of interdependencies in the world leading to the world becoming "compressed" along with the consciousness and realization of this compression (Giddens, 1990; Robertson, 1992; Beck, 2000), challenges the main premises of the nation. These challenges may be summarized as economic, political, socio-cultural, and environmental. Specifically, the post–Second World War Bretton Woods system, which established a global governance of finances through institutions such as the IMF and the World Bank, actively undermines the ability of the nation to govern its own economy. This is even more so in the case of the Eurozone countries, whose financial policies are already decided upon not by their voters, but by the supranational institutions of the EU. In addition, the capitalist dynamic of expansion requires that nations expand beyond their borders in order to prosper, while at the same time they are increasingly reliant on imports from other nations. These developments appear to undermine the autonomy of nation-states.

Politically too, nations are losing sovereignty: the decreased ability of nations to dictate policy, which is the result both of the rise of supranational institutions and the growing interdependencies in the world. While nations rely on borders and territorial control, global media and transnational communication networks operate beyond borders, while increased human mobility transforms borders into porous formations. These movements of media, ideas, and persons, which Arjun Appadurai (1996) has called mediascapes, ideascapes, and ethnoscapes, offer different bases for identity undermining the one-culture character of the nation. Finally, environmental and eco-logical issues spread across nations, demanding concerted and multilateral action beyond the power of the nation-state.

In the midst of all these challenges, will the nation-state survive? Answers to this question depend on the theory one holds of the nation. Thus, perennialists might argue that globalization might affect the current form of the nation as an autonomous political community, but the community which formed the nation will never cease to exist. Similarly, ethnosymbolists might argue that the ethnie will remain for as long as it circulates myths of its existence. As evidence for this position one might cite the continuing power of ethnic identities to mobilize action, as seen in various independ-ence movements – for example, Kurds, Basques, Chechnyans, and North Ossetians. Marxist modernists such as Gellner and Hobsbawm might assume a more cynical or perhaps functional perspective, arguing that nations will remain for as long as they can serve capitalism, mobilizing and inventing symbols and narratives only secondarily in order to coat the economic basis of this (and indeed any other) form of community. A modified modernist position following Anderson might hold that nations will sur-vive in a changed form: if the nation is imagined as a community inhabiting and ruling over a certain territory and sharing certain values, then it can be reimagined along different lines. This position, which may be termed "tranformationalist," is shared by important contributors to the debate on globalization, such as David Held (1999). They would welcome a cosmopolitan world order, where we would be citizens of the world rather than parochial citizens of a nation-state. This, in political terms, would empower all of us and enable us to take decisions for the best not only of our region and territory but of the world as a whole. Clearly this position requires that the nation-state is transformed into something else, losing much of its "nationalistic" core. But does this also mean that problems of ethnocentrism and racism will become obsolete? Much as we would want this to happen, it is unlikely. A world organization would emphasize and amplify the challenges of living with and recognizing diversity, and of finding just ways of managing conflict and issues of wealth distribution.

2.3 Conclusions

Understanding the nation, its past, present, and future, is not an easy feat. Evidence for the hold that the nation, and of course the underlying ethnie, has over us are abundant. These range from the ridiculous to the tragic: they include the various nationalisms of the Eurovision Song Contest, flag waving in the Olympic Games, acts that some define as terrorism and some as independence movements, such as those in

Table 2.1 Theories of nationalism

Theories of the nation	Main arguments	Provision for diversity	Role of the media
Primordialism (van den Berghe, 1967)	Nations are bound together by blood ties and culture	None: the nation as an exclusive community	None: the media merely serve as platforms for the expression of the nation's will
Perennialism (Hastings, 1997)	Ethnie always present	None: the nation as the "chosen people"	As above: the media represent and express the national community
Modernism I: nations and industry (Gellner, 1983)	Nations, as a result of need to industrialize; serve capitalist functions	None: nationalism responsible for genocide	The media help construct the nation; the media's language and style are more important than the message
Modernism II: invented traditions (Hobsbawm and Ranger, 1983)	Nations are built on invented traditions which hold them together in order to serve capitalism	Only insofar as difference can be assimilated and subsumed in invented tradition	The media help disseminate and reproduce invented traditions; the media's role is crucial in maintaining the nation
Modernism III: imagined communities (Anderson, 1983/1991)	Nations are the outcome of print capitalism and operate as imagined communities	Yes: nations can be reimagined across different lines	The media are the catalyst for the creation of the nation: the convergence between print technology and capitalism led to imagined communities
Ethnosymbolism (Smith, 1998)	Past-present continuity on the basis of shared myths and symbols	Some, but discriminatory: those not sharing the myths cannot be part of the nation-ethnie	The media as disseminators of founding myths and symbols

Spain by Basque separatists, in Israel by Palestinians, in Turkey by Kurds, in Chechnya and in Tibet, to name but a few. But this is not enough to help us explain what the nation is and how it has come about. The main line of disagreement is the extent to which the nation is a recent form of political organization coinciding with the advent of modernity.

While the various positions are summarized in table 2.1, it must be said from the outset that all positions have interesting and convincing points to make, and it is not easy to dismiss any of them out of hand. However, we are concerned here with the accommodation and management of diversity; hence, we must identify the perspective that is more likely to lead to ways in which difference can be accepted. And this, we have argued in this chapter, is more likely to be a modernist perspective because it allows for the dynamism of the nation and the way in which it is imagined and, crucially, disseminated. It is only within a dynamic, fluid, and ever-changing environment that difference can not only survive but flourish. If we theorize the nation as a primordial or perennial community that continues in a more or less similar form throughout history, then the role of diversity in contributing to the nation's character is denied. On the other hand, the role of the nation's history and political and economic context must be taken equally seriously in determining the treatment of diversity. This is the topic of the next chapter.

3
Varieties of Multiculturalism

Each nation-state, characterized by sovereignty over its territories, drafts its own laws and policies that dictate who belongs to the nation and under what circumstances, and what their rights and responsibilities are. From this point of view, immigration and integration policies are very closely linked with modes of citizenship. More specifically, as we noted in our earlier discussion, sovereign nation-states have to come up with rules of belongingness: these correspond directly to citizenship laws. Such laws determine who is a citizen of which state, and what rights and responsibilities they enjoy. In many countries, such laws have been inherited from the past, often long before the current wave of immigration, long before "globalization" became part of our everyday life, and long before the rise of supra-national institutions and global politics. Such laws, moreover, draw upon what Adrian Favell (1998) has termed "public philosophies," or commonsense understandings of what the nation is about, and who has the right to claim citizenship. They represent, in other words, deeply enshrined beliefs and views regarding the nation. Some of these may be seen as corresponding to the theories we discussed above, showing an interaction between theories and practices – commonsense beliefs and actions – which in turn are coded into policies. Finally, we should note that, although these are resilient and resistant to change, they can and do change as a result of shifts in public opinions, beliefs, and actions, and as a function of shifts in global politics.

3.1 A Typology of European Multiculturalism

To speak of European multiculturalism as a single variety is somewhat misleading. Despite efforts by the European Union to harmonize immigration and integration policy across all its member states, to this date these remain diverse and variable across Europe. In a well-known publication, Adrian Favell studied the historical and political background of immigration policies in Europe, arguing that diverse "public philosophies" lead to diverse practices and policies vis-à-vis multiculturalism. In his *Philosophies of Integration* (1998) Favell focused on the UK and France as providing two opposing models of integration – we may term these the pluralistic and republican models respectively. In a similar vein, Christian Joppke compared the logics and the resulting policies of the US, Germany, and the UK. While we shall discuss the case of the US in the next section, Joppke's discussion of German multiculturalism provides yet another label: we may term this the "ethnic" multicultural model.

3.1.1 Multiculturalism in former empires: UK and France

Beginning with the two former empires, the UK and France, their obvious differences in their philosophies, practices, and policies are very clear and may help us frame our discussion. Precisely because of their past as colonial powers, the European metropolises of London and Paris met an influx of people from across the globe. Arriving first as slaves, servants, or even as exotic curiosities, people from across the world ended up settling in the great cities of Britain and France, eventually forming sizeable groups. In addition, Britain accepted refugees from various revolutions, upheavals, and wars, from the French Revolution to the Jewish pogroms in Russia, as well as Irish settlers fleeing poverty. However, the great big wave of migration took place after the dissolution of the former imperial powers, following the Second World War. In Britain the symbolic starting date was June 21, 1948, with the arrival in London of HMS *Empire Windrush*, following an 8,000-mile journey from the Caribbean, carrying about 500 Caribbean men and women. This marked the beginning of a wave of immigration from the Caribbean in the 1960s, followed by immigration from South Asia in the 1960s and 1970s, firmly establishing the UK as a mosaic of cultures. Until the late 1960s, settlement in the UK had been straightforward, with members of the so-called Commonwealth, i.e. the territories that formed part of the British Empire, having the right to settle in the UK, as they carried a British passport. A series of successive changes in the immigration laws, however, made it harder and harder for new immigrants to settle, especially those of a different ethnicity. The Immigration Act of 1971 gave the right to settle only to those who had a parent or grandparent born in the UK, excluding most of those who had no ethnic connection to Britain.

In these terms, successive legislation on immigration firmly shifted membership towards an ethnic model and placed more and more restrictions on new immigrants. At the same time, however, these restrictive immigration policies were accompanied by a very generous set of integration policies aimed as successfully integrating newcomers in the British society. Thus, the three most salient aspects of the UK case include, firstly, a shift from a civic to an ethnic model of membership; secondly, very strict immigration controls based on the assumption of zero immigration; thirdly, well-intended and thought-through policies aimed as removing discrimination and establishing equal opportunity. Joppke (1996) argues that the key to understanding British immigration and integration policies is to locate them in the context of Britain's devolution from an empire to a nation-state. At the end of the Second World War, about 800 million people had the status of "British subject" with the right to settle in the UK. As Joppke rightly points out, the decision to move from a membership based on allegiance to the crown towards a national-territorial model was not only a pragmatic one, but also one corresponding to the defining right of a nation-state to control its boundaries. But the result of this shift was to divide Britain across racial lines, since it was now formed on the basis of a "white" centre and a "black" periphery. Immigration control then essentially amounted to a control along racial lines; highlighting the racism of this approach, *The Economist* wrote in 1982 that "Britain preferred white immigrants" (quoted in Joppke, 1996: 478). The mantra repeated by successive British governments was that Britain was not an immigration country and that it accepted zero immigration. Tough controls were established, often landing Britain in trouble for breaching human rights. But, on the other hand, these stringent controls were accompanied by serious attempts to integrate immigrants. In sum, the specificity and logic of the UK policy is clear in the words of the British politician Roy Hattersley in a 1965 Labour Government White Paper: "Without integration, limitation is inexcusable; without limitation, integration is impossible" (cited in Joppke, 1996: 497, n. 124).

But how was integration conceived in the UK? This is a central issue in understanding the British variety of multiculturalism, and its crucial lines of difference from other European countries. Perhaps because of its rules of devolved government within its empire, in which local governments ran things and reported to the colonial authorities, Britain saw no need to assimilate difference and to make it conform to a single model common to all. In a remarkable statement, Roy Jenkins, the Home Secretary in 1966, defined integration "not as a flattening process of assimilation but as equal opportunity, accompanied by cultural diversity, in an atmosphere of mutual tolerance" (cited in Joppke, 1996: 480). The outcome of this was the establishment of a "race-relations" industry, consisting of publicly financed professionals who oversaw the application of the relevant race-relations legislation and consulted various public bodies on their anti-discrimination policies. A cornerstone of this policy has been the ethnic monitoring of various bodies and organizations to ensure equal representation of minorities. Although not instituting positive discrimination policies, as we shall see in discussing the US, the bottom line of the British legislation was to ensure equal opportunity while maintaining cultural pluralism. Thus, it made concessions such as allowing different codes of dress to some groups (e.g. turbans, shalwars, hijabs, etc.) and more controversially allowing different schooling, through religious schools for Catholics, Muslims, Jews, and other groups, while also widening the curriculum to include the histories and cultural practices of the various groups that comprised multicultural Britain.

Although this policy was to a large degree commendable in its acknowledgement of cultural difference, Joppke rightly points to several problems associated with it. Firstly, despite, or perhaps because of, its insistence on cultural difference, it ended up reifying cultural difference and establishing firm boundaries between groups. One could not think of oneself as British, but rather as South Asian, Irish, White, Other, etc., reflecting the classifications used in forms of "ethnic monitoring." In addition, civil unrest, with race-related riots almost every decade in the past forty years, has shown that this version of multicultural policy has failed in its quest to resolve tensions between communities. Moreover, the shock of the so-called "home-grown" terrorists" and the London bombings of 2005 by British citizens, products of years of multicultural policies, forced a debate on, and rethink of, the notion of multicultural Britain. Thus, as a well-known report has argued, what Britain needs is more social cohesion. The Cantle Report into Community Cohesion (2001), following a series of rioting in Oldham and other cities in Northern England, highlighted the dangers of a "divided Britain" and suggested policies aimed at creating a common framework and set of values which would contribute to overcoming divisions across communities. The Cantle Report certainly signalled a change in both policy and rhetoric in the UK, which sought to move away from "divisive multiculturalism" to policies establishing social cohesion.

The debate on multiculturalism in Britain shifted therefore from a recognition and acceptance of cultural difference within a frame of mutual tolerance towards emphasizing commonality, cohesion, overcoming divisions, and a return to so-called "British values." British intellectuals such as Yasmin Alibhai-Brown (2004) and Kenan Malik (2005), but also Trevor Phillips (2005), the chair of the Commission for Racial Equality, held official multicultural policies responsible for creating group enclaves and segregation, for supporting what was at best ineffective and conservative community leadership, and ultimately for failing to address the continued inequalities between communities in Britain. Parallel to this line of argument, several British commentators underlined the role that multicultural policies played in creating a victim mentality, whereby personal failures and failures of community leadership were attributed to racism and discrimination. And, in addition, multicultural policies were branded as illiberal and undemocratic because they expected community members to be represented by unelected community leaders, making self-representation outside the community difficult if not impossible. However, we must make a distinction here between the rather conservative calls for a return to (which?) British values and calls to reform official multicultural policies, usually associated with the left, and also with British descendents of foreign-born parents. While the former call for a firm establishment of a core set of values to which one must conform or else, the latter seek to open up a debate about what are the best ways to re-engage an alienated generation of mostly British Muslim and black young people and how best to ensure equality.

While in Britain the debate is now moving to the issue of social cohesion and a united Britain, in France, the debate started from a core republican France, to which everybody belonged in the same way. The Fifth Republic, the current constitution of the Republic of France, was established in 1958, following the governmental collapse after the Algerian war of independence. The establishment of the Fifth Republic was the culmination of several centuries of turbulent history in which France alternated between republicanism, monarchy, and imperialist expansion, and suffered defeats and losses but also rebirths and regenerations. Like Britain, France was an imperial power that had to rethink itself as a nation-state. Unlike in Britain, however, the form that this rethinking took was one of unity and fraternity, in which loyalty to the Republic and equality before the law led to the formulation of an assimilationist policy vis-à-vis not only newcomers to France, but also towards those inhabitants of territories ruled by France. Thus, unlike Britain's more loose system of imperial government, the French empire was oriented towards the export of French language and culture, and the assimilation of all inhabitants of colonies into France. Revolving around the ideals of the French Revolution, equality, fraternity, and liberty, imperial France sought to export and spread these indeed universal ideas across the world, and to socialize all natives into becoming French.

If this corresponded to the ideal behind French assimilationism, there were more pragmatic reasons for it as well. Both Silverman (1992) and Collett (2007) point our that France has had the greatest number of immigrants in the last 200 years, due to low birth rates, labour shortages, wars, and so on. It therefore needed to understand itself as a nation based on voluntary association and commonality rather than on common descent. Most clearly, this attitude is captured in the philosopher Ernest Renan's 1882 speech to the Sorbonne with the title "What Is a Nation?" Renan responds to this question by posing the nation as a voluntary association of people, who daily affirm their shared values and ideas, and their common past, present, and future. These aspects, voluntary association and commonality, formed the basis for French assimilationism, which then sought to impose French culture across the territories it controlled, often at the expense of local cultures. This "*mission civilisatrice,*" "civilizing mission," was the justification for much of France's colonialism, which saw the forced "Westernization" of natives as civilization. On the other hand, by "civilizing" natives, it accepted them as equals, offering them the same rights and responsibilities as any other French citizen. Upon the collapse of the French empire and faced with increased immigration both from Europe and especially from North Africa and Asia, France followed the same model internally. Any foreign-born newcomer would enjoy the same rights as a French citizen, provided that they fully accepted, and were assimilated into, the French culture. Notwithstanding the patronizing aspects of these ideas, they come across as fair, at least insofar as they offer equality to new settlers. Moreover, people are assimilated on an individual basis, rather than as part of a community. Nevertheless, as Silverman (1992) is quick to point out, the assimilation policies of France betray a badly hidden racism, with foreigners tacitly classified into those easy to assimilate and those who resist assimilation. And those who "resist" assimilation just happen to be those whose race or religion differs. Silverman (1992: 105) cites a 1945 speech by the then President de Gaulle, who spelled out his parameters for the ethnic constitution of the immigration that France was to receive, based on ideas about ethno-cultural proximity. According to this ideal scenario, 50 percent of the new immigrants would come from Northern Europe, followed by those from South and East Europe, followed by those from North Africa, and so on in decreasing quotas in order to achieve an "ethnic balance." More recently, during the 2005 riots in the Parisian suburbs, or *banlieues*, the then Minister of the Interior (and current President) Nicolas Sarkozy suggested that the "immigrants" participating in the riots be deported. But, as Collett (2007) points out, these "immigrants" were in fact French citizens and the reference to them as "immigrants" is a covert reference to their identification as non-white. Thus, the French assimilation policy, ostensibly based on individuality and equality, is evidently not as color blind as some of its supporters insist.

In practice, assimilation policies meant that although people were allowed to practice their religion, customs, and so on (insofar as those did not clash with French values and customs), they enjoyed no special treatment or indeed any concessions. At the same time, children born to foreign parents had, until 1993, automatic rights to French citizenship. In 1993 and then in 1998, the law was amended in order to offer the right to choose to become a French citizen, thereby affirming the voluntary basis of belonging to the nation. One of the most controversial French policies is that of public secularism. The well known French laïcité resulted in the banning of any religious symbols at schools, effectively forbidding Muslim girls from wearing headscarves. But behind such equalizing policies lies continued resentment, inequality, and discrimination, culminating in severe civil unrest, not unlike that encountered in the UK. The most recent riots of 2005 were considered as symptomatic of the social problems faced by second- and even third-generation immigrants, who, according to

French policy, had to be fully assimilated. But to insist that all French citizens are equal fails to pay attention to the continued bigotry and racism faced by some of these citizens. It fails to address problems and needs specific to this segment of the citizenry, and masks the high rates of unemployment and chronic lack of opportunity concentrated among those communities. Collett argues that France needs to rethink political equality alongside economic and material differences. The debate on multiculturalism in France is therefore still marked by a widespread acceptance of the principles of equality and liberty, but alongside an increasing need to address the material, social, and cultural conditions that sustain such principles.

3.1.2 Blood and soil: multiculturalism in Germany

The French insistence on the voluntary nature of the nation, which clearly resonates with the modernist ideas of the nation as a constructed community, is in stark contrast with the German Romantic idea of the nation as *Volk*, denoting an organically connected community of people sharing not only a blood line, but culture, language, and territory as well. Germany's history of migration began with emigration. In the nineteenth century, Germans massively emigrated from Germany, mostly destined for the US, but also heading for Canada and Australia. Germans formed the second-largest immigrant group in the US after the English, moving to the States primarily as economic migrants, but also to avoid political and religious prosecution (Kivisto, 2002). Around about 1885, the situation was reversed. Germany was establishing itself as an industrial nation and experiencing increased demand for labor. This was resolved through immigration mainly from the East, with Polish workers moving in, but also through Jewish settlement in German cities.

Despite the contribution of immigrants to the regeneration of the pre-Second World War German economy, they faced hostility and a restrictive legal regime that prevented them from claiming citizenship. This was, as Kivisto documents (2002), a result of the dominant understanding of what it meant to be German. For Germany, citizenship and ethnicity are fused, so that one can only claim citizenship if one can claim a German bloodline or lineage. This is known as the principle of *jus sanguinis* – the right of blood – according to which national membership is determined by blood line. This principle is opposed to the principle of *jus soli* – the right of the soil – which refers to the right to claim national membership if one was born in the territory of a given nation. Germany has been considered the example *par excellence* of *jus sanguinis*, which points to an understanding of the German nation as an ethnically homogenous community, corresponding directly with primordial conceptions of the nation. Foreigners could never therefore claim belongingness to the German nation, notwithstanding their cultural proximity. The implications of this definition of the German nation, based on a notion of exclusion of others, were made tragically clear in the Nazi era, during which Jewish inhabitants of Germany were rendered stateless, thereby legally opening the way for their internment in concentration camps.

Under the weight of this history, post-war Germany sought to reformulate both its laws and its commonsense understandings of what it means to be German. In common with other Western European nations, divided West Germany invited immigrant labour to deal with labour shortages. Guest workers, the famous *Gastarbeiter*, began to arrive from East and Southern Europe, but also from Turkey, and Northern Africa.

These guest workers helped achieve the German economic miracle, contributing to the rise of West Germany as the strongest economy of Europe. But they were understood to be temporary settlers, who would subsequently leave the country. By the 1970s it was clear that this was not the case. Having lived in the country for at least ten years, many of these guest workers felt settled, brought in their family members, and had no intention of returning to their country of origin. Germany had made no provision for the long-term integration of these people into Germany. While they were allowed permanent residence, they had no citizenship or political rights. The second and third generations, the children of the initial immigrants, born and raised in Germany, were culturally German but were not offered citizenship rights. Joppke (1996) argues that this situation, coupled with Germany's history of persecution of foreigners, led to a heated and polarized debate in which "friends of foreigners" stood up against "enemies of foreigners," defending an idealized image of foreigners. Joppke (1996: 470) quotes a slogan of the early 1990s that shows both the polarization and also the paradoxical nature of the debate in Germany: "Foreigners, don't leave us alone with the Germans!"

The complexity of the German case was further compounded by the reunification of Germany in 1990, and by the return of hundreds of thousands ethnic Germans – *Aussiedler* – who were granted automatic citizenship rights, betraying the ethnic basis of German citizenship laws. Finally, and under considerable pressure from the political left, in 1999, the Bundestag, the German Parliament, passed a new immigration law, finally recognizing that past immigration to Germany was permanent (Kivisto, 2002). The new law finally granted citizenship rights to children of immigrants born on German soil, but still precludes dual citizenship after the age of twenty-three years (Kivisto, 2002). But for Germany, this signalled an official recognition of a movement towards a multiethnic, multicultural and multi-faith country (Benhabib, 2002).

These three cases represent the three main varieties of multiculturalism in Europe, and other European countries may be seen as falling in one or the other. For instance, while the Netherlands and Sweden follow a multicultural policy based on the recognition of difference that resembles the British model, Greece follows a *jus sanguinis* model of citizenship. However, most of the countries that have received immigration relatively recently, such as some of the Southern European countries, have sought to legislate against immigration, focusing on strict border controls, but without any provision for dealing with the integration of those who live in the country. Immigration into such countries is characterized by high levels of illegality and irregularity with periodic amnesties and regularizations, which in practice encourage more illegal migration (Geddes, 2003). The lack of provision for the integration of immigrants and their children in the host country betrays the refusal of some countries to wake up to the realities of globalization and global migration flows. At the same time, this refusal is a time bomb, waiting to explode: how sustainable is it in the long run to have a segment of a population deprived of political rights, or the right to have their cultural specificity and needs recognized?

On the other hand, immigration and integration policies in Europe are increasingly influenced by the European Union, pushing towards a harmonization across its territories. Although this implies the adoption of the EU anti-discrimination policy, which is one means of protecting migrants, it has also resulted in a partial loss of the variety that we observed above. But what is the direction that this harmonization is taking? Joppke (2007) suggests that this convergence is taking the form of a civic integration process which, while differing from assimilation, emphasizes similarity and commonality. In November 2004, the EU agreed on a set of common basic principles underlying the immigration and integration policies of its member states. These include, among others, that integration is a two-way process, with both migrants and host societies mutually adapting themselves to each other; that migrants should respect the EU political principles of liberty, democracy, and respect for human rights; that employment is a key part of the integration process; that there is a necessity to have a basic knowledge of the host society; and that migrants have the right to be treated equally (in Joppke, 2007: 3–5).

In these, Joppke sees a shift from the requirement to assimilate to the culture of the host country to the endorsement of a political liberalism while respecting different cultures. This has echoes of Jürgen Habermas' concept of constitutional patriotism, which we will discuss in the next chapter, but it also means that the host country is under no obligation to support immigrant cultures. Similarly, Joppke points out that there is an overall shift of the burden from the state to the new citizens themselves, who must be proactive in learning about the new culture, adopting its political principles, finding and maintaining employment, and so on. Autonomy and self-sufficiency are the new keywords of this integration. The host society, on the other hand, needs to set some procedures of civic integration to measure and test the levels of integration.

Thus, the Netherlands has implemented a Newcomer Integration Law (1998), comprising a twelve-month course in Dutch language, culture, and politics, as well as preparation for employment. The revised 2006 version further requires that migrants pay in full for this course. Joppke (2007) notes that this type of civic integration is becoming increasingly common, and sees in it a shift towards the obligations of migrants rather than their rights. This, in turn, he associates with the repressive side of liberalism, in which people must govern and control themselves: they are obliged, as it were, to reinvent themselves in terms dictated by liberal individualism, in order to survive in what Joppke calls a global competition state. We can understand this as a shift towards neoliberalism, which, although containing some of the main political principles of liberalism, also has a dark, repressive side.

3.2 Multiculturalism in Immigration Countries: US and Canada

While most of Europe exists in a kind of denial of immigration, countries such as the US and Canada explicitly understand themselves as immigration countries. They were formed by immigrants, who fled their countries of origin because of poverty or political or religious persecution. They were formed on a voluntary basis, on the basis of a "contract" between citizens and the state, a constitution that codified and enshrined the basic and important rights and obligations of citizens. Another important characteristic of these countries is that, while they understand themselves as nations of immigrants, they both contain groups of indigenous people, whose rights over territory, culture, and history are at once accepted and marginalized. Because they were formed on the basis of immigrants and because they had to address the needs of the indigenous people, these countries have a long history of policies related to immigrant and indigenous groups. However, while both Canada and the US were formed under similar circumstances, their approaches differ. The US approach is famously known as the "melting pot" approach, while Canada has the distinction of being the first country to mobilize the term multiculturalism in public policy usage, as well as to draft and implement multicultural policies.

As many commentators have noted, successive waves of immigration have shaped the constitution of the US. In the early nineteenth century this was primarily immigration from North and Western Europe. From about 1880 until the immigration restrictions of 1924, the second wave of immigrants arrived from East and South Europe, while the third wave, which followed the Immigration and Nationality Act of 1965, comprised immigrants from Latin America and Asia (see *inter alia* Castles and Miller, 1993/2003; Joppke, 1996; Kivisto, 2002). These waves of immigration into the US required a construction of an identity beyond ethnic commonalities. In the US, this was accomplished through invoking an overarching American identity based on the political criterion of loyalty to the constitution. This meant that new immigrants were offered political rights, while their descendants acquired American citizenship automatically if they were born on American soil. The political basis of American identity led to the creation of a somewhat paradoxical situation, whereby American society comprised several ethnic groups which retain their cultural distinctiveness while at the same time holding a strong identification with the US. As Joppke (1996) indicates, the ethnic constitution of American society has served the unique purpose of holding together, organizing, and controlling groups of newcomers, while allowing them political representation, through lobbying and ethnic voting.

However, the dominant metaphor characterizing American society was that of the melting pot, which referred to the creation of a new kind of culture, representing a fusion of all the nationalities and cultures that went into forming the US. Kivisto (2002) writes that the melting pot metaphor was most clearly articulated in a theatrical play by Israel Zangwill in 1908, which captured the popular ideas on immigration in the early twentieth century. However, the melting pot metaphor was subsequently used in order to justify a series of "Americanization" campaigns, in which newcomers were in fact assimilated into the dominant WASP (White Anglo-Saxon Protestant) culture. Names were changed, languages were forgotten and bypassed in favor of English, and new immigrants were encouraged to adopt American cultural practices. Underlying such attempts was a divide between those considered easy to assimilate and those seen as "unmeltable" (Kivisto, 2002). The two factors determining assimilation were race and religion. Careful readers will note here the similarity between these ideas and practices and Ernest Gellner's idea of the so-called "inhibitors of social entropy." Thus, the dominant ethno-cultural groups in the USA in the early twentieth century felt that the US should recruit immigrants that were easy to assimilate; in practice these were immigrants whose culture resembled the WASP culture of America, hence those originating from North-west Europe. This preference was codified in the Immigration Act of 1924, which introduced national quotas. While not explicitly prohibiting immigration from South and East Europe, the Act limited the number of immigrants from these regions to only 2 percent of the number of those already settled in the USA. In addition it prohibited immigration from Asia, on the basis that "non-whites" could not become naturalized Americans as per the Naturalization Law of 1790, which only allowed "free white persons" to be naturalized.

While these racist laws form the historical background to American immigration, Kivisto argues that things changed in the 1960s, as a result of both the civil rights movement and the 1965 Nationality Act, which abolished national quotas and repealed the racist character of the 1924 legislation. The result was that multiethnic and multiracial immigration to the USA increased, alongside an increase in the awareness of ethno-cultural distinctiveness. In the words of Nathan Glazier's and Daniel Patrick Moynihan's classic work *Beyond the Melting Pot* "the point about the melting pot … is that it did not happen" (quoted in Joppke, 1996: 464). What Glazer and Moynihan were suggesting was the failure of "Americanization" policies to succeed in replacing ethnic cultures with an American one. This may be attributed to the persistent nature of ethnic identification (see the discussion of "primordialist" theories in Chapter 2). Alternatively, it may be seen as a kind of "return of the repressed," with a resurgence of ethnic cultures following the explosion of the civil rights movements that allowed for the free expression of thoughts and ideas and encouraged pride in one's identity. Whatever the origin of this resurgence and reaffirmation of ethnic identities, the end result was a multiculturalism that led to a quest for "public status" for ethno-racial identities (Joppke, 1996). Thus, while the American model of national citizenship only allows for the concurrent existence of ethnic and particularistic identities insofar as these remain private, multiculturalism requires the public recognition of these identities, thereby undermining the universalistic basis of citizenship.

In other words, as a number of commentators, including Glazer (1975), Joppke (1996), and Kivisto (2002), argue that the issue of race is pivotal in the debate over integration and immigration in the USA. Joppke argues that the US situation is a paradoxical story in which a society that began as an egalitarian, color- and ethnicity-blind society ends up as one of the most colour conscious ones. The most straightforward way of retelling this story is that the intense racism and segregationist "Jim Crow" laws of the USA led to the black civil rights movements that sought a redress in the form not only of equal access policies but also policies explicitly seeking to counter previous or hidden discrimination. These are known as affirmative action policies, and they are based on the assumption that, in order to equalize society, the previously discriminated-against minorities need a helping hand both in education and employment. These policies, also known as positive discrimination policies, allow for the preferential treatment of people coming from certain ethnic backgrounds when it comes to applying for higher-education institutions or seeking employment. But in order to implement, monitor, and regulate these policies, the state had to reinforce race-related segregation or at least fragmentation of society. The US does not have merely American citizens, but African-American, Hispanic-American, Asian-American, and so on. Moreover, because of the privileges offered by these programs, ethnic groups are incentivized in thinking of, and modeling, themselves as minority groups, seeking to benefit from affirmative action policies.

Notwithstanding the necessity to counter racism and recognize ethnic and cultural distinctiveness, as Joppke argues, the end result in the USA was a top-down elite-driven culture alongside a certain political opportunity structure that sustains this version of multiculturalism as the demand for group rights. Fundamentally, continues Joppke, the problem is that there is a clash between the American (and more broadly immigrant) tradition of "never looking back" and of "forging a new identity," and the interpretation of multiculturalism as particularistic rights and entitlements based on one's ethno-cultural origin. And perhaps we could add here that another pressing problem for this version of multiculturalism is that a look in the current statistics in education achievement and employment will show that discrimination persists, and that affirmative action has failed in its objective to eradicate racism.

What is the future for American multiculturalism? It certainly has its share of critics. Nathan Glazer rather fatalistically observes that "we are all multiculturalists now" (1997), while Arthur Schlesinger (1992) contends that America is disunited precisely because of such policies. For the respected liberal historian Arthur Schlesinger, multiculturalism means the "disuniting" of America, the loss of the melting pot dream, which would signal a new, stronger, and united society forged out of a fusion between newcomers and those already settled. Instead the "new tribalism" that has replaced the melting pot dream will, for Schlesinger, end up in conflict. People are classified on the basis of ethnic and racial criteria, not as individuals, thereby undermining the individualism that has long fed American culture. Multicultural education results in segregation along ethno-cultural lines, with blacks being taught at black-only schools, Hispanics taught in Spanish in Hispanic schools and so on: this is the disuniting of America, which Schlesinger argues will lead to conflict. His remedy is to return to a model revolving around the idea *e pluribus unum*: out of many cultures one. But Schlesinger is quick to point out that the old melting pot idea was indeed racist, that there were mistakes made, which needed to be addressed through changes in educational curricula and in other spheres of life to redress the Anglo-Saxon hegemony. On this basis, Nathan Glazer (1997) suggests that there is no going back to a period when there was a single American history, culture, education, and so on. For him multiculturalism is the price America is paying for its racism and its failure to offer equal opportunities and recognition to black Americans. His remedy is to rethink the American ideals of liberty and equality for all in a non-racist way, rather than to implement a divisive version of multiculturalism.

Critiques of multiculturalism take on a rather more shrill tone in Samuel Huntington's *Who Are We?* (2004), in which the author of the controversial *Clash of Civilizations* argues that America's core Anglo-Saxon Protestant ideals and cultures should remain firm against both the Hispanic-Catholic and Muslim and Asian cultures that seek to relativize if not overwhelm them. If nothing else, Huntington's book betrays the fears of (part of) "white" America and shows the hidden aspects of the American debate on multiculturalism.

On the other hand, Canada appears much more certain as to the positive effects that multiculturalism has had on Canadian society. Canadian history mirrors in many ways the history of the USA, with new settlers displacing indigenous people, and with relatively generous immigration laws designed to address the labor and population shortages of the country. However, as Kivisto (2002) notes, there are important differences between these two countries. The most relevant of these for our purposes is the concurrent existence of two prosperous ethno-cultural communities: the Anglophone and Francophone communities. Relations between these communities have always been tense, with the result that no "melting pot" ideal ever emerged in Canada. Rather, both communities were keen to retain their cultural and linguistic heritage. Although the Anglophone community soon outnumbered the French one, recognition of the latter's specificity was granted as early as 1774, with the Quebec Act establishing its religious and linguistic rights, while it was also allowed to use French civil law. Until the middle of the twentieth century the three main groups that comprised Canada were the Anglophone and Francophone groups and the Canadian First Nations people – which represent about 3.7 percent of the total population. However, things changed as successive waves of immigration began to arrive in Canada, comprising the so-called third force in Canada. While initially Canada practiced a "whites only" immigration policy, the 1960s saw the liberalization of relevant laws, paving the way for Asian and African immigrants.

Thus, Canada had to reconfigure its ethnic relations on the basis of the continued existence of the Francophone community and its separatist movement, known as Quebec nationalism; the inflows of immigration from across the world; and the rise of indigenous movements, seeking redress for past wrongs and recognition of their rights over Canadian land (Kivisto, 2002). Multiculturalism – the term was first used by the Canadian Senator Paul Yuzyk in 1964 and it was implemented as a state policy in 1971 – was meant to replace policies that considered Canada a bilingual and bicultural society with policies that accord equal validity and respect to all the ethnicities and cultures encountered in Canada. Given the precedent of the Francophone community, and the advocacy of the First Nations groups, Canada was prepared to draft policies that were asymmetrical and aimed towards the preservation, rather than the assimilation, of cultures. This preservation of the "mosaic" character of Canadian multiculturalism has been seen as a guarantee of loyalty to Canada since its inclusiveness and equal respect of all cultures safeguards stability and promotes tolerance.

But such asymmetrical policies have proved controversial, especially when they concern recent immigrant groups rather than indigenous communities. A recent controversy concerns the application of Sharia law to Canadian Muslims. The controversy began in 2004, when the former Attorney General, Marion Boyd, suggested that, as with Jewish and Catholic groups in Ontario, some family disputes among Muslim couples could be resolved through voluntary resort to Sharia courts. This suggestion met a very vocal opposition because Sharia law treats men and women on an unequal basis. More importantly, it was seen as undermining the common basis of Canadian society. Eventually, the recommendation was rejected in September 2005 by the Premier of Ontario, Dalton McGuinty, who moreover said that he will ban all religious family courts in the Province (CBC, 26 May 2005; BBC, 12 September 2005).

Thus, Canada has one of the most clearly articulated policies of multiculturalism, leading to a vibrant debate whose positive effects in providing the basis for recognition and respect for identities alongside equal opportunities are well documented (Taylor, 1994; Kymlicka, 1995). However, alongside support for Canadian multiculturalism there exist a number of vocal critics, who are mainly concerned with the divisive effects of treating different groups in different ways. Authors such as Neil Bissondath (1994) and Kenneth McRoberts (1997) argue that multiculturalism has impeded rather than facilitated integration and that the everyday experience of Canadian citizens is one of ghettoized communities with little interaction. The problem for these critics is that Canada needs to draft policy that unites citizens and fosters a common identity rather than adopt policies that encourage people to think in terms of their ethnic identities.

Both the US and Canada, as well as Australia, whose policy we cannot cover here, but which follows similar dilemmas (see for instance, Castles and Miller, 1993/2003; Zappalà and Castles, 2000; Kivisto, 2002) illustrate the important issues involved in the processes of forging an immigrant nation, and creating an open yet circumscribed identity. All the cases covered so far in Europe and America locate the issues of multi-culturalism in dealing with relative newcomers, with the immigration of new groups into host societies, be they immigration nations or established ethno-national states. What happens in the case of nations that are constitutively multicultural, which have, from the very beginning of their existence, to recognize and deal with difference? This is the case of India and Nigeria, which we will cover next.

3.3 Constitutively Different: India and Nigeria

In some respects, the cases of India and Nigeria may not be seen as deserving separate treatment. Canada understands itself as a constitutively different nation, comprised of two charter groups, the Anglophone and the Francophone, as well as the First Nations group. In addition, the UK is also constituted by different nations: England, Wales, Scotland, and Northern Ireland. Indeed, the mono-cultural ethnic nation-state is more fiction than reality, since most nations encompass different ethno-cultural groups, be they recognized or not. But the cases with which we will deal here are unique in that they are explicitly acknowledging difference at the core of their exis-tence. Moreover, this difference is multiple and crosses over several areas: we are deal-ing with ethnic, cultural, linguistic, religious, tribal, caste, and class differences that somehow succeed in existing within unique and united states. How is such difference managed in these countries?

In September 2007, Shashi Tharoor, one of India's most prolific and well-known authors, and in 2009 Minister for External Affairs, began his speech to New York University with the following anecdote, encapsulating the uniqueness of India's multiculturalism. During celebrations of the forty-ninth anniversary of Indian Independence, Prime Minister Deve Gowda addressed the nation in Hindi, Indian's national language. But Deve Gowda was a Southern Indian from Karnataka, who couldn't speak a word of Hindi! The speech was written in his native Kannada script so that he could read it out. More recently, Tharoor related, a Roman Catholic Indian political leader of Italian origin, Sonia Gandhi, made way for a Sikh Prime Minister, Manmohan Singh, who was sworn in by a Muslim President, Abdul Kalam, in a country the population of which is 81 percent Hindu (Tharoor, 2007).

These anecdotes show the degree of diversity that characterizes India, which, with a population of 1 billion, is not only the world's most populous democracy, but also socially and culturally the most diverse. While the majority ethnic group is the Hindus, they occupy geographically diverse regions, hold multiple beliefs, and have different practices, forming an internally diverse group, which is also divided by castes and languages. In addition, India's population also includes Muslims (about 12 per cent), Sikhs, Buddhists, Christians, and Jains. India is the home of almost 100 languages and dialects, of which eighteen enjoy official recognition and protection (Bhattacharyya, 2003). Given the extent of India's diversity, how does it manage to remain a united state while safeguarding this diversity? The answer is both simple and complex.

Following the violence of the partition of the subcontinent between India and Pakistan in 1947, the Indian state decided to make multiculturalism the cornerstone of its existence and the most important basis of its legitimacy (Mitra, 2001). Multiculturalism was based on the twin principle of individual rights and protection of minorities, in a context in which there is no hegemonic religion. The Indian Constitution enshrines this twin principle, establishing India as a secular state, practicing neutrality vis-à-vis religious practices and beliefs, all the while protecting both individual and group rights (Mitra, 2001). When it comes to the regulation and management of the different communities, each group is – to a certain extent – self-governed, operating within its own religious and cultural frameworks, and administering its own personal law. This, argues Benhabib (2002), is a legacy of India's colonial rule. Warren Hastings, the Governor-General of India, required in 1772 that in matters of "inheritance, marriage, caste, and other religious usages, or institutions, the laws of the Koran with respect to the Mahometans, and those of the Shaster with respect to the Gentoos, shall be invariably adhered to" (originally in Mansfield, 1993: 145, cited in Benhabib, 2002: 93–4). When conflict arises, matters are dealt with by higher courts, but, by and large, India practices a kind of legal pluralism, religious tolerance, and coexistence that has gone far beyond anything that any Western nation has dared implement. This pluralism has certainly contributed to the well-being of India.

Mitra (2001) attributes this success to a fuzzy definition of both the Indian nation as such and multiculturalism itself. The founding fathers of India, he argues, evaded a very precise definition in order to avoid narrow interpretations that would lead to the exclusion of certain groups and to the hegemonic rise of others. For India to be truly multicultural, its own self-understanding must be fuzzy enough to allow for its various groups to imagine themselves as its members. Others, such as Bhattacharyya (2003), take a more institutional view, holding that India's multicultural success is due to the political decision to form a federation comprising different states. These states, in turn, correspond to territories which coincide with certain ethnic and especially linguistic groups. Often these states are the result of movements struggling for recognition of their distinctiveness. For Bhattachanyya the readiness with which India is prepared to accommodate such demands for recognition and autonomy further supports and firmly establishes its multiculturalism.

But behind these attempts to create a multicultural India one finds the ever-present specter of communal violence, which periodically erupts. Examples include the destruction of the Babri Mosque at Ayodhya in Uttar Pradesh by Hindu nationalists in 1992, rioting in Mumbai in January 1993, as well as, more recently, the Gujarat violence in 2002. Most of these events took place between Hindu and Muslim communities, although such violence has also affected the Sikh community as well. It is easy to attribute such violence to the failure of multiculturalism (see Embree, 1990), and several voices are critical of the possibility of India existing as a multicultural nation. Mitra (2001) attributes such pessimism to authors such as Salman Rushdie, who, in his novel *Midnight's Children* (1982), deplores India's inability to develop a common culture, remaining instead a "chutney," an eclectic mixture of unblended materials. However, communal violence in India may be seen as evidence of the attempt to create a "society" in India, rather than evidence of its failure (Chakrabarti, 2007). In Chakrabarti's Foucauldian argument, "society" exists only when it manages to banish internal wars to its outer limits. In these terms, post-colonial India is still in the process of creating this society, and periodic eruptions of violence are not an indication of failure but rather an indication that this construction is an ongoing process. Certainly, as Mitra argues, one can chose to be pessimistic or optimistic regarding the future of India as a united multicultural nation. Here perhaps we can side with Mitra and Tharoor, in adopting an optimistic view of the future of multicultural India.

Communal violence is also encountered in another post-colonial state, Nigeria, a country whose ethnic and religious diversity closely parallels that of India. An oil-rich country, Nigeria is a federation of some thirty-six states, which gained its independence from Britain in 1960. Since then, with the exception of the years 1979–1983, it was ruled by military juntas until the election of President Olusegun Obasanjo in 1999. Home to several ethnic groups, of which the Yoruba, Hausa, and Igbo are the largest, Nigeria also has the distinction of having the largest Muslim population west of the Persian Gulf, while striking an approximate demographic balance between the Muslim and Christian faiths (Paden, 2008). To complicate matters even further, the oil reserves of Nigeria are the subject of an intense struggle between ethnic groups, the federal government, and oil companies (Obi, 2001). Given these various ethnic, linguistic, and religious groups, and the competition for resources, the main challenge for Nigeria is to develop a political system that can accommodate its ethnic and religious diversity while also relying on the democratic values of rule of law and justice (see Jega, 2007; Paden, 2008).

This is by no means an easy task. With a history of political and communal violence, corruption, and nepotism, Nigeria might be seen by many as an example of how not to do things. Yet despite these problems, Nigeria not only manages to stay united, but also to enjoy relative stability and prosperity. Far from collapsing under violence and the pressures of managing diversity, Nigeria emerges as the locus of a unique experiment in multiculturalism, based on multi-jurisprudence and the "zoning" of power.

Following independence, Nigeria's constitution established a national criminal and corporate law, with Islamic (Sharia) and customary law applied in civil contexts. However, when Ahmed Sani won the gubernatorial elections in the predominantly Muslim state of Zamfara in 2000, he established, as per his pre-election manifesto, Islamic law in criminal matters. Other states followed suit, applying Sharia law in criminal matters to Muslims only. Although the harsher parts of Sharia law, such as stoning and amputation, are usually overturned in appeals, Sharia remains controversial and divisive within Nigeria. More recently, reforms to make the application of Sharia law more transparent and accountable and less harsh and idiosyncratic made the move more popular in states such as Kano, and contributed to the normalization of the application of Sharia. Paden cites the re-election of Kano's governor as evidence for the popularity of the Sharia reforms. The application of this type of multi-jurisprudence is certainly a novel experiment, which is seen as reflecting several underlying tensions. The first of these tensions concerns the relationship between state and federal law: Paden reports that as of 2007 no Sharia case was heard by the Nigerian Supreme Court, which is made up equally of Muslim and Christian judges. At the same time there are persistent questions regarding the constitutionality of Sharia law for criminal cases (Nmehielle, 2004). In addition, there is the question of the Christian population living in states where Sharia law applies: since it concerns wider aspects of social behaviors it may be seen as illiberal. The broader issue of human and individual rights is also at stake here, given some of the excesses of Sharia law such as stoning, as well as the treatment of women. A further issue concerns the more general "right to exit," i.e. the right to be treated as an individual rather than as part of a group. Finally, in the cases of Canada and India, where we saw some instances of multiple jurisprudence, albeit in personal or civil matters rather than criminal, the overall context was one of state secularism. The application of Sharia in criminal matters certainly challenges any assumed state secularism in Nigeria. These tensions have not been resolved and appear to feed the broader debate of the form that a multi-faith and multiethnic Nigeria should take.

While Sharia law remains controversial, the question of how best to divide federal power among the various religious and ethnic groups stirs up even more controversy. While the Constitution has no relevant provisions, there is an informal understanding within all parties that presidential candidates should rotate in a manner which leaves no religion or ethnicity out. In practice this meant that, following Olusegun Obasanjo's (a Yoruba Christian) two-term rule, most political parties put Muslim candidates forth for the 2007 election. In the end, the ruling People's Democratic Party candidate, Umaru Musa Yar'adua, a Muslim of Fulani descent, won the election. While this zoning arrangement appears to be a fair means by which ethnic and religious balance is achieved, it is not without its problems. One of the most serious problems is that zoning may be counter to the requirements of meritocracy. Thus, the candidate may not be the best candidate but the only candidate of appropriate background. Moreover, the informality of the approach does not guarantee its continuous application. Indeed, Alhaji Umar Gana, a Nigerian politician and PDP campaign coordinator, said in a 2004 interview that zoning was an ad hoc agreement to stabilize Nigeria that need not be repeated in the future (Anon., in *Nigerian Newsday*, August 11, 2004). However, without this zoning agreement what are the possibilities for a minority candidate to be put forward? Without, in other words, some sort of institutional arrangement, as for instance found in some countries on the issue of gender, there is no guarantee that Nigeria's diversity will be represented adequately in the country's Senate and House of Representatives. Conversely, the existence of such an agreement does not safeguard democracy. Thus, the 2007 Nigerian election was marred not only by violence, but also by accusations of fraud and disenfranchisement (McGreal, 2007).

How might we assess Nigerian multiculturalism? Given the violence and accusations of corruption, one might be tempted to see failure. However, as with India, this may be a quick and superficial conclusion. As with India, Nigeria's problems might not be seen as a result of its diversity but rather as the culmination of various factors: the colonial legacy, the years of military rule, and, perhaps most importantly, the widespread poverty of the nation despite the vast oil reserves all combine to create a combustible situation that periodically erupts. Paden (2008) argues that, without economic development and without some degree of just redistribution of wealth, the problems of Nigeria will persist.

3.4 Conclusions

We reviewed in this chapter several models of multiculturalism, summarized in table 3.1 (opposite page).

This wide variety of multicultural policy, rhetoric, and practices shows that an assessment may be a difficult task. In every case we discussed there were numerous

Table 3.1 Varieties of multiculturalism

Varieties of multiculturalism: rhetorics and policies	Main characteristics	Country
Ethnic model ("public philosophy," rhetoric, and policy)	*Jus sanguinis*, ethnic descent, no citizenship for foreigners	Germany (until 1999)
Pluralistic model ("public philosophy," rhetoric, and policy)	Equal opportunities structures, multicultural educational curricula, citizenship rights, emphasis on integration	UK, Spain
Republican model ("public philosophy," rhetoric, and policy)	Emphasis on assimilation into mainstream culture, no special provisions for foreigners, full citizenship rights	France
Civic integration ("public philosophy," rhetoric, and policy)	Emphasis on learning and tolerating mainstream cultural and political values; degree of coercion: newcomers must conform to these values	Netherlands, but also endorsed by most EU nations
Melting pot (mostly rhetoric and contested ideal)	Creating of a new type of culture; fusion and overall loyalty to the political values of the state; full citizenship rights to those born on US soil (*jus soli*)	USA
Affirmative action (contested policy)	Discriminating in favor of disadvantaged groups until they become equal	USA
Mosaic (rhetoric) and asymmetrical rights (policy)	A composite of cultures remaining more or less intact; policies aimed at preserving cultures	Canada
Constitutional multiculturalism (policy and rhetoric)	Preservation of diversity, self-rule, and autonomy; both individual and group rights; personal law different according to community	India
Zoning and multi-jurisprudence	Rotation of main groups and power sharing; different jurisprudence according to one's community (Sharia law for Muslims in some Nigerian states)	Nigeria

problems associated with the inception of new communities, with the host and indigenous communities, and with the historical, political, and economic contexts of each country. The first conclusion we can draw, therefore, is that there is no such thing as "one size fits all" when it comes to multiculturalism. Secondly, however, we observe that time and again similar dilemmas emerge: are group rights more important than individual rights (as in the case of applying Sharia law)? Is equality more important than acknowledging diversity (as in the French republican and in the US affirmative action models)? Does multiculturalism lead to fragmentation or is it a guarantee of unity? In many ways these dilemmas are common to all countries discussed above. The next chapter will discuss the normative basis and proposed solutions given to these dilemmas in political philosophy.

4

Theories of Multiculturalism

4.1 Multicultural Dilemmas

This chapter is concerned with normative and theoretical approaches to multiculturalism. To some extent, multicultural policies and politics are dictated by pragmatic concerns and issues; yet they are also influenced by normative understandings of how a society ought to deal with ethno-cultural diversity. The central question here is, to use Pnina Werbner's (2002) words, how to deal with heterogeneity. We saw in earlier chapters that this question arises in contexts where the predominant socio-political organization is that of a nation-state, which revolves around the idea of ethno-cultural homogeneity. Thus, when confronted with ethno-cultural diversity, such nation-states must find ways to deal with the issues that arise. We saw the different policies assumed by different countries, which reflect their particular histories and cultures. However, we still need to understand the issue of dealing with diversity in normative and theoretical terms as such an understanding will provide guidance on what is just and fair. At the same time, it is impossible to address the question of cultural diversity in an "objective," non-politicized manner. This is because it is virtually impossible to stand outside society, to step out of any identity, and decide on what is "better" without reflecting or invoking certain positions, group interests, and values. In these terms, multicultural theories are necessarily politically contentious. In responding to issues pertaining to cultural diversity, therefore, it is necessary to achieve both theoretical clarity and a political compromise.

Typically, theories of multiculturalism are understood in terms of certain dilemmas, reflecting the ongoing debates and various political approaches to difference and cultural diversity. These dilemmas involve values and ideas that prioritize certain aspects over others, and which are central to different theories and political approaches. Three such dilemmas emerge as the more central for multiculturalism. These involve the dilemma of essentialism or fluidity; universalism or particularism; and recognition or redistribution (Siapera, 2006a). Each pole holds that it must prevail over its "adversary" for a politically satisfactory solution to multiculturalism. But these dilemmas do not tell the whole story: in dealing with cultural diversity in terms of dilemmas they are locked into a fruitless battle, which overlooks the dynamic nature of cultural diversity and its shifting position in society. Moreover, from our point of view, they tend to ignore the role of the media and of the mediation of cultural diversity. This mediation means that cultural diversity is produced, represented, and received through the various media of communication; at the same time, cultural diversity itself participates actively in this cycle by producing and representing itself, and by responding to its representations critically or otherwise. This, in turn, implies that cultural diversity cannot be conceived or apprehended in a "direct" manner but rather only through its many media traversals.

Although we will discuss mediation in more detail in the next chapter, the idea that cultural diversity exists through a dialectic with the media means that none of these positions can be held as more valid than the others. This is because, firstly, cultural diversity is far too dynamic to be forever contained in a certain "solution"; and, secondly, because democratic politics is premised on the idea that societies remain open and responsive to contestations and struggles. Another problem with normative theory is that it tends to overlook everyday practices and focus on either pivotal cases or on abstract concepts. It is dictated more by notions abstracted from the context of "prosaic," everyday encounters, thereby ending up somewhat wooden and removed from the actual terrains within which cultural diversity exists and flourishes. All these point to the need for a theoretical and normative perspective that pays attention to the mediated nature of cultural diversity, and which is informed by the everyday mediated practices of cultural diversity. In this chapter, we will critically discuss these dilemmas and the role they allocate to the media, before arguing for the necessity for more nuanced and less polarized approaches to the question of dealing with heterogeneity.

4.2 Essentialism or Fluidity?

Essentialism entails an understanding of community identity as stable and fixed, linked to certain traditional practices, which remain relatively unchanged through time, and assume a central position and role within the community. In contrast, fluidity of identity entails an understanding of community identities as unstable and dynamic, characterized by permeable and porous boundaries, changing across time and contexts, and subjected to contestations within the community itself. Although at first glance there is no question that fluidity of identity is a more appropriate understanding, this dilemma is not that easily resolved. This is because for a community to be offered recognition and redress of any injustices, it must be characterized by a stable core set of characteristics which will determine who belongs to it, and which will determine the identity to be recognized and offered respect. In other words, for a proper politics of multiculturalism or for a minority politics, it is necessary for communities to mobilize relatively fixed identities that will allow them to participate and compete in the public arena. To elaborate more on these arguments, this section will focus on two important works that have advanced the respective poles of essentialism and fluidity: these include the work of Charles Taylor (1994) and Bikhu Parekh (2000).

In 1992, Charles Taylor, the renowned Canadian political theorist, wrote an article that has, in many ways, kick-started the discussion on multiculturalism. Titled "Multiculturalism and the Politics of Recognition," the essay tackled the demands for recognition of all identities, and the attribution to them of equal dignity and respect.

Taylor's essay has in fact addressed all aspects of the dilemmas of multiculturalism, as it made clear the conflicts between universalism and particularism, equality and difference, recognition and redistribution. While Taylor's positions on other matters will be discussed elsewhere, it is his conception of identity that is of interest here. Taylor formulates an argument against liberalism and its view that identities are achieved by individuals, thus becoming a more or less personal matter. But Taylor's rejection of the liberal view of identity, no matter how justified or well argued it is, ends up supporting an essentialist view of community identity.

Specifically, Taylor takes issue with what liberal theory, and in particular the strand associated with the philosopher Immanuel Kant, considers central for modern identity: that individuals construct their identity on their own, through exercising their reason and choosing some aspects over others. The political implications of this view are crucial: the political system must on the one hand allow individuals to pursue their goals free of coercion and on the other to treat these identities equally. The problem, however, argues Taylor, is that identities are constructed in dialogue with others. Influenced by the philosophy of Georg Hegel and the social psychology of G. H. Mead, Taylor argues that we form our identity not on the basis of individual choice but rather through interaction and dialogue with other identities and especially significant others, whose identities count more for us. This dialogue also includes conflict, disagreement, and struggle. Taylor sees in this dialogical construction of identity dependence on others as well as reciprocity. For Taylor, in order for any identity to be achieved, it must be recognized by others as a good and valid identity. Misrecognition leads to wounded identities and requires redress (see Fanon, 1967).

From this point of view, one's identity is built upon foundations that borrow from, debate, contend, and reflect on, other identities. Reliance or dependence on other identities shifts the onus for identity construction from the individual to society. It is not the individual who must be allowed to choose, but society that must ensure that all cultures are preserved and allotted equal dignity, because they are important sources for self-definition and self-identification. Put in a different way, one's identity cannot be truly recognized and respected unless one's community is allowed to exist and survive as a distinct and respected community. This gives rise to another demand that accompanies the demand for equal recognition and equal rights: the demand for group rights, offered to cultures that are misrecognized and/or marginalized. These group rights, such as for instance the right to have French as the official language in Quebec, ensure that individuals are allowed to develop their self-identities in their appropriate contexts. Politically, therefore, there is a significant difference between a procedural liberal model, which focuses on procedures that ensure equal treatment for all individuals, regardless of their religion, race, culture, etc., and a group rights approach, which differentiates between cultural groups and offers some rights to some groups.

Taylor's contribution has developed a convincing account of a politics of recognition which is based on a politics of difference rather than equality. His emphasis on communities as sources of identity, esteem, and pride provided a useful corrective to the purported color blindness of procedural systems, which ultimately end up further marginalizing certain cultures as well as leading to their assimilation and homogenization by the dominant, hegemonic cultures. However, problems arise when we consider how one's identity is forever bound to one's community; any rights are contingent upon group membership, which in this way might trap individuals in certain groups, even if they want to exit these. Although Taylor sought to justify rights offered to communities as a whole, recognizing the irreducibly social nature of the self, the result of his argument is that firm boundaries are built between communities, which then determine who belongs and who doesn't. Individuals are, in these terms, refused choice over belongingness and identity. For example, being born into a French Quebecois community means that one will have a French education; however, there may be some French Quebecois citizens in Canada who would prefer to have a choice over the language of their children's education. This choice will be denied them so long as their identity is determined by membership into the Quebecois community. Similar problems arise with, for instance, the application of Sharia family law to all those belonging to a Muslim community, regardless of whether they would accept this or not.

Bhikhu Parekh (2000) recognizes these problems and focuses on the internal diversity of communities. He agrees with Taylor that communities and cultures form the basis for a meaningful and worthwhile life, but argues that a community's identity is in constant flux, and under constant discussion within communities. On the one hand, Parekh rejects cultural monism, or the view "that only one way of life is fully human, true or the best" (2000: 16); this kind of cultural monism results in either avoiding all contact with other cultures, or in attempts to assimilate them, peacefully or otherwise. Clearly cultural monism in the end rejects any possibility of coexisting with cultural difference. On the other hand, however, Parekh rejects cultural pluralism, because it falls into the trap of attributing far too much power to culture for individuals' identity, thereby overlooking the contributions made by individuals in shaping cultures. Because of this, cultural pluralism ends up assuming that cultures are closed and unchanging, internally homogenous, and autonomous from any economic, political, and other structures. This results in a kind of misguided multiculturalism that ends up trapping people into static group memberships – just as we have seen in Taylor's work.

Instead, Parekh argues, we need a theory of culture and cultural identity that attributes an appropriate weight and meaning to tradition, change, and individuality. Parekh then moves on to define culture as a set of beliefs and practices that is historically constructed and that serves to organize and attribute meaning to the common life and the experiences of members of a given group. Culture, in this respect, is both constitutive of and constituted by individuals: individuals acquire identity and meaning through membership of particular groups, while cultures themselves only exist insofar as they continue to provide individuals with meaning. But membership of a particular group is not a case of all or nothing: individuals might accept only certain beliefs, or differ in their interpretations of core cultural ideas. In these terms, resulting identities are variable even if they fall under the same group membership. This, in turn, means that cultures are always internally variable and heterogeneous, "never settled, static and free of ambiguity" (Parekh, 2000: 148). Individuals then can be critical towards their own cultures, seek to reform them, or reach out to other cultures. As a result of this dialogue, identities are fluid, boundaries between communities porous, and cultures are constantly evolving. Any conflicts that arise between and within communities can be resolved through a dialogue, conducted under conditions dictated by the "operative public values" of the society at large – which are themselves subject to change, contestation, and periodic readjustment (Parekh, 2000: 436).

Although this is a powerful and persuasive account it faces two main problems. Firstly, it cannot address the demands of groups that seek to cut themselves off from society, and to operate in an autonomous and independent manner (Tempelman, 1999; Shachar, 2001). These groups refuse to participate in a dialogue, but seek to barricade and seclude their members rather than engage in a re-creation and reinterpretation of their beliefs. Secondly, because of the insistence of this understanding on the permeability of borders between communities, there is a general failure to grasp that separatist, or more broadly identity, politics emerges in conditions where such borders are clear and distinct rather than porous and fuzzy. In other words, the problem is that a group may seek autonomy precisely because it feels it has been discriminated upon by other, hegemonic cultural groups (Baubock, 1999). In this case, speaking of a minority politics, in which a group seeks rights and recognition, depends upon clear definitions of membership and needs to formulate an equally clear case of internal homogeneity and commonality across its members, in order to justify its claims. An example here may be that of gay groups, which seek rights and recognition for their members: in order to make such claims, they must impose certain criteria for membership, which might exclude some persons who might otherwise understand themselves as gay. In order, therefore, to conduct a minority politics groups need to mobilize more or less essentialized identities. This has echoes of Gayatri Spivak's (1996) argument on strategic essentialism, in which she argued that groups must contest representations from within an imputed identity but with full cognizance of the political purpose of this mobilization (see also Chapter 10).

More broadly, the dilemma of essentialism versus fluidity of identities foregrounds the distance between political and analytical understandings of identity, which prioritize different elements: distinct borders and clear identities and porous boundaries and fuzzy identities respectively. However, to argue that essentialism is more expedient in political terms overlooks the ways in which it is used in order to police and control communities. On the other hand, to insist on the fluidity of identities overlooks the reality of particularly ethnic and racial identities in everyday contexts – a reality in which borders exist both materially and symbolically.

Beyond the actual difficulty of resolving this dilemma, another problem here concerns the role of the media in the construction of identities. While essentialism presupposes an almost primordial identity, shaped by the traditions of the community, fluidity implies that people play with identities almost at will. The essentialist position seems to imply that the media act as mere channels for the transmission of culture or platforms for cultural expression. On the other hand, the position of fluidity is caught in an impasse. It can either claim that the media reflect the dynamism and diversity of identities, thereby contributing to the ongoing construction of identities; or that they do not, in which case they are irrelevant to any identity process, since the latter are anyway always dynamic and diverse. The problem is that the role of the media is not theorized properly, resulting in somewhat naive positions regarding a complex relationship between media and identity processes. Under-theorizing the media further implies a broader failure to take into account mediation, which is a crucial aspect of contemporary, late (or for some post-) modern societies. Overlooking mediation, in turn, may end up overlooking important processes and dynamics in the relationship between cultures and identities. But this under-theorization of the media is not found only in this dilemma: it is common also in the universalism or particularism debate.

4.3 Universalism or Particularism?

The main question here concerns the extent to which communities must accept a common set of values in order to coexist. Some theorists argue that societies can only function if they operate on the basis of a set of common values, often inscribed in their constitutional and legal systems. Indeed, this dilemma is at the heart of multicultural politics: must we come up with several sets of laws to apply to different communities and which reflect their own traditions and values? If so, what happens in cases of conflict between traditional values and practices, as for instance, in the case of female circumcision or honor killings, to name two of the most contentious and controversial practices? On the other hand, must we impose a singular law and an overarching set of values that ultimately iron out differences? If so, how can we protect and preserve cultural diversity?

It is in the procedural and deliberative model of democracy proposed by Jürgen Habermas (1994) that we find the most articulate and convincing account of universalism. Habermas has attempted to create a framework that accepts difference while also operating in a context that endorses a set of universal values. In doing so, he divides the political from the cultural sphere, arguing that, while cultures can and should be different, the political sphere must be the same for all, and it must adhere to values and principles endorsed by all, regardless of their cultural background.

Specifically, Habermas sought to address the problems associated with the classical liberal and the social welfare (or communitarian) models, and their failures to deal with difference. These failures are due to the liberal tendency to accept only individuals, thereby rejecting the relevance of culture; and to communitarianism's disregard of the special role and significance of culture for the development of autonomous persons. He therefore proposed a circular link between individual and collective rights and autonomy. This circular relationship implies a coexistence of private and public autonomy, which means that while rights must apply to all in the same manner, they must also include a recognition of the different ways in which individuals develop: "A correctly understood theory of rights requires a politics of recognition that protects the integrity of the individual in the life contexts in which his or her identity is formed" (1994: 113).

Although feeding into each other, this idea implies a separation of these "life contexts" from the domain understood as properly political, which is seen as universalistic and based on equality. Habermas argues that the political domain must remain ethically neutral if it is to protect such cultural contexts, and of course, if a political community is to sustain itself as such: "The ethical substance of a political integration that unites all the citizens of the nation must remain 'neutral' with respect to the differences among the ethical-cultural communities within the nation, which are integrated around their own conceptions of the good" (1994: 137). In other words, for different cultures to exist the overarching political and legal system must be neutral, i.e. it must not a priori support or prioritize one kind of culture over others. This neutrality is basically the entrenched predominant political culture of the nation itself, which comprises different ethical communities, i.e. communities with different understandings of what the "good life" is.

This separation of the political from the cultural leads Habermas to argue that there are two levels of integration, the political and the cultural one. Political integration requires "assimilation to the way in which the autonomy of the citizens is institutionalized in the recipient society and the way the "public use of reason" is practised there" (1994: 138). In other words, political integration requires that all citizens accept the main political values as enshrined in the politico-legal institutions and systems of the country. Cultural integration, on the other hand, requires a full endorsement of "the way of life, the practices, and customs of the local culture" (ibid.). As such, cultural integration is not a necessary condition for multicultural societies, which allow for the existence of many cultures; political integration, however, is a necessary condition for multiculturalism. In other words, political integration is crucial for the functioning of a multicultural democracy, as it operates as the condition on the basis of which such a society can incorporate a multitude of communities. This type of political integration is referred to as *constitutional patriotism* and it requires the loyalty of citizens to the political system whilst allowing for cultural heterogeneity.

It is difficult to underestimate the contribution of Habermas to this debate. Constitutional patriotism is a unique concept, which allows for the development of political stability in societies characterized by diversity. Moreover, it displaces loyalty from nationalistic contexts, which are characterized by emotion, and places it in the realm of reason and intersubjective agreement, whereby citizens are loyal because they agree with the political system and find its decisions legitimate. However, this emphasis on constitutional patriotism appears to overlook the "politics of culture," or the political relevance of culture. Constitutional patriotism implies that cultures coexist more or less harmoniously, leading parallel lives as it were, and enjoying the protection of the state and its constitutional principles. But is this the case?

Habermas argues that preserving cultures and upholding their traditions and values is not an obligation of the state, but rather falls on the shoulders of the communities themselves, which should subject their claims to the principles of rational justification. In this manner, their survival and vitality is ensured, and their dynamism safeguarded rather than preserved in terms of fixed and ascribed identities. This aspect of Habermas' argument is crucial in that it widens the applicability of the "discourse principle" (see box 4.1) to include cultural alongside political communities. In this sense, although the separation between politics and culture appears in the first instance to render culture politically irrelevant, a closer look reveals that in fact culture is politicized, in the sense of becoming subject to political or deliberative processes. But this politicization ultimately favours the dominant culture, the norms and values of which are entrenched and hegemonic, and which therefore appears to make more sense. In other words, constitutional patriotism ultimately results in the imposition of one set of values, thereby suppressing and dominating difference.

Patricularism, on the other hand, seeks to preserve the integrity of different cultures in prioritizing value pluralism over the acceptance of a single overarching, universalizing set of values. Habermas' universalism is misplaced, according to some critics, because it assumes a universal subject, a rational and sovereign individual, who can take decisions and make choices exercising his/her reason. This, however, overlooks the role played by culture in constructing individual identities, and also the ways in which arguments and ideas are themselves subject to cultural contexts. From this point of view, it is not a case of "the most reasonable argument wins," but rather, the winning

> ## Box 4.1   Multiculturalism and the discourse principle
>
> According to the discourse principle, "[j]ust these action norms are valid to which all possibly affected persons could agree as participants in rational discourses" (Habermas, 1996: 109). Action norms are understood as "generalized behavioural expectations" (ibid.). In Habermas' discourse ethics, all decisions must be taken in common by all those affected by them. Different cultures must therefore subject their claims to this principle. In practice, this means that, if, for example, a community wants to operate its own legal system or to practice certain traditions, all those affected by these must explicitly agree. This, however, presupposes that individuals are willing and able to participate in such decision-making processes, and to apply their reason freely, without coercion or pressures of any kind. But can we guarantee that this is the case? Moreover, some religious cultural practices are a matter of belief rather than reasoned argument. What might happen in this case?

argument is the one enjoying a wider consensus because it comes from a hegemonic culture, which dictates what is reasonable. Equally, we cannot argue that, if the procedures are in place, then we must accept the outcome of a deliberation, because the procedures are themselves dictated by the dominant culture and its values. Arguing that what is claimed to be universal is in fact hegemonic, dominating rather than recognizing other cultures as equal, theorists have pointed to the need to allow for pluralism to seep through the whole polity, including its institutions and legal system.

Theorists such as John Gray (1997) argue in favor of value pluralism. In short, value pluralism rests on the idea that contemporary societies are characterized by deep cultural diversity, which is reflected in their values and traditions, and which needs to be recognized by the legal, political, and cultural institutions of states. It posits "that there is an irreducible diversity of ultimate values ... and that when these values come into competition or conflict there is no overarching standard or principle, no common currency or measure, whereby such conflicts can be arbitrated or resolved" (Gray, 1997: 69–70). In other words, it reflects the particularism of values, traditions, and cultures, and it accepts that there is no basis on which to argue that some of these are better, more correct, or more valid than others. While sharing some affinities with liberalism, value pluralism accepts communities or ways of life, rather than individuals, as the bearer of rights, thus leading to mixed systems. At the same time, a pluralist political order does not and cannot dictate how states negotiate issues such as exit from a community, or conversion, or dealing with a mixed heritage, precisely because it operates on the premise of value pluralism: this is something that different communities negotiate differently, on the basis of their constitutive communities and their values. In general, however, within such a system, there is no requirement that all communities adhere to an overarching set of values. In addition, such pluralism also acts as a guarantee that cultural diversity is upheld: pluralization of values guarantees its continuation since all have a stake in its preservation – preserving plurality is in the end self-preservation for cultures and communities (cf. Waldron, 1999).

Value pluralism appears, therefore, a better option for multiculturalism than universalism, which ultimately negates difference. However, value pluralism and the particularism to which it is linked leads to important questions regarding common life. Taken to its logical conclusion, value pluralism leads to a kind of "apartheid" regime, whereby communities exist in separation from each other, each operating with its own values and traditions. Where and how can they coexist, act together, communicate, and even seek redress for perceived injustices? How, and where, can arbitration take place when differences arise between communities? There are no immediate answers to these issues.

As with the former dilemma, universalism or particularism appears to disregard the role of the media in creating common worlds as well as in sustaining pluralism. As we shall see in the next chapter, the media exist in a dialectical relationship with society, its members and its institutions: they contribute to the construction and the (re)imagining of new and old communities, which in turn contribute to the construction, maintenance, or dissolution of institutions and the media themselves. The media, in these terms, literally act as mediators between and within communities; in this manner they create new bridges and connections between communities, helping to create new commonalities and to rethink relationships between universal and particular values (cf. Georgiou, 2005b; Siapera, 2007). Theorizing the role of the media may therefore contribute to a better insight into how multicultural societies actually operate across dichotomies between universal and particular values. On the other hand, such theorization requires that we think about the main demands of cultural diversity. This takes us to the next and final dilemma: recognition or redistribution?

4.4 Recognition or Redistribution?

What Women Want (Meyers, 2000) is the title of a popular romantic comedy film, which purports to know, or at least speculate on, what the female population may want out of life. We might pose the same question concerning cultural diversity: what do culturally diverse groups actually want? Do they want recognition of their particularity, their specificity, and full redress of the misrecognition, misrepresentation, and insults they have suffered? Or do they actually seek a fairer share of collective assets, a more equitable redistribution of wealth and power? Both, one might say. However, this dilemma is actually more complex than it appears because these claims rest on different, and contradictory, principles of justice. Redistribution rests on an idea of justice as equality, which requires that people are treated in the same way. Recognition, on the other hand, requires an acknowledgement of difference and cultural specificity, which leads to differential treatment. This debate has been at the centre of the work of two important political theorists, Nancy Fraser and Axel Honneth (2003). While Nancy Fraser argues that claims for recognition and claims for redistribution must both be honored in different ways, Honneth argues that recognitive justice is in fact a super-ordinate category, which includes redistributive justice: honoring claims for recognition therefore precedes and frames claims for redistribution. Social democracy, linked to an egalitarian distribution of resources, is, according to this formulation, antagonistic to multiculturalism, which requires differential treatment.

Nancy Fraser (1997; 2000; Fraser and Honneth, 2003) has eloquently formulated the problem as involving a shift from demands to address material inequality to demands to address cultural domination. This involves a shift from class interest as the main means for political mobilization to group identity. "Race," ethnicity, and often also gender and sexuality act as the new foci for political struggle, and this struggle does not necessarily involve demands to address material inequality. Rather, these identities formulate claims against cultural domination, against offensive and insulting representations, and against the violence of mono-culturalism. Fraser then moves on to articulate some of the questions emerging: "what should we make," she asks, "of the rise of a new political imaginary centred on notions of 'identity,' 'difference,' 'cultural domination,' and 'recognition'? Does this shift represent a lapse into 'false consciousness'? Or does it, rather, redress the culture-blindness of a materialist paradigm rightfully discredited by the collapse of Soviet communism?" (1997: 11–12).

None of these positions can be right, she claims, because they both leave out many questions and because they leave some demands unaddressed. We need to reformulate social justice in ways that accommodate both kinds of demands, and we need to develop concepts of cultural recognition and social equality that support rather than undermine one another. Fraser's solution and reformulation is to propose a so-called *perspectival dualism*, which acknowledges an analytic but not a substantive division between the economy and culture, underpinning redistribution and recognition respectively.

Fraser views the division between the economy and culture as one imposed by historical circumstances, and specifically by the requirements of capitalism, which required increased specialization. But this separation between the economy and culture does not reflect the complex reality, in which these two are "interpenetrated," i.e. mutually depending on, and influencing, each other. To argue that one should take precedence over the other overlooks this complex relationship between them. Perspectival dualism then seeks to restore this complexity, by always posing a dual question: does a practice under question undermine or support both the objective and intersubjective conditions of life for groups and their members? Social justice, according to Fraser's perspectival dualism, must ensure that the economic aspects of cultural misrecognition are addressed at the same time as the cultural aspects of maldistribution. Using perspectival dualism, for example, we can examine the economic costs of, for instance, heterosexist misrecognition which forces gay people into the closet; and the effects of chronic maldistribution on the identities of single mothers (Fraser, 1999). In practical terms, Fraser's solution requires that we apply a process of deconstruction on misrecognized identities in order to restore them; and a process of socialist redistribution of resources to redress material inequalities.

When it comes to conflictual demands raised by recognition and redistribution claims, Fraser proposes the mobilization of the norm of participatory parity: according to this, "justice requires social arrangements that permit all (adult) members of society to interact with one another *as peers*" (Fraser and Honneth, 2003: 36). Participatory parity rests on two elements: an objective one, which relates to the material resources that ensure parity, and an intersubjective one, which refers to the symbolic resources, status, and value that equally ensure parity. Claims for recognition and redistribution should be honored in order to ensure participatory parity, while participatory parity provides a means of adjudicating between these. For instance, in the notorious case of the ban of the Muslim headscarf – the hijab – in educational establishments in France, Fraser argues that we must assess this ban on the following points. Firstly, the ban is justified on the basis of egalitarianism: all groups, religious, ethnic, or other, should be treated in the same manner, and therefore none of their members are allowed to wear religious symbols at school. But does it constitute an unjust imposition of the majority to the minority, thus erecting barriers to educational parity for Muslim girls? Secondly, those seeking to restore the practice through mobilizing the right to difference should be questioned as to the extent to which this practice exacerbates female subordination, thus erecting a barrier to female participatory parity.

There is no doubt that Fraser's account is an ingenious attempt to reconcile apparently contradictory conceptions of justice. Perspectival dualism and participatory parity allow for the formulation of clear gauges or yardsticks by which all kinds of claims can be assessed and honored. At the same time, by keeping intact the analytical separation between claims resting on economic injustices and those resting on cultural injustices, Fraser's theory avoids either economic or cultural reductionism. On the other hand, however, it inevitably comes across certain conceptual problems. For Axel Honneth, the main problem is that this dualism overlooks the way in which economic divisions in fact are premised on moral ("right") and ethical ("good") understandings of justice and the rights of groups and individuals. Honneth (1995; Fraser and Honneth, 2003) has developed a theory of social justice which places recognition at the centre and which views conflicts of distribution as struggles for recognition.

More specifically, Honneth draws on the philosophy of Georg Hegel on recognition, but modifies it by combining it with the social psychology of G. H. Mead. Hegel had considered intersubjective recognition as crucial not only for the development of individual identity and self-awareness, but also for the moral and ethical development of society: for Hegel, a society would morally progress on the basis of the widening of claims for recognition placed by different identities and aspects of identities (Honneth, 2001). Honneth builds upon Hegel's insights by arguing that there are three levels of recognition: love, rights, and solidarity. He further draws on Mead's psychology, according to which people come to understand themselves through recognition by others; if they fail to have their choices and ideas recognized, or if they are consistently misrecognized, then these injuries will fuel conflict and struggles. Failures of recognition therefore cause injuries, denigration, or insults, and they can occur at three levels. At the level of individual's affective development, if one's needs are consistently met (i.e. recognized), then one develops self-confidence. At the level of rights, recognition is offered to a larger group: one's rights can only be recognized if one is seen as a member of a wider community that deserves, claims, and gets respect and recognition in terms of rights. Finally, in solidarity one demands recognition of one's or one's group special traits and abilities; failure to attribute esteem to one's community results in a kind of injury which can only be restored a kind of solidaristic recognition by other groups. The positive mode of recognition at these three levels creates self-confidence, self-respect, and self-esteem respectively.

Honneth sees the demands for just distribution as deriving from demands for recognition. He argues that "the rules organizing the distribution of material goods derive from the degree of social esteem enjoyed by social groups, in accordance with institutionalized hierarchies of value, or a normative order" (2001: 54). In other words, you will only receive what the society in which you live believes you are worth. Divisions of power, wealth, and status, divisions of labor, and access to goods and resources are all determined by cultural values and ideas about worth and entitlement. To demand more then implies that one's identity feels devalued and that it should receive more. Misrecognized identities have been given a distorted sense of worth, thereby depriving them of a fair share of society's wealth. If they are properly recognized, then the result will be a fairer redistribution. For example, access to top jobs by women or ethnic minorities is restricted precisely because they are devalued in society – being properly recognized implies and requires that they are offered a fairer deal. There is no need, therefore, for a bifurcation of demands into symbolic (recognition) and material (redistribution) as they are both conjoined by the superordinate category of recognition, which is sufficiently expanded to include the levels of love, rights, and solidarity. Recognitive justice is then considered to include redistributive justice, which can only be justified and honored on the basis of offering recognition to individuals and their communities.

Honneth's account of recognition provides a unique insight into the social movements of recent years and the continued struggles of ethnic and other groups, such as gay and lesbian communities, as well as women's groups. These struggles are motivated not by a utilitarian self-interest but rather by a sense of injustice that has deep moral roots. By uniting and locking together these two kinds of claims, Honneth avoids both the kind of dichotomous thinking evident in Fraser and the reductionism of either culturalism or economism. However, it is not clear how a society can assess demands of recognition, and determine which ones are legitimate or not (Thompson, 2006). Moreover, it does not necessarily follow that recognition will lead automatically to the redistribution of resources: to deconstruct identities, in other words, does not automatically and inevitably lead to just distribution. A look at the ongoing struggles of both ethnic minorities and women's groups shows that this is a long and complicated process.

While this debate cannot be resolved here, it presents a clear case for the role of the media. Specifically, demands for recognition directly engage the public sphere and the cultural hierarchy of identities as it appears publicly. In these terms, the media is one of the most important arenas for struggles of recognition, where groups and individuals can formulate, present, and justify their claims. Studying media representations, far from being a futile semiological exercise, has an important political goal: to examine which representations actually misrecognize which groups, and if possible to redress such misrepresentation. From this point of view, this emphasis on recognition provides a crucial normative yardstick by which to assess the media: do they allow for access and the publication of all kinds of voices? Do they provide fair and balanced representations, or do they merely repeat stereotypes? On the other hand, this perspective implies a straightforward relationship in which the media are held to be the mirror in which society is reflected. But, as we shall see shortly, the role of the media is much more involved than this: the "mirror" is taken to play a much more direct role in constituting society and hierarchies of values and identities. For now, our task of examining the main normative approaches and dilemmas of multiculturalism is done.

4.5 Conclusions

Understanding multiculturalism and more broadly the position and role of cultural diversity in contemporary societies requires that we examine the normative and theoretical approaches to the issue of living with difference. We need not only understand the reality of the treatment of cultural diversity across the world, we further need to understand how we ought to think and about it and what kinds of policies we ought to draft. But normative perspectives are not only multiple, they also involve contradictory positions. Which one should we choose and why? This chapter presented some of the main dilemmas involved in thinking normatively about diversity. However, it stopped short of offering a definitive solution to these dilemmas: this is not the task of theory, but a political task to which different societies may want to give different solutions. However, by way of conclusion, this section suggests that, while we must keep on debating and thinking about these normative approaches both theoretically and politically, any solution must be temporary and provisional: it must be continuously reassessed and changed if and as necessary. Thus, theoretically, it was argued here that failure to consider the constructive role of the media in multiculturalism has resulted in somewhat simplified and naive positions. In political terms, multiculturalism requires that the poles that constitute these dilemmas are involved in continuous struggles without the imposition of a permanent closure.

Specifically, the dilemma between essentialism and fluidity overlooks the role of the media in identity construction. It seems to assume that identities are either predetermined on the basis of existing traditions, in which case the media can play no role; or alternatively that they are fluid and porous, and that people can move from identity to identity almost at will, in which case the actual conservative and reactionary role of the media in repeating stereotypical and often even racist representations of cultural identities is overlooked. Similarly, the dilemma of universalism versus particularism creates a polarization that may not be necessary; in addition, it overlooks the role of the media as standing in-between: constructing bridges and commonalities holding people together, or conversely divisions and separations keeping people apart. Hannah Arendt used the metaphor of the table as a mediator in a similar manner: the table across which we sit, she said, connects us but also keeps us apart (1958/1998): it simultaneously relates each of us to others, and keeps us separate as individuals because we are uniquely positioned in our seat on the table. Failure to theorize the role of the media as mediators of relationships between and within communities results in a failure to grasp the complex interplay between universal and common values and the specific values particular to certain groups only. Finally, in the recognition– redistribution debate, the role of the media is that of a transparent medium, which reflects society: if a group is generally misrecognized, then that is how it will be reflected in the media. This view, however, overlooks the constructive ways in which the media actually build up representations according to logics specific to them – representations which subsequently circulate in society only to be contested and questioned. In short, in theoretical terms we need to consider the role of the media as cultural identities, cultural particularities, values, and demands exist in contemporary societies primarily in mediated forms.

Box 4.2   Key issues and definitions

Essentialism: the view that communities have a stable "essence," often codified in certain traditions and practices that remains unchanged and that should be unchallenged.

Fluidity: the view that identities develop in discussion and in relation with others, that borders between communities are porous, and that communities are dynamic, evolving across time.

Universalism: the view that certain common values should prevail for societies to be able to function.

Constitutional patriotism: the idea that loyalty should be based on endorsement of a set of common political values and principles, which is decoupled from the majority culture (Habermas, 1998).

Value pluralism: the position that the diversity of values encountered in multicultural societies must be preserved (Gray, 1997).

Participatory parity: the idea that all members of society should be able to interact with each other as peers (Fraser, 2003).

Recognitive justice: justice that is based on the recognition of identities, their particularity, and their demands. It also refers to freedom from cultural domination, nonrecognition, and disrespect – see below.

Cultural domination: "being subjected to patterns of interpretation and communication that are associated with another culture and are alien/hostile to one's own" (Fraser, 2003: 13).

Nonrecognition: being rendered invisible in representational, communicative, and interpretative practices.

Disrespect: being routinely maligned or disparaged in stereotypical representations and in everyday life.

Redistributive justice: justice that is based on an equal distribution of material resources.

In political terms, the formulation of theoretical propositions in polarized and dilemmatic terms creates false antinomies, and pressures for solutions that will privilege one understanding against others. Although, of course, societies need to decide which type of policy and law they want for themselves, they must also allow for an ongoing contestation, debate, and struggle between these positions. From this point of view, societies need to keep open the means by which such struggle between positions can take place: in short, we return to the media understood as institutions in the public sphere, within which contestation, as well as presentation of views, images, and positions, can take place. Rather than deciding on a particular position, societies must ensure that they remain open both to the antagonisms between different communities, their values, and ideas, but also to the competing claims that living with such heterogeneity entails. To quote James Tully, multicultural societies should not aim "to discover and constitutionalize the just and definitive form … but to ensure that ineliminable, agonic, democratic games … can be played freely and with a minimum of domination" (2000: 469).

5

Media Theories
and Cultural Diversity

This chapter will address the relationship between media and cultural diversity by using the media as a starting point. Typically this relationship is posited in terms of media effects, whereby the media are assumed to have certain effects on cultural diversity. Indeed, the "media question" more generally is interpreted as a question of "effects." Most accounts of the history of research into the media note that concerns over the effects of the media arose almost as soon as the mass media made their appearance (McQuail, 2005). Often, the main reason for studying the media is precisely an assumption of their effects. From this point of view all media theories are, to an extent, media effects theories. There are, however, several and important differences between these theories. One of these is the extent to which they consider that the media have powerful effects. One of the most common ways of discussing media theories is to divide them into those that consider that the media have powerful effects on audiences and those that maintain that they have negligible effects. The former view often dominates in periods of anxiety and instability, and the latter in periods of stability and prosperity (McQuail, 2005; Silverstone, 2005). Here, however, we will assume a different perspective, which we hope does justice to the complexity of all the theories; this involves a classification of media theories on the basis of their level of analysis.

Early theories focused on the individual, and empasized the socio-psychological effects of media consumption on people who were considered especillay vulnerable. These studies were concerned with the direct effects of the media on people, their behaviors and attitudes – the focus here was on the audiences and their responses to media stimuli (e.g. Katz and Lazarsfeld, 1955/2006). The difficulty of proving such direct effects led to shifts in perspective from the socio-psychological to the macro-sociological. Social theories of the media attempted to capture the wider influence of the media, and to place them in their particular political, social, and economic context. Two types of theories can be identified here: firstly, so-called medium theory, which viewed communication media as determining the world around them (McLuhan, 1964); secondly, political-economic studies, which viewed the media as part of a capitalist organization (Adorno and Horkheimer, 1947/1997; Herman and Chomsky, 1988). These studies looked at both the production and the contents of the media, highlighting the links between media ownership and capitalism, while also exposing the ways in which texts support dominant ideologies and understandings. The linear relationship posited by these theories was questioned by theorists who argued that communication media are already embedded in society and must not be considered as mere epiphenomena of capitalism. This gave rise to another shift towards a cultural model of communication, which viewed the media not as merely transmitting information but as part and parcel of rituals that create society (Carey, 1989). This position, however, might imply that media power is too widely diffused or even non-existent. What appears necessary is a perspective that recognizes media power, while also paying attention to the nuanced ways in which this works. This is the perspective of mediation, which views the media as embedded in society, making use of it, while also being used by it. In this perspective the different "moments" of the cycle of communication (Hall, 1980) – production, circulation, text, and reception – are seen as equally important, each contributing to the mediation of cultural diversity. At the same time, however, there is an overt recognition of the asymmetry between these moments: to the "strategies" of media production, to the formal and structuring aspects of media circulation and text we can only juxtapose the "tactics" of media reception (see de Certeau, 1984). But the significant contribution of mediation as a perspective is that these moments must all be examined if we are to understand the process of communication in its entirety.

These perspectives and arguments will unfold in the first section of this chapter, which will begin with socio-psychological approaches to the media, then move on to discuss medium theory, before finally examining political-economic and socio-cultural approaches. Mediation as the emerging theory will be discussed separately. Throughout the discussion we will consider the implications of each perspective for the relationship between the media and cultural diversity.

5.1 Socio-Psychological Approaches to Media

Some of the earliest studies of the media focused on the level of the individual or small groups and sought to identify the effects that media consumption and use had on individual behaviors, choices, attitudes, and habits. The rise and rise of the mass media in the early twentieth century, including radio and film, had created a lot of anxiety as to their effects on society, but especially on those deemed vulnerable, namely women, children, and for some also certain ethnic groups. The underlying assumption was that mass media would have direct and pernicious effects on those groups, especially on their morals and behaviors. The main anxiety was that such groups would not be able to control their urges, leading to behaviors that would have a detrimental effect on society as a whole. The successful use of the media for propaganda in the First World War lent some credence to such fears. Indeed, the great propagandist films of the first part of the twentieth century, such as *Battleship Potemkin* (Sergei Eisenstein, 1925) and *Triumph of the Will* (Leni Riefenstahl, 1934), were created precisely in order to elicit certain responses in audiences.

However, when it came to actually proving a direct relationship between media consumption and shifts in attitudes and behaviors, things became more complex. Lacking appropriate methods, studies were concerned with inventing the necessary methodological tools for capturing media effects. Such methods included keeping diaries, conducting personal interviews, running case studies, designing experiments to measure attitudes and responses before and after watching films, and focus group discussions, all of which sought to gauge audience reactions to media use. While certainly innovative, such methods in the end produced a mixed bag of findings. For every study that showed a certain effect there was another showing no such effects. All these led Joseph Klapper (1960) to conclude that the media had no significant effects on people – at most they reinforced existing beliefs and attitudes. This shift from powerful media to powerful audiences was reinforced by functionalist theories, such as the uses and gratifications approach, according to which audiences use media in order to accomplish certain goals, ranging from seeking information to entertainment (Blumler and Katz, 1974).

One of the earliest studies on media effects concerned the effects of the media on young people. This was in fact a series of studies commissioned by the Motion Picture Research Council, collectively known as the Payne Fund Studies, which took place in the USA in the years 1929–32 before eventually leading to the publication of eight volumes in 1933–5. In their review of the history of the Payne Fund Studies, Jowett *et al.* (1996) report that there were links between the studies and the University of Chicago, then the cradle of social scientific research. Research at this time had a clear policy agenda, seeking to improve people's lives through applying scientific findings and recommendations. Thus, the Payne Fund studies wanted to find the impact of "motion pictures" on American youth. At the time, children would go to the cinema unsupervised and watch any film that was on, leading to serious concerns regarding their moral well-being.

Some of the most dramatic findings of these studies concerned attitudes to race. Two of the Payne Fund researchers, Ruth Peterson and L. L. Thurstone (1933), specifically looked at children's social attitudes before and after exposure to films. In general, they found a moderate but consistent effect of movement towards a favorable or unfavorable attitude, depending on the film. For example, they measured attitudes to Germans before showing the film *Four Sons* (John Ford, 1928), which is a sympathetic portrayal of a German family's troubles during the First World War. When they administered the attitude questionnaire again, they found a small but significant shift towards a more favorable attitude. These small effects became really dramatic when Peterson and Thurstone administered a similar questionnaire on attitudes to blacks before and after D. W. Griffith's racist paean to the Ku Klux Klan, *Birth of a Nation* (1915), which was re-released in 1930 with sound. The questionnaire was administered to schoolchildren in a small town in Illinois, most of whom had never seen any black people. Their attitudes, according to Peterson and Thurstone, were then seen as being influenced almost completely by the film. Before watching *Birth of a Nation* children's attitude to black people was rather favorable, scoring 7.46 on a 10-point scale. Following the film the mean score went down to 5.95, leading the researchers to conclude that the film had a considerable effect on the children's attitude, which was by far the most striking of their study, and which was also a persistent one: five months later, the researchers found that the negative attitude towards African-Americans was still present.

Such findings are very significant for many reasons, both scientific and socio-political. American blacks protested against *Birth of a Nation*, but the standard response they received was that there was no evidence to suggest that the film had any negative effects. In a letter to the black American intellectual W. E. B. Du Bois, William Short, one of the chief scientists of the Payne Fund Studies, wrote that the NAACP (National Association for the Advancement of Colored People, of which Du Bois was a founder and Short a member) would finally have the ammunition it required (Stokes, 2007). Scientifically, the studies showed that the relationship between media and cultural diversity was one in which the former played a determining role. Short's triumphant tone, however, was short-lived: the Payne Fund studies did not enjoy any widespread respect and support, while politically they were used to justify censorship rather than to advance social justice (see Jowett *et al.*, 1996).

While Jowett *et al.* cite several reasons regarding the failure of the Payne Fund studies to generate the interest they deserved, one of the factors that could have contributed was the inability of other studies to replicate the findings in a consistent manner. Although work on media effects was undertaken during the Second World War by the Yale psychologist Carl Hovland and his colleagues (Hovland *et al.*, 1949), it was a study by Paul Lazarsfeld and Elihu Katz that left its indelible mark on the history of media research. In their book *Personal Influence*, Katz and Lazarsfeld (1955/2006) made the empirically backed argument that the effects media messages have are mediated by a variety of factors. Such factors include the role played by influential others – the so-called opinion leaders. For Katz and Lazarsfeld, media effects are always mediated by the personal and small-group context in which they are received. If, therefore, the micro-social context within which the media messages are received is hostile to a specific message or representation, then this will be rejected.

The importance of Katz's and Lazarsfeld's work lies in making clear that media messages and representations do not occur in a vacuum, but are received in a social context that is already saturated with certain beliefs, opinions, and attitudes. Media representations are then mediated by these. Katz and Lazarsfeld cite other social psychological work on attitude change, according to which deeply entrenched attitudes, such as prejudice against certain groups, persist despite messages to the contrary. They cite Cooper and Jahoda (1947) as well as Hyman and Sheatsley (1952), whose work has shown that people misinterpret or reject (media) messages in a manner that supports the views they already hold (in Katz and Lazarsfeld, 1955/2006: 23). In these terms, the media can have little or even no effects – and the effect they do have is mediated by other socio-psychological factors. People therefore cannot be persuaded to be more or less racist, to accept or reject cultural diversity, because of relevant media representations. They are already racist or tolerant, and, following the premises of Katz and Lazarfeld's work, there is little the media can do about it.

There is no room here to discuss the controversies of socio-psychological research into media effects (see McQuail, 2005 for a broad overview). However, the above studies suggest that, if there are no strong opinions or attitudes held on a matter, then the media may play an important and influential role in bringing about prejudice – this seems to be the conclusion of Peterson's and Thurstone's study. The media cannot, however, be used to remove it, as by then such an attitude – if indeed we can see it as an attitude – is already held, hence disempowering any new media messages that seek to correct the old racist messages.

We can therefore retain three elements found here: firstly, the emphasis on the receiving part of the communication process: the audiences or people themselves.

Secondly, the important finding that media messages and representations do not fall in a vacuum but form part of a broader nexus of relationships, social and symbolic. Finally, that it is very difficult to validate empirically any direct media effects. But while these studies were looking at the level of the individual or the small group, others were looking at the structural level, and specifically at the role played by the media in the construction of the world around us. We will discuss this position next.

5.2 Medium Theory

"The medium is the message" is by far the most famous statement of the Canadian theorist Marshall McLuhan, the main exponent of this approach (McLuhan, 1964/2001: 7). Notoriously and perhaps purposely opaque, this statement can be interpreted in several ways. Firstly, McLuhan argues that specific media of communication institute certain fundamental changes in society. Secondly, he argued that the content of any new medium is the media that preceded it. McLuhan was directly influenced by Harold Innis (1950; 1951), another Canadian scholar, for whom the media form was credited with the institution of particular models of power. We will in this section discuss McLuhan's work, as it is characteristic of medium theory. We should note, however, that in this general category we can also classify the work of Walter Ong, as well as Benedict Anderson's implicit media theory, and Derrida's approach to communication as always-already mediated. Specifically, Walter Ong (1982) argued that the shift from oral to written and then print cultures signalled fundamental shifts in thought and action. For Benedict Anderson, as we have already discussed, print capitalism made possible the construction of the nation as a singular and imagined culture and community. Finally, the French philosopher Jacques Derrida's concept of logocentrism was proposed in order to criticize the assumption that speech is the most direct way to pure thought and that unmediated communication or "pure thought" is possible.

McLuhan followed and developed Harold Innis' main arguments, which revolved around the idea that different media lead to different kinds of social and political organization. In general, McLuhan accepted the crucial role of the media in structuring the world around us, and took the argument even further. For McLuhan, media not only determine forms of socio-political organization, but also what will be perceived and how. They structure our perception of the world, since they emphasize one of our senses over others. Thus, radio emphasizes sound and television vision. One extends our body in terms of sound, the other in terms of vision. But in extending our bodies, the media construct another world, which requires different degrees of involvement, and highlight different aspects of our environment.

The crucial distinction that McLuhan introduces is between "hot" and "cold" media: the former leave little room for interpretation and "filling in," while the latter allow our mind to wander over them, to fill in gaps, and add to them as we see fit. McLuhan classified photographs, lectures, radio, and print as hot media: these allow less participation, as they require audiences only to pay attention to them. Hot media are sequential and linear and rely on logic, while cold media invite more participation, as they require simultaneous apprehension of several parts at once. Cold media, and here McLuhan classifies speech, the telephone, and television among others, are characterized by low resolution and as such they involve more effort in order to be understood, as audiences need to fill in the gaps caused by low resolution. Although this classification appears somewhat counter-intuitive in this era of HDTV, the distinction may be used to high-light the space for interpretation created by different media: the more the space left, the more likely it was that audiences would actively interpret and engage with the media. High-resolution media, on the other hand, render audiences passive as they ask noth-ing of their minds other than directly apprehending the media messages.

Written in an abstract manner, McLuhan's prose might perhaps be thought as an example of his cool media, as readers are required to make connections and interpret-ations in order to fill in gaps. However, McLuhan's focus on the media form is an important corrective of the focus on the media message as the all-important variable in the communication process. And here McLuhan draws attention to the extent to which print – a typical hot medium – is a form which leads to homogeneity, uniform-ity, and repeatability. In a chapter that must have inspired Benedict Anderson, McLuhan argues that typography was in fact the architect of nationalism. Nationalism, which McLuhan (1964: 93) defines as an "image of group destiny and status," can more abstractly be understood as "continuity and competition" in a space that print has helped homogenize through the simultaneous circulation of ideas, news, prose, and so on. Radio, on the other hand, signals a return to "tribalism," in that it perme-ates people's lives and calls them to action in a way that harks back to the tribal drum. McLuhan in this manner anticipated the role played by radio in the mobilization of people and eventual genocide in Rwanda in 1994 (see Thompson, 2007).

Television, finally, is a cool medium which requires active participation and there-fore engages audiences more; McLuhan describes television as a mosaic, which engages the senses and the imagination. It therefore rejects the uniformity imposed by print and radio – the so-called mechanical media – in favor of a sensual attention to diversity and uniqueness. The electronic age, according to McLuhan, will usher in new approaches to questions of difference, and these will lead not to the eradication of all diversity but to its acceptance:

> The entire approach to these problems [i.e. racism and other forms of prejudice against difference] in terms of uniformity and social homogenization is a final pressure of the mechanical and industrial technology. Without moralizing, it can be said that the electric age, by involving all men deeply in one another, will come to reject such mechanical solu-tions. It is more difficult to provide uniqueness and diversity than it is to impose the uniform patterns of mass education; but it is such uniqueness and diversity that can be fostered under electric conditions as never before. (McLuhan, 1964: 345)

This passage is remarkable for its optimism and the reversal of widespread ideas on television: for McLuhan the novelty of the television is that it engages all our senses as well as our imagination. Rather than the passive audiences – the couch potatoes of later years – we have active participants in the world as shown on television. For this pur-pose, the "logical" uniformity characteristic of the mechanical era of nationalism will be replaced with the "synaesthetic" diversity of the electronic era. It is hard to resist this optimism, which was symptomatic of the time that McLuhan was writing – the 1960s civil rights movements demanded an end to 1950s mass production and uni-formity and fought for the right to difference and diversity.

Was McLuhan right in attributing such developments to the new perceptions cre-ated by electronic media such as television? Certainly, the outcome of the 1960s for part of the West was precisely the development of multicultural practices as detailed in earlier chapters. On the other hand, we also saw that full recognition of diversity is yet to be accomplished. For a long time nationalism seemed to be the natural way of organizing communities; we can therefore trace a line connecting it to certain media such as print and the radio. On the other hand, multiculturalism never achieved a similar status despite the spread of electronic media across the planet. If the media are to have the kind of structural relationship that McLuhan is claiming, then we would have expected a fundamental shift in ethno-political organizing as a result of the rise of the electronic media. Since this is not the case, and since nationalism still prevails, we may want to question such views. However, it can equally be said that such shifts evolve over time, and that our current historical period may be a transitional one from nationalism and the nation-state to a kind of global society – or what McLuhan would call a "global village." If indeed we consider our time as a transitional one, then both nationalism and globalization (understood here as its opposite) can be observed at the same time.

Whichever is the case, the contribution of such views to understanding the relationship between media and cultural diversity must be acknowledged. Firstly, the links between particular media and particular historical epochs reveal the deep involvement of communication in political, social, and historical processes. It is difficult, if not impossible, to prove whether this relationship is "causal" – it has caused certain historical shifts – or "epiphenomenal" – it is the outcome of, or concomitant with, these shifts. It is nevertheless clear that different forms of communication are associated with different forms of socio-political organizing. From this point of view, if we accept the shift from print to electronic media then we should expect changes from the nation-state to some other form of political organizing. Secondly, the emphasis on the structural level constitutes a useful corrective to the somewhat more narrow emphasis on contents and audiences. We are thus able to grasp the broader picture rather than focus on narrowly conceived media effects. For cultural diversity this means that its relationship to the media is not merely one in which media contents determine attitudes to cultural diversity, but one where particular media forms allow more or less space for diversity. It is, however, very difficult to determine this empirically, thereby limiting these theories to abstract discussions rather than concrete illustrations. Political-economic theories, on the other hand, require close attention to empirical reality, and emphasize concrete cases of power differentials and hierarchical structures. To these we turn next.

5.3 Political-Economic Theories of the Media

If social psychological approaches focus on audiences, and medium theory on media forms and macro-structures, political-economic theories, broadly speaking, address the production side of the media. The main premise of such approaches is that the media (as institutions and contents) are the outcome of dominant forms of economic organizing. Since the dominant form of economic organizing is capitalism, the media are considered to be determined by the capitalist mode of production. The media as institutions are then seen as functioning in ways that maximize their profits, while media contents are seen as ideologically supporting the dominant and ruling classes.

In addition, media companies tend towards an oligopolistic model, that is, media institutions are controlled by a few media corporations. It is therefore hard to find alternative views in the media. The role of the media according to this model is one of direct media influence and control of contents, which exclude alternative, potentially subversive views. Some of the most well-known exponents of this position include Adorno and Horkheimer (1947/1997) and Herman and Chomsky (1988). This perspective is Marxian in its approach: it combines political and economic analyses of the media, with a view to illustrating how these "conspire" to support and sustain dominant ideologies and modes of production.

It may be considered an oversimplification to refer to Adorno and Horkheimer as political economists, since the breadth of their work is such that defies easy classification. Nevertheless, it was their famous chapter "The Culture Industry: Enlightenment as Mass Deception" in their hugely influential publication *Dialectic of the Enlightenment* (1947/1997) that signalled a shift from the analysis of contents and reception towards an explicit link between capitalism and mass culture. As such, they may be considered as the founders of the political-economy approach, which contextualizes culture and especially mediated culture as part of capitalist relations.

In *Dialectic of the Enlightenment* Adorno and Horkheimer set down the main premises of what is currently known as Critical Theory. The main argument of this publication is that the Enlightenment, instead of producing freedom and the "disenchantment of the world," has led to a new kind of barbarism. They attribute this to the internal dialectic of the Enlightenment, which is based on the dichotomy between nature and society. The result is that the Enlightenment will lead to self-destruction because it seeks to control nature through the application of scientific and instrumental reason, forgetting that the nature–"man" dichotomy was an arbitrary one, posed by the Enlightenment itself (see also Jay, 1996). While this problematic is illustrated in several spheres, such as the separation of science from practical everyday life and the formalization of morality, considerable emphasis is placed on the role of mass culture. Specifically, Adorno and Horkheimer argue that the uniformity of mass culture is the only possible outcome of the advent of the mass media and mass audiences. The work of art is unique and therefore subversive: its uniqueness is subversive precisely because it "sticks out", and, in doing so, it questions established patterns, thoughts, and practices. But the mass products of the media are the exact opposite: they manipulate and control minds rather than lead them to question things. And "[t]his is the result not of a law of movement in technology as such but its function in today's economy," argue Adorno and Horkheimer (1947/1997: 121). Because culture has become a commodity and hence dependent on the economy – it has to be produced and consumed – it fails to fulfill its function as a means of alerting the world to its own failings. It can now only fulfill its economic function as a commodity on the one hand, and as a means of deceiving or manipulating minds on the other.

Because of this, nothing can escape the totalizing effects of mass culture; even distinction between low and high culture is dissolved into mass culture's obligatory uniformity. Nothing is left outside, everything is included, regurgitated, and repeated. This is how the culture industry works: through the subsumption and homogenization of everything under banner of entertainment, on the basis that "this is what audiences want and like." This is for Adorno and Horkheimer the very ideology of mass culture: "Business is their ideology" (p. 137). And this is why "amusement is the prolongation of work": the mechanized repetition that one finds in factory work is also found in the formulae of the pop song, the "blockbuster" film, the popular TV program – they are all part of the same totality.

The implications of this position for cultural diversity are clear: its only option is to be subsumed under mass culture, to be stripped of any meaningful difference and sold to mass audiences. And, moreover, there is no escape, as anything that passes through the media is immediately contaminated: it becomes mass culture even if people can actually see through it. If it cannot be subsumed under mass culture, then it will be aggressively destroyed or kept on the margins. In a chapter on anti-Semitism, Adorno and Horkheimer spell out the function of cultural diversity: it is used to conceal domination. In blaming the "Jews," or the "blacks," or the "Muslims," the real reasons for frustration and exploitation are occluded, thereby in practice perpetuating domination. This is because the "logic" of the Enlightenment is one of eradicating everything that contradicts it, and everything that is defined as "other" to it. The role of cultural diversity is therefore to be used as a scapegoat, and the role of mass culture is, on the one hand, to attempt to preserve "harmony" (or the status quo) through coopting difference and, on the other, to point a finger to those who inhibit social harmony.

The pessimism of this work is perhaps commensurable with the period in which it was conceived and written. Following the horrors of totalitarianism, the Holocaust, and the specter of nuclear disaster, it is perhaps difficult to be optimistic about the future of humankind. But its general message still resonates: capitalism as the form of economic, social, and political organization demands a uniformity in thought, behaviors, and ideas which is served by the culture industry. Audiences are powerless to act, either because they have been manipulated by the culture industry, or, for those belonging to culturally diverse groups, because they have been marginalized and dominated. The only solution, as Adorno argued in his later work *Negative Dialectics* (1990), is to accept otherness and diversity through highlighting contradiction, paradox, and strangeness in cultural forms: but it must never be dictated as a positive program because of the danger of cooptation. Critique, in other words, is the only means of preserving some form of true individuality in the days of uniformity.

Following along similar lines, Edward Herman and Noam Chomsky highlight the actual processes by which the mass media and in particular journalism serve capitalism. In their book *Manufacturing Consent* (1988), they argue that, while in totalitarian regimes the media are directly controlled by governments, in the "free world" they are more subtly controlled through the unifying logic of capitalism and the market, and the eternal quest for profit. They formulated the "propaganda model," in which the argue that media contents are determined by a set of five factors which interact with each other and which in the end apply as "filters" through which all media contents must go through. These are: "(1) the size, concentrated ownership, owner wealth, and profit orientation of the dominant mass-media firms; (2) advertising as the primary income source of the mass media; (3) the reliance of the media on information provided by government, business, and 'experts' funded and approved by these primary sources and agents of power; (4) 'flak' as a means of disciplining the media; and (5) 'anticommunism' as a national religion and control mechanism" (Herman and Chomsky, 1988: 1).

In short, this model posits that, because the media are controlled by a few profit-seeking corporations, which rely on advertising for income, and because they are oriented towards institutions of power as sources of news, their contents are such that they never actively question established patterns and relationships, effectively serving powerful interests. Rather than the so-called "fourth estate," the function of which is to watch and criticize the powerful, the media have become a servant of powerful interests. At the same time, if any of these media dares to provide something that breaks the mold, it receives so much flak – i.e. negative responses either by audiences or by politicians and even media owners – that it is forced to get back in line.

At the time when Herman and Chomsky first published their book the American media operated within a climate dominated by the Cold War, one that was therefore virulently anti-communist. This led to the media censoring themselves in case any of their contents could be interpreted as supporting communism. We could perhaps update this, substituting the word "communist" with "terrorist" or "Islamic funda-mentalist" – in both cases, the argument is the same: the media operate within an ideological climate that supports only certain views while tacitly censoring alternative or contradictory views and opinions.

For cultural diversity, the implications of this model are rather straightforward: at best it will be ignored, as it will not be newsworthy or considered "sexy" enough to sell. At worst, it will be scapegoated as the "other" or "enemy." As for general audi-ences, these are socialized into becoming good and obedient citizens: to accept their lot as natural and just, and never to question the way things are. At the same time, media workers must learn to conform to dominant models, and to suppress their criti-cal and investigative abilities in the service of the media corporations. The role of the media in this sense is clearly ideological: they help to maintain capitalist order by spread-ing "false consciousness", i.e. preventing people from critically apprehending the world. This points to an emphasis within this perspective on research that shows the economic interconnections of media corporations and political actors, as well as the ways in which media corporations induct their workers into the logic of media work. In short, this perspective focuses more on the production side of the media, as it is there where all the work is done, while audiences merely sit passively on their couches.

These two elements, the focus on one side of the media process and the assumption that audiences are passive recipients of media contents, point to a kind of reduction-ism in this perspective. Specifically, in its quest to explain the broader context within which the media operate, it reduces their operations to a result, or an epiphenome-non, of capitalism. Although it is both useful and necessary to place the media within a social, political, and economic context, we must not overlook the processes that belong to the media as such, or the difficulties in controlling and predicting audience reactions. In other words, the problem here is that this perspective does not pay enough attention to the "media logic" itself, as something that is unique and specific to the media, over and above their function within capitalism; this can be formulated as the question of what have the media brought to capitalism. Secondly, the passive audience view is unwarranted: while perhaps it is clear that there is no widespread subversion of capitalism, there is no reason to assume that human beings are "cultural dupes" (Hall, 1980) ready to lap up whatever the media serve. Notwithstanding the efforts of more recent theorists to rethink this paradigm in non-reductionist terms (e.g. Mosco, 1996; Golding and Murdock, 1997), the dissatisfaction with the priori-tization of economic and production factors led to the formulation of alternative approaches, termed here socio-cultural approaches.

5.4 Socio-Cultural Approaches to the Media

One of the main characteristics of this approach is the positioning of the media within their socio-cultural environment. While previous approaches emphasized the psycho-social attributes of audiences, structural and formal features of the media, and economic determinants of media functioning, socio-cultural perspectives seek to identify the specific role played by the media in current societies. Moreover, socio-cultural approaches reject the transmission view of communication, which understands communication as a linear process, beginning with a source transmitting a message via a channel to a receiver. Rather, communication is seen as an integral part of society, functioning as a means of sharing and maintaining beliefs and ideas (Carey, 1975/1989).

Specifically, communication is understood as the process par excellence for the construction and maintenance of society: James Carey defines communication as "a symbolic process whereby reality is produced, maintained, repaired, and transformed" (1975/1989: 23). This means that the role of communication is necessarily an "ideological" one, in the sense not of leading to a "false consciousness" but of constructing, (re)presenting, and (re)producing understandings and ideas of the world around us. Building upon such a view, theorists then move on to specify the ways in which such construction and representation take place in the media. This should not be taken to imply that such construction is "innocent" or free of power differentials. Rather, the media are involved in *hegemonic* processes, whereby certain ideas, views, and opinions take precedence over others.

The best-known example of such a view, and one of the most influential, is found in an essay by Stuart Hall titled "Encoding/Decoding" (1980). Hall was concerned with elaborating a model of mass communication which would take into account the complexities of modern society: the various symbols and definitional struggles, as well as the various power asymmetries. Beginning with the message, Hall argues that it constitutes a discursive form, which is comprised of certain codes. In some ways, these codes that form a discursive message might be seen as existing in a kind of suspended state. This is because the message is "encoded", that is put together on the basis of certain codes shared by those who produce the media contents. These codes may include professional codes and conventions, as well as understandings of the world based on media workers' educational and class backgrounds. While these codes in a sense determine the message that will be circulated, they do not predetermine its reception. Rather, at the receiving end, the codes inscribed in the message may be rejected, negotiated, or fully accepted as a function of the codes shared by those decoding the message. Groups that share the educational and class background of the media workers are more likely to fully accept the media message, while those at the exact opposite educational and class position are more likely to fully reject the message. Those found in between the "dominant" and "dominated" groups are likely to accept the basic frame of reference of the message while rejecting some of its positions – this is what Hall calls a negotiated reading.

Hall divides the process of mediated communication into what he calls determinate moments. These include the production, circulation, and reception of media messages. Each of these moments is relatively autonomous, but must be studied in conjunction with the other processes, as together they form the circuit of communication. In addition, since these coexist in the same context, they feed back into each other. Thus, media messages become encoded in ways commensurable with the knowledge frameworks of media workers, and form a meaningful discourse; these are subsequently decoded, interpreted, or deciphered by groups which are themselves informed by knowledge frameworks. The extent of correspondence between the knowledge frameworks of encoders and decoders determines the reception or "reading" of the media message: it may be accepted "full and straight" (Hall, 1980: 171), rejected, or negotiated. At the same, potential discrepancies in codes, interpretations, and frameworks of knowledge show that the media are not so much involved in total domination (as the Frankfurt School implies) as in hegemony.

Hall is borrowing the term hegemony from the Italian Marxist theorist Antonio Gramsci. Gramsci, concerned with explaining the reasons why dominated groups accept their position, came up with the concept of hegemony: they accept their lot because they think it is natural and commonsensical. Dominant classes dominate precisely because they have somehow managed to "usurp" common sense, so that it justifies and naturalizes their position. Hegemony (leadership or domination) is not exercised through outright coercion but through a consensus based on dominant commonsense understandings. At the same time hegemony can never be total: there is always room for alternative views, however marginalized these may be. But hegemonic cultures will continue their dominance for as long as they control commonsense understandings. Gramsci's work (see Gramsci, 1971) constituted an important revision of classical Marxism in showing that cultural aspects, previously considered "ideological" and hence "superstructural," i.e. depending on the economic base, are in fact much more directly implicated in sustaining capitalism. This elevation of the significance of culture is shared by all cultural theorists, for whom the media exert their power precisely because they are involved in the reproduction of hegemonic cultural ideas.

In these terms, Hall views the relationship between media and cultural diversity as one caught up in hegemony. On the one hand, the media will make use of dominant codes and frames of reference, reproducing the ideas and discourses that contribute to the domination of certain ethno-cultural groups. As the history of colonialism shows, these groups are typically African and Asian – at any rate non-Western European. On the other hand, however, such groups have their own codes of reference and frameworks of knowledge, which lead them to reject and resist dominant meanings and discourses, while they also contribute to the creation of alternative networks of mediated communication, themselves then participating in a parallel communication circuit. This is precisely why several theorists have highlighted the importance of minority media (a. o. Husband, 1994; 2000; Georgiou and Silverstone, 2005): they allow the (re)creation, circulation, and representation of alternative discourses on cultural diversity, which in turn help sustain the cultural and moral integrity of marginalized groups.

It is hard to underestimate the significance and influence of Hall's essay. Despite some conceptual ambiguities, this essay has led to a shift from studying media texts towards studying audience reception. One of the first studies following Hall's model was David Morley's (1980) study *The Nationwide Audience*. Morley tested the premises of the model by showing a BBC program called *Nationwide* to different audience groups – separated in terms of class, education, and race. His findings supported Hall's ideas on the various decoding positions. Thus, black further education students, one of Morley's groups, produced an oppositional reading, rejecting the program's message. Eventually, this model led to a prioritization of the "moment" of audience reception and ideas of the active audience. Several studies supported the active audience thesis, according to which audiences are active interpreters of media messages, mobilizing their own frames of reference and rejecting or negotiating dominant or preferred meanings.

Followed through, this position implies that ethnic and culturally diverse audiences are producing their own readings of media messages. At the same time "mainstream" audiences do not buy wholesale representations of cultural diversity – in other words, viewing racist or problematic portrayals of diversity does not mean that audiences agree with them or that they turn racist. However, this leads to two problems: firstly, the problem of "essentializing" ethnic audiences; secondly, the issue of ultimately absolving media from their responsibility for racist or problematic portrayals. "Essentializing" ethnic audiences means that they are seen as a homogenous whole, acting and reacting in a uniform manner; in addition, to attribute an "essence" to a certain identity means that it possesses a set of unchanging features that characterize it as a whole. The problem here is that the diversity that exists within cultural groups is overlooked, as they are considered to be internally homogenous. There is no reason to assume, for example, that black audiences all produce the same – oppositional – readings of mainstream media; there is great diversity within these groups that leads them to a number of different interpretations of media contents, possibly unrelated to their "racial" identities. The second problem here is that ultimately this perspective ignores the media contents themselves, since it prioritizes audience interpretations of these. The question posed by this view is: what does it matter that media representations are problematic, potentially racist, biased, etc., since audiences in any case produce their own readings of such representations, readings which are likely to be oppositional? To pose this question, however, overlooks the ways in which media representations are part and parcel of the cycle or circuit of communication. And in addition, it removes any responsibility from the media for the perpetuation of stereotypical images and even racist representations and places the onus on audiences. But is this appropriate? Can we view audiences or the processes of audience interpretation of media messages as cut off from the whole process of communication? By focusing on audience reception at the expense of the processes of production and representation, this view ends up in the paradoxical situation of ignoring the media as such. These problems gave rise to the formulation of another perspective, that of mediation.

5.5 Mediation: The Difference Media Make

Although the term mediation has a long genealogy in sociology (see Couldry, 2008), it was first linked to the media by the Colombian theorist Jésus Martín-Barbero. In his book, *Communication, Culture and Hegemony: From Media to Mediations*, which was translated into English in 1993, Martín-Barbero attempted to produce an understanding of the role of the media that does not reduce them to outcomes of economic processes, that examines their wider implications and power, and that accepts that audiences are actively involved in the appropriation and interpretation of media materials. Moreover, Martín-Barbero wanted to take into account the institutional dynamics of the media, and their technological attributes and historical specificity. In other words, he attempted to develop a non-reductionist approach to the media, their power and their effects. While Martín-Barbero was writing specifically about Latin America and the social history of its media, Roger Silverstone (2005) sought to theoretically develop the concept of mediation into something approximating a new theory of the media. Both emphasize the domain of everyday life as the terrain in which the media "work," and both equally emphasize the interaction or dialectical relationship between media as institutions and their socio-cultural and political contexts. Before we examine the implications of this perspective for cultural diversity, we need to elaborate on its main premises.

Martín-Barbero's main concern was to avoid the elitist conception that mass-mediated popular culture is merely a means for dominating the "masses". On the other hand, he wanted to avoid the opposite contention that the media and dominant representations have no power at all. His theory, drawing on the work of Michel de Certeau, Gramsci, and others, is that processes of production, representation, and reception are locked in a particular kind of dialectic, whereby audiences creatively appropriate and resignify materials and representations they encounter in the media. They do so in terms of practices meaningful in their own lives. Thus, the homogenizing impulse found in the mass media –which is due to processes of production and dominant discourses – meet with the actual complexity and diversity of position, experience, and location found in audiences. The result is a complex dialectic, an appropriation of media contents that neither blindly reproduces dominant ideologies, nor subverts them or opposes them totally. Rather, it gives rise to something else, a hybrid culture – Martín-Barbero uses the term *mestizajes* or mixtures to refer to the cultures that emerge out of the encounter between the mass media and popular cultures. To study the media from the perspective of mediation more broadly refers to the study of the media in terms of the specific mixtures that emerge when different logics meet: when the logic of production meets that of representation, and when both meet the logics of reading, use, and interpretation by differentially placed social groups.

It is precisely this dialectic that Roger Silverstone insisted upon. Silverstone attempted to clarify and elaborate on the theoretical premises of mediation in order to provide a clear theoretical statement. He defines mediation in the following terms:

> Mediation is a fundamentally dialectical notion which requires us to address the processes of communication as both institutionally and technologically driven and embedded. Mediation, as a result, requires us to understand how processes of communication change the social and cultural environments that support them as well as the relationships that participants, both individual and institutional, have to that environment and to each other. At the same time it requires a consideration of the social as in turn a mediator: institutions and technologies as well as the meanings that are delivered by them are mediated in the social processes of reception and consumption. (Silverstone, 2005: 189)

Silverstone is here enriching the cycle of communication through incorporating technological and institutional dimensions alongside those of media production, representation, and consumption or use. But more fundamentally, Silverstone explicitly wants mediation to refer to the changes instituted by the media in our social environments, thereby acknowledging media power. However, the relationship is a dialectical one, thereby paying attention to the ways in which reception, consumption, or use (all these terms used here interchangeably) feed back into media institutions, technologies, and outputs. Silverstone (2005: 191) further specifies the main premises of this paradigm or media theory: (i) all media processes or moments interact, and no single process (e.g. production) can be said to determine another (e.g. consumption); (ii) flux and fluidity characterize both production and consumption, and consumption does not spell the end of the communication process; rather it feeds back into it in numerous ways; (iii) "media power exists as a generalized resource of symbolic definition" (Silverstone, 2005: 191), which involves all of us, producers and audiences, although our involvement is not equal. This understanding, as Downing (2000) points out, also includes alternative media, which must also be seen as involved in struggles for media power; (iv) there is a need for a broader social theory, which will locate the media and the process of mediation in its proper place and which will acknowledge its historical specificity.

In short we can see in Silverstone's account a synthesis of many of the elements we encountered earlier in this chapter in an isolated form. Processes of production, institutional and technological development, textual dynamics, and media use and reception are all involved in a dialectic which takes specific forms at specific historical junctures and which constitutes the process of mediation of meanings. In this manner, this account acknowledges the role played by technological evolution (as McLuhan does), the role played by forces of capitalism and modernity (as Adorno and Horkheimer do), the role played by dominant players and corporations in determining media outputs (as both the Frankfurt School and Herman and Chomsky do), while finally taking seriously audiences themselves, their psycho-social, cultural, and historical contexts (as Katz and Lazarsfeld, Hall, and the active audience paradigm do).

While this perspective presents a unique synthesis that can become very fruitful in guiding empirical studies, it is rather too vaguely conceived, giving rise to important conceptual and methodological openings. Mirca Madianou (2005), who has conducted one of the first empirical studies within this paradigm, points out that because of the emphasis on the fluidity of meanings, it is hard to empirically locate meaning: is it to be found in the text, in producers' discourses, or in audience interpretations? The point here is that meaning in mediation becomes elusive, especially since, as Silverstone put it, "mediated meanings are not exhausted at the point of consumption" (2005: 191).

Another opening here concerns the question of power. Silverstone clearly acknowledges the complexity of this issue, arguing that media power is located in the power to provide definitions of symbols and signs, which involves all the participants in the process of communication. However, this may lead to the inappropriate conclusion that they are equally endowed with the same degree of power. In other words, the problem of power asymmetry is not very clearly articulated. Couldry (2008) makes the point that this is a problem inherent in viewing mediation in dialectical terms. Specifically, he argues that to speak of mediation as a dialectic appears to mask power asymmetries between different media actors, overlooking the fact that some groups cannot influence the media process at all. Couldry then proposes to view mediation as capturing a variety of dynamics (rather than a dialectic) within media flows of production, circulation, interpretation, and so on. In these terms, some of these reinterpretations or appropriations might end up influencing the general process while others become lost or ignored. Although Couldry may have a point in arguing for discontinuity to be seen as part of mediation, perhaps we could point out here that even such discontinuity ends up "structuring" the whole process by omission if not by commission.

Whether viewed as a dialectic or specific dynamic, the point raised by a theory of mediation is that mass-mediated communication is an ongoing, dynamic, and fluid process involving several sets of actors, and operating at several levels at once. The question from our point of view is to identify the implications of a theory of mediation for the relationship between media and cultural diversity. We need, firstly to think of this relationship in terms of a mediation of cultural diversity: this implies not only a non-linear process, but a more dynamic – even dialectical – relationship, in which cultural minorities are not seen as the passive victims of racist representations. Yet, paying attention to the issue of asymmetrical power, we need to think about the institutional contents and logics that feed into the forms that the mediation of cultural diversity will take. These in turn are met with a varied set of responses, some of which end up influencing the media environment in direct or indirect ways. Moreover, these processes have to be located in particular socio-historical contexts. This means that we should not look for the "effects" of the media on culturally diverse groups, or for particular, negative or positive, media representations of cultural diversity, or, finally, for ways in which audiences (minority and majority) resist or appropriate these. Rather, a mediational perspective means that we need to incorporate *all* of these in order to fully understand mediated cultural diversity.

Following through this perspective, the remainder of this book will examine processes of media production, representation, and consumption as they engage with cultural diversity. The main argument in this investigation is that cultural diversity in this particular historical juncture must be seen as mediated, that is, traversing processes of the production, circulation, representation, and reception/consumption of meaning that characterize late modern, technologically evolved societies. In this manner, we will examine the mediation of cultural diversity as it emerges in all those areas and as found in the work of relevant theorists and researchers. Some of these processes inscribe cultural diversity as essential, while others allow its dynamism and ever-shifting aspects to predominate. The main argument underlying a theory of mediation is that understanding the position, role, and status of cultural diversity in late modern societies requires that we understand the multiple ways in which it is mediated.

5.6 Conclusions

This chapter reviewed several media theories, and examined their position on the relationship between the media and cultural diversity. The following table summarizes these theoretical approaches, their main arguments and views vis-à-vis difference. All approaches have made valuable contributions to our understanding of cultural diversity and the media, with each focusing on and prioritizing different elements. All of them essentially deal with the question of media power (or effects), but make different arguments. However, most theories have faced the problem of reductionism and determinism; they seem to explain media power on the basis of one factor: economics, or technological innovation, or cultural factors, and so on. This is where a theory of mediation gains an advantage.

Table 5.1 Media theories

Approach to the media	Main aspects and arguments	Position/findings on cultural diversity
Socio-psychological approaches	• Communication a linear process of transmission; • media influence located at the individual, psychological level; • focus on audiences or the "receiving" part of communication	Mixed findings: • Racist media contents lead to racist attitudes (Peterson and Thurstone, 1933); • Racists will always interpret media contents in racist ways – thus, if society is already racist, then there is little the media can do (Katz and Lazarsfeld, 1955/2006)
Medium theory	• Media influence located at the structural level; • emphasis on media technologies; • different media sustain or even lead to different forms of political, social, and cultural organization	Different media lead to different relationships: • Print→homogenization (McLuhan, 1964; see Anderson, 1983/1991) • Radio or the "tribal drum" (McLuhan, 1964)→polarizing people • Television→the "mosaic": accepts and promotes diversity (McLuhan, 1964) • Internet→unknown (see Chapter 12
Political-economic approaches	• Media influenced by the economy and their influence determined by economic factors; • emphasis on media economics (questions of ownership, concentration, etc.)	• Cultural diversity ignored, coopted or scapegoated according to needs of capitalist media corporations (Adorno and Horkheimer, 1949; Herman and Chomsky, 1988); • the culture industry imposes homogenization of all styles (Adorno and Horkheimer, 1947/1997)
Socio-structural approaches	• Contextualization of media in socio-cultural terms; • a cyclical, non-linear view of communication (Hall, 1980); • media audiences active; • media power diffused (and for some defused as well)	• Ethnic or culturally diverse audiences produce their own readings of media texts, often oppositional to dominant ones (Morley, 1980); • mainstream audiences may accept, reject, or negotiate media messages on cultural diversity depending on their cultural and socio-structural background (Hall, 1980); • media have limited power over cultural diversity
Mediation theory	• Communication as a dynamic and dialectical process located in concrete socio-historical circumstances; • No single "moment" determining outcomes, but asymmetrical relationship between processes of production, representation, and consumption (Silverstone, 2005; Couldry, 2008)	• The relationship between media and cultural diversity is determined by a complex interaction between historical, political, socio-cultural, and economic factors, alongside media institutional logics; • To understand this relationship all processes involved in mediation (i.e. media production, representation, and consumption) must be examined (see Martin-Barbero, 1993; Madianou, 2005; Silverstone, 2005; Couldry, 2008)

A theory of mediation understands the process of communication as a non-linear process: no one component can be privileged, and power is understood as diffused across the elements of this process. Everything counts, albeit in an asymmetrical way; unpredictability, dynamism, and flux characterize media communication, but this should not be taken to mean that anything goes. Rather, the research direction in which a theory of mediation is taking us is informed by social history and concrete political, economic, and socio-cultural circumstances. Thus, in terms of cultural diversity, this means that its relationship with the media is a dynamic one: in concrete settings, mediated communication interacts with political, socio-cultural, and economic factors, leading to different relationships. The relationship between media and cultural diversity is therefore not already given, or the same across the world. Different media systems in different countries interact with the specific circumstances of each country, giving rise to different outcomes: cultural diversity may be encouraged, debated, ignored, marginalized; it may fight back, respond, resist, represent itself, and/or all of these at the same time. We cannot, therefore, predict a single trajectory for mediated cultural diversity, but we can study the products of the various circumstances in different settings. The following chapter will begin with the process of media production, before moving on to the processes of representation and reception.

6

Media Production and Diversity

6.1 Media Production and Mediation

In a theory of mediation, the process of media production plays a crucial, albeit non-determining, role in mediating diversity. Even if we accept that mediated communication is a non-linear dialectical process, this process must begin somewhere. The examination of mass-mediated communication can therefore begin with the process of production, as this is what sets in motion – but does not determine – media communication. Thinking about media production processes, we need first to locate these in their appropriate social, political, and economic context. In addition, the media work within a specific organizational context that influences their operations. Professional values, as well as, more generally, the cultural backgrounds of the media communicators themselves may contribute towards the process of media production. These are some of the issues that this chapter will address.

Specifically, the first part of this chapter will examine the media within capitalism but also within different regulatory contexts. Capitalism may be globally the dominant form of socio-economic organization, but different countries follow different trajectories or paths in adjusting to capitalism. In the same vein, the media in different countries operate in different regulatory frameworks that in turn influence their operations. Secondly, we need to examine the specific logics that characterize the media as institutions, as production is often thought to be the result of such institutional logics. Altheide and Snow (1979) were among the first to identify what they called media logic, referring to the specific way in which the media address and intervene in public debates. Of relevance here is Pierre Bourdieu's sociological approach to the media and journalism as a field, while more recently the concept of "mediatization" has been proposed as a means for capturing the specificity of the media and the ways in which they affect and reproduce the world (Schulz, 2004). Thirdly, we need to know about the communicators themselves: who are they and how do they influence the media production process? Production values and journalistic ideologies are some of the ways in which such influence is exerted. In addition, theorists have attempted to explain the general lack of fair portrayals of cultural diversity in terms of a general lack of ethnic and cultural minority media workers. Following multicultural policies with an emphasis on equal opportunities, we might ask if this has made any difference in terms of increases in the numbers of minority workers. Finally, in the concluding section we will review all these aspects from the point of view of a theory of mediation.

6.2 Media Corporations

Media means business – media corporations exist in order to generate profits, notwithstanding the crucial ethical, political, and socio-cultural role played by the media. The existence of public-service media, such as the BBC, constitutes the exception that proves the rule. And even public-service media are, as we will see, increasingly subject to the rules of the market. The consequences of the media operating as corporations are (at least) twofold. Firstly, the media must be seen as operating in conditions of (globalized) capitalism; while, as we will see shortly, there are certain differences in regulatory contexts, overall the media must be seen as involved primarily in a quest for profit. Secondly, in thinking about the process of media production, we must incorporate the role played by a capitalist mode of production: we must not only "follow the money," but also see how the media as institutions are shaped by capitalist conditions of existence (commodification).

What does it mean in practice to say that the media operate in conditions of globalized capitalism? It means that more and more power and control of the media is concentrated in the hands of few large corporations that operate across borders. Typically, this is thought to occur primarily via three main processes (see Murdock and Golding, 1974 Mosco, 1996): (i) integration; (ii) diversification; and (iii) internationalization. To begin with integration, also often referred to as concentration, in its more simple sense this means that more and more media are owned by the same owners. In the early twentieth century, in the UK, the first media "barons" – and many of them were actually granted peerages, such as Lords Beaverbrook, Northcliffe, and Rothermere – owned chains of newspapers, and yielded considerable political power. Similarly, in the USA, William Randolph Hearst, who was famously the basis of Orson Welles' character in the film *Citizen Kane* (1941), owned several newspapers. Integration can be horizontal and vertical. Horizontal integration means that more and more producers of similar products form part of an integrated media corporation. In simpler terms, it means that more and more media forms are concentrated in the hands of a single owner (or corporation). Thus, News Corporation owns not only newspapers (e.g. the *Sun* and *The Times* in the UK), but also cable broadcasting channels (e.g. Fox in the USA), satellite television (e.g. BSkyB), book and magazine publishers (e.g. HarperCollins and Inside Out in Australia), film production companies (20th Century Fox), as well as web formats such as MySpace. More often than not, media corporations are also vertically integrated: they own producers of goods or services across different phases of the production system. For example, within a media conglomerate, a film production company may have signed certain actors to work with, and it may own talent agencies and film studios, DVD-manufacturing companies, movie theaters and so on (Croteau and Hoynes, 2003).

Diversification is another process contributing to increased media power. This refers to the expansion of media corporations across other industries, mainly through mergers and acquisitions. Thus, Vivendi, a European-based media corporation, owns telecoms companies (Maroc Telecom), music production companies (Universal), as well as games companies(Vivendi Games), film production companies and studios (StudioCanal and Universal Studios), broadcasting channels (Canal +), and utility companies (e.g. the UK train company Connex).

Finally, internationalization refers to the increasing expansion of media corporations in other countries through export and investment. This trend has been amplified in more recent years and is considered both a result (e.g. Doyle, 2002) and one of the causes of globalization (see, for instance, Appadurai, 1990). Most notoriously, Rupert Murdoch and his News Corporation own and control several media across different continents.

The focus on media ownership is justified on the basis that powerful media owners have a direct influence on the way in which media organizations are run and, crucially, on what they have to say. First and foremost, media owners will support their own interests, rather than serve the public good. More broadly, however, the operation of media companies as for-profit corporations has had wider implications. Thus, Mosco (1996) following the work of Smythe (1981) and other political economists of the media (e.g. Adorno and Horkheimer, 1949; Murdock and Golding, 1974), suggests that the operation of the media in a capitalist context results in the commodification of media production. This term, found in Marxian political economy, refers to the transformation of use value (what we use a thing or product for) into exchange value (what we get by selling or exchanging this product). For the media, this means that production has become a process whereby the media are transformed from something that has use value – that people enjoy using per se – to something that is valued only insofar it can be exchanged and can generate income. In other words, the media production process is such that issues of profit and income generation will always assume priority over issues of quality, ethics, and fairness. In these terms, trends such as the concentration of media ownership are not only contributing to the control of the media by a few powerful people who exert direct control over media organizations, they are also contributing to the spread of capitalist social and economic relations, which include the unfettered pursuit of profit.

In many ways the domination of this model of large and global media corporations has been the result of years of liberal and neoliberal policies adopted initially by the US and later by other countries. Such neoliberal policies sought to abolish state regulation and control over media practices, leaving the "free market" and "competition" to take care of things. Thus, the continued rise of neoliberalism in the last thirty years or so has led towards a convergence in the regulation of the media across different countries. In a recent book covering Europe and North America, David Hallin and Paolo Mancini (2004) identify three media systems which are correlated with three distinct regulatory models: the Mediterranean or polarized plural model, the North/Central European or Democratic Corporatist model, and the North American or Liberal model. In the polarized plural model, which is found in countries of South Europe, such as Italy, Greece, Portugal, and Spain, state regulation tends to be tighter and more controlled, while the media tend to be closely involved in party politics, and commercial media have developed only relatively recently. In the Democratic Corporatist model, prevalent in North/Central European countries, we find the coexistence of commercial media and media tied to the interests of organized social and political groups, while state regulation is discreetly present at all times. Finally, the

Liberal model, found in the USA, Ireland, and the UK, is characterized by the dominance of commercial media and the relative absence of state regulation. Despite the existence of different regulatory regimes, Hallin and Mancini point out that the pressures of globalization and the rise of neoliberalism have led to a tendency towards the homogenization of media systems, which tend to converge to the Liberal model.

The upshot of the prevalence of the neoliberal model is that media corporations are able to prioritize the pursuit of profit for their shareholders. One of the most common criticisms of the corporatization and conglomeration of media companies is that media pluralism is destroyed. As more and more independent media companies merge to form large media conglomerates, alternative views and interests, and creative but not overly commercial artistic work, are sacrificed at the altar of profit. For cultural diversity, this means that it will be taken into account only insofar it fits into the broader plans of media corporations. Furthermore, it implies that entrance into the media world will lead to commodification: cultural diversity will only be valued insofar as it has some exchange value. Indeed, as we shall see in Chapter 9, this commodification can be linked to a new representational regime that commodifies cultural diversity. But what does commodification actual mean for the production process and media organizations themselves? Theorists have argued that commodification and more broadly the relationship of the media to the economy have resulted in a distinct set of characteristics or "logic"; conversely, this "logic," or distinct way of doing things, is considered to be contributing to the commodification of the media. To understand this, we need to understand media organizations themselves and the context in which they operate. This will be considered next.

6.3 Media Organizations and Media Logics

Understanding the way in which media organizations operate is crucial in order to capture the relationship between cultural diversity and media production. Following upon a theory of mediation, the main argument here is that, although (or for some theorists, because) the media operate within a capitalist social organization, they have developed their distinct way of doing things, which in turn feeds into the current phase of capitalism. At the same time, observing and theorizing the way in which media organizations operate will provide important insights into the way in which the media create and sustain specific types of social relations. Three distinct but related approaches will be considered here: Altheide and Snow's (1979) media logic, Pierre Bourdieu's field theory (e.g. Bourdieu, 1999; Benson and Neveu, 2005), and the more recent concept of mediatization (Schulz, 2004). All these rest on the premise that the media have developed a set of distinct operations, functions, and characteristics which subsequently feed into the social world.

6.3.1 Media logic

In an early but influential work, David Altheide and Robert Snow (1979) argued that media organizations have developed a distinct logic. Specifically, media logic refers to the assumptions and processes that inform the production of media outputs within particular media. This logic includes certain formats and grammars. Media formats – or

genres – refer to the rules for defining, selecting, organizing, and recognizing information. Grammar refers to the ways in which different materials and media products
are put together, the kind of sequence they follow, and the relationships between
them. Altogether these elements constitute a distinct way of perceiving (or constructing) the world. According to Altheide (2004), media organizations employ this logic
widely, with the result that they transform every aspect or issue that goes through
them in ways compatible to their logic. For instance, journalism is transformed by this
media logic: from the pursuit of information, journalism has become more an entertainment format. More broadly, the wide application of media logics has given rise a
media culture that has become increasingly pervasive in recent years. This media culture is characterized by an emphasis on novelty, immediacy, personalization, dramati-
zation, conflict, and so on (McQuail, 2005: 332). Media organizations therefore
consciously or unconsciously make use of this media culture, which then becomes
even more entrenched. Here we can also classify work in news values (Galtung and
Ruge, 1965; Gans, 1979). Relevant studies have shown that media organizations
select and present news following certain pre-determined values and criteria, such as,
among others, conflictual, personalized, or dramatized news stories.

   Altheide's main argument is that media logic is transformative: the media transform
everything that goes through them, on the basis of their own logic. This implies that,
when issues concerning cultural diversity enter the media production process, they
will end up being transformed into issues characterized by this media logic. Following
this argument, issues of equality and recognition will end up personalized, dramatic,
conflictual, etc. We will examine in more detail the actual media contents or representations in later chapters. It should be pointed out here that Altheide and Snow (1988)
refer to this process as "mediation." This use of the term is quite different to the one
outlined in Chapter 5. For Altheide and Snow, mediation implies the one-way or linear imposition of a certain media logic onto the world, while the way in which we use
the term here implies a more dialectical process whereby the media are both altering
and are themselves altered by the world (see also Couldry, 2008). Thus, although the
notion of a distinct media logic is useful in understanding the ways in which media
organizations function, this uni-directional flow of influence seems somewhat simplified, leaving several unanswered questions.

6.3.2 The field of media and cultural production

One of these concerns the issue of where this logic actually comes from. The work of
Pierre Bourdieu is instructive here. Bourdieu argues that the social world is structured
into fields or arenas of life, such as education, art, the economy, sport, and so on. Each
of these is characterized by its own rules of engagement, its dominant and dominated
"classes," and its own capital (Bourdieu, 1984; 1991; Bourdieu and Wacquant, 1992).
All fields are relatively autonomous, but are influenced by the operations of a kind of
"meta-field," the field of power. This determines the relations between fields, but also
the amount of capital circulating within each field. At the current historical juncture,
this meta-field of power is determined by capitalism and the power relations it engenders. While Bourdieu's field sociology is far too complex to be described here, his
arguments have important implications for understanding media production and have
to be considered at least in a summary form.

Bourdieu has considered the media in more detail in a slim volume titled *On Television and Journalism* (1999), but he has also written about the media in *The Rules of Art* (1996) and *The Field of Cultural Production* (1993b) (see also, Benson and Neveu, 2005; Couldry, 2003; Hesmondhalgh, 2006). More specifically for the field of cultural production, Bourdieu argues that it contains two subfields: small- and large-scale production. The former refers to small and artistic projects, and is characterized by a high degree of autonomy vis-à-vis the field of power; here production follows the logic of "art for art's sake" and thus enjoys a high level of symbolic capital, or recognition of its value by others. Large-scale cultural production is perhaps better understood as mass production and is characterized by a low degree of autonomy, although it is high in economic capital; journalism and other kinds of mass media production belong to this subfield. Because of their relatively low symbolic capital, journalism and media production are considered to be dominated by the small-scale subfield of the production of *avant-garde* and other artistic works, in the sense that they enjoy much less prestige and status. Nevertheless, journalism and mass media production exert important power over other fields because they dominate the means of public expression. And because this (sub)field is dominated by the field of power (determined by the market and economic capital) it imposes its own rules and principles over the public aspects of other (sub)fields.

For Bourdieu, the whole field of cultural production, of which journalism is a subfield, is in a tension produced by two opposing principles of legitimation: peer recognition and public recognition as expressed by sales and ratings. For Bourdieu (1998) the problem is that the latter has come to dominate media production almost totally. Media production, in other words, is "permanently subject to trial by market" (Bourdieu, 1999: 71), through competition for ratings or for advertising income. This competition has two effects: an emphasis on novelty, "scoops," and "exclusives" which have the aim of attracting large audiences, and a constant preoccupation with what other media producers are doing, in order that no major news or themes are missed. Ultimately this results in uniformity, a general lack of diversity and alternative views, as all media producers are after the same news.

The main point in Bourdieu's account is that the subfield of media production is articulated with the field of power, which at the current historical juncture is dictated by capitalism, thereby leading to a set of market-driven characteristics. The only way of escaping this is to reinstate journalistic autonomy, allowing journalists and other media producers to develop their own rules and principles of legitimation free from the demands of the market. Indeed, this argument has certain commonalities with arguments emphasizing the crucial role played by public service broadcasting in ensuring a degree of autonomous media production (e.g. Curran, 1998).

For the relationship between cultural diversity and media production, Bourdieu's view implies that the logic of the market and ratings will apply here too: thus, issues pertaining to cultural diversity will only be covered insofar as they may lead to increased ratings or advertising income. At the same time, when such issues are given media time, they are likely to be transformed into something sensational, as this is the way in which ratings are generated: for instance, race riots or other forms of ethnic conflict are guaranteed air time. On the other hand, so long as the field of small-scale production keeps on existing, cultural diversity finds a small but autonomous space for expression. More broadly speaking, ensuring that the media can operate autonomously from the market might lead to the creation of more and more diffuse autonomous spaces for communicating and expressing aspects and experiences pertaining to cultural diversity which may eventually lead to an overall fairer and more equitable relationship to cultural diversity. In Chapter 12 we will discuss the extent to which the new media allow for the operation of such autonomous media spaces. On the other hand, however, Bourdieu's account appears somewhat deterministic in that it does not allow for multiplicity, creativity, or exchange between fields. Market domination seems to be an irresistible, one-way force determining more or less everything else. While rich in insights, this work focuses almost exclusively on the structuring role of power understood as dictated by the requirements of global capitalism. The specificity of the field of the media appears lost in this theoretical version; this specificity and the multiple forces structuring the media are considered in the perspective known as mediatization.

6.3.3 Mediatization

Thus, Bourdieu's emphasis on autonomy and the domination of media production by market concerns seems to overlook characteristics specific to the media, which subsequently feed into and determine the kind of relationship the media acquire with other fields, or institutions. Specifically, Bourdieu's work on the field is rightly characterized as "work in progress" (Benson and Neveu, 2005) as it has failed to consider either the media producers themselves (Hesmondhalgh, 2006) or those characteristics, technical, symbolic and economic that make the media "field" what it is. It is here that we may consider Schulz's (2004) work on mediatization. Although this notion may be seen as competing with that of mediation (see Couldry, 2008), we use it in this context to understand the process of media production because of its consideration of a combination of factors and characteristics specific to the media.

Schulz argues that the media function through three processes: firstly, they operate through the *relay* process, which rests on their specific technological attributes that enable the transmission of "code." The relay function, moreover, rests on the media ability to overcome and bridge temporal and spatial distance. Secondly, the *semiotic function*, in which media messages are "encoded," that is, they are constructed on the basis of certain rules, formats, styles, and so on; Altheide and Snow's media logic can be located here. Finally, *economic processes* must be seen as part of the overall media production process, but perhaps not as determining as implied in Bourdieu (1999). All these characteristics circumscribe and determine the production process, which then must be seen as having technical, semiotic, and economic aspects, all equally contributing to the final outcome.

Such a position may be seen as having important implications for cultural diversity. Firstly, in terms of the relay function and the technological elements of media production, we might say that these allow cultural diversity to overcome limitations of time and space. This is important particularly because difference is always seen as belonging somewhere else in terms of time (consider so-called "primitive" cultures) and of space (consider the notions of indigenous and "host" cultures). In technological terms, the ability of the media is crucial in providing bridges that connect the here and the there and the then and the now. In these terms, we find here a promise that does not exist in any of the previous accounts. Mediatized cultural difference may therefore link time and space, providing new configurations and dimensions for diversity.

However, the semiotic or symbolic elements enter the equation: these are notoriously involved in reproducing dominant ideas and opinions about things; we can expect, therefore, the media to engage cultural diversity within codes, formats, and symbols that belittle, dominate, or marginalize it. Finally, the economic aspects point to the elements of commodification and competition discussed above: cultural diversity will be given air time only insofar as it makes economic sense. Moreover, when and if airtime is given, this will necessitate that cultural diversity conforms to the profit-driven imperatives of media production processes. Articulated together these elements imply that the relationship between cultural diversity and difference is one in which the latter emerges distorted or ignored. Clearly, mediatization has gone a long way towards connecting previously disparate elements, such as technological and semiotic codes, along with economic factors. On the other hand, however, it appears to overlook the creative and unexpected elements of the production process, focusing primarily on structural factors. An additional problem is that mediatization implies a series of more or less identical transformations brought about by the media; but, as Nick Couldry (2008) has argued, the relationship of the media and society is more complex and more reciprocal. We cannot predict the ways in which the media will influence the world, nor can we foretell the ways in which they themselves are subject to the social-transformative forces of culture and history.

6.4 Media Workers

In most of the approaches discussed above, media workers' role is already given: they consciously or more often unconsciously reproduce media logics, thereby sustaining a problematic and heteronomous media system. Given that the media system indeed suffers from a number of problems, and given its general resistance to change, such views may well be seen as justified. When, however, media producers are considered as individuals, research has focused on questions of imbalance, bias, and the influence brought by individual and idiosyncratic factors in the process of media production. What might be this perspective bring to our understanding of the relationship between media production and cultural diversity? In the first instance, this has led researchers to argue that mainstream media producers are more likely to cover and select stories that reflect their backgrounds and interests and to ignore those of other groups.

One of the earliest studies on media communicators has focused on their role as "gatekeepers." David Manning White (1950) studied "Mr. Gates," an editor of a daily newspaper in the US of the late 1940s, in order to understand the role played by the individual background of media communicators in the selection of news stories. "Mr. Gates" was anti-Catholic and did not support Harry Truman's (the US President at the time) economic policies. White found that his selection of stories broadly reflected these views, thereby concluding that editors subjectively select stories based on their own attitudes and opinions. Later studies have sought to address the claim that journalists in the US tend to be liberal in their personal opinions, and hence to report and interpret the news from their personal perspective. However, an analysis of fifty-nine studies of US presidential campaigning coverage by D'Alessio and Allen (2000, cited in

Whitney and Ettema, 2003) concluded that there was no evidence to support the claim that communicators had introduced a liberal or conservative bias to their reporting.

While theorists such as Michael Schudson (2005) examined media organizational culture as a factor influencing the production of news, others focused on the role played not by beliefs but by identities, such as gender and ethnic identity, held by professional communicators and media producers. The main idea involved here is that women and ethnic minority communicators will choose and present news and other media products from their point of view. The relative lack of such communicators may therefore be responsible for the under-representation of stories concerning cultural diversity (e.g. Gilliam, 1991). However, empirical studies have failed to support the view that such communicators select more relevant stories, or indeed that they report from a "minority" point of view (Bleske, 1997 cited in Whitney and Ettema, 2003). Given the question of essentializing ethnic and gender identities – that is, attributing a stable and core "essence" to those identities – perhaps we should not expect the identity of the communicators themselves to make any difference.

On the other hand, to have diversity in the newsroom is a value in its own right, especially given the equal opportunity policies of recent years. But is this the case? To what extent are minorities employed in the media? Findings are mixed here. ASNE, the American Society of Newspaper Editors, has pursued an equal opportunities policy as reflected in their Diversity Mission Statement and strategic goals or benchmarks (see boxes 6.1 and 6.2). The main idea here is that, every three years, ASNE reviews the situation on the basis of the benchmarks and adopts new resolutions or revises its goals according to new evidence. 2008 marked the thirtieth anniversary of ASNE's employment census, and ASNE happily reported that things had moved on significantly. In 1978 an estimated 43,000 full-time journalists worked as editors, reporters, copy editors, and photographers; of this 3.95 percent were minorities. In 2008, the census found 52,600 full-time journalists of which 13.52 percent are minorities (www.asne.org). However, this still falls short of ASNE's mission statement, since ethnic minorities make up about 34 percent of the US population according to the US Census Bureau (reported in www.asne.org). In addition, most US broadcasters have adopted equal opportunities policies, but there are no published reports regarding the extent of their success, signalling that their rhetoric might not always be in line with their actual practices.

In Europe, the European Broadcasting Union has a special group on cultural diversity – the Intercultural and Diversity Group – encouraging and promoting pluralism and diversity in all areas of broadcasting. Broadcasters from across Europe implement a series of strategies in order to achieve minority representation in the workplace, but so far the results of these are unknown. In 2007, both the BBC and France Télévisions reported that they had commissioned research on the ethnic constitution of their workplace, but by late 2008 the results had not been published. Further, the BBC reported its plan to recruit 12.5 percent of its workforce from minority communities by December 2007, but again, we have no evidence to assess the success of this initiative. In the UK, a 2002 study by the Journalistss Training Forum reported that about 96 percent of UK journalists working in the media industry as a whole were white. This shows very clearly that the media workforce is not representative of the diversity more broadly encountered in Britain – the 2001 census puts the number of non-white British people at 7.9 percent (see http://www.statistics.gov.uk). To some extent this

Box 6.1   ASNE's diversity mission statement

To cover communities fully, to carry out their role in a democracy, and to succeed in the marketplace, the nation's newsrooms must reflect the racial diversity of American society by 2025 or sooner. At a minimum, all newspapers should employ journalists of color and every newspaper should reflect the diversity of its community.

The newsroom must be a place in which all employees contribute their full potential, regardless of race, ethnicity, color, age, gender, sexual orientation, physical ability or other defining characteristic.

Box 6.2   ASNE three-year benchmarks

- Increasing overall newsroom minority employment;
- increasing the number of minority interns;
- increasing the number of minority supervisors;
- reducing the number of newspapers with no minorities on staff; and
- measuring whether newspapers have achieved parity with their communities.

is a result of the failure to address discrimination in the workforce. However, media industries are required to operate within the legal system of their countries; thus, in countries such as France, where it is illegal to discriminate in any way, employers cannot invite applications specifically from ethnic minority applicants, since that would constitute discrimination. A first barrier to a diverse workforce might therefore be that minorities are not encouraged to apply for media positions by the employers themselves. To counter this, media employers in countries with explicit multicultural policies have introduced a vocabulary that seeks to actively recruit minority workers (see box 6.3). As a second step, media employers have cooperated with schools and other institutions, setting up mentoring and training schemes, thereby giving a taste of media work to people from diverse backgrounds, as well as offering them a path to media employment. Box 6.4 details some of these schemes.

Ethnic minority workers, however, may face a different kind of barrier. In 2006, the British Commission for Racial Equality reported that, although a relatively large number of young people from an ethnic minority background had considered a media career, in the end they decided against it, or, if they had entered it, had decided to leave it, as they thought that the media workforce was "too white." Another barrier faced by ethnic minority media workers is therefore the lack of awareness of diversity in media organizations. Similar concerns are expressed by Wilson (2000), who discusses the dilemmas faced by African-American journalists. Wilson argues that, when African-American journalists find employment in mainstream media, they have to either conform to the media organizational ethos, thereby acting as "whites," or else resign. For instance, a black journalist working for the *Washington Post* argued that the newspaper "frequently seems to interpret equal opportunity as meaning that if minorities and

Box 6.3   Encouraging culturally diverse applicants

- In 2005 WDR (Germany) stated: "WDR promotes cultural diversity in the company, therefore we welcome candidates with migration backgrounds," thereby actively encouraging minority communicators.
- SVT (Sweden) adds to its announcements that "experience or knowledge about different cultures and religions and language are valuable."
- NPS (Netherlands) defines itself as the multicultural broadcaster of the Netherlands, and thereby looking for multicultural talents.
- The human resources aims of the BBC regions are: recruitment, retention, and progression. Job advertisements include the requirement "an understanding of diverse communities needed."

Box 6.4   Diversifying the media workforce: training
and mentoring schemes

- Move On Up events, organized by BECTU, a UK-based independent union of broadcasting and entertainment workers, organizes events that allow talented professionals who want to make contacts and seek new opportunities to meet senior executives from a range of organizations. http://www.bectu.org.uk/news/gen/ng0291.html
- CREAM Plus is a pan-European project to promote education and research in the field of media and diversity, and one of the main activities is the organization of a Day of the Media for students of secondary schools. For one day every year participating broadcasters open their studios to students, who can attend different workshops. Parallel workshops on media education are also organized for teachers and school coaches. http://www.olmcm.org/
- Digi-tales is a storytelling project involving young people from across Europe, who make short films about their lives and so learn to write a script, record voiceovers, and edit photos or drawings. http://www.digi-tales.org
- VRT (Flanders, Belgium) encourages young people to think about careers in television and radio by organizing "reaching-out" days for pupils in their last years of secondary school. http://www.vrt.be/vrt_master/over/overdevrt_diversiteit_schermen/index.shtml
- Every year the diversity cell at VRT organizes positive action to give people from minority groups the opportunity to get experience in a media job. The placements are in activities such as research or production assistance in an editor's office from one of the mainstream TV, radio, or online programs.
- The Finnish YLE Mundo project, funded by the EU ESF Equal Programme, included a two-year media education and work-training program for ethnic minority youth. Its overall aim was "to blur, or even erase, the borders between native Finns and immigrants." http://ec.europa.eu/employment_social/equal/practical-examples/employ-07-mundo_en.cfm

• Since 2005, the "WDR-grenzenlos" (WDR-boundless) project in Germany has introduced young journalists with migration backgrounds to WDR and to broadcasting. Every year, ten young talents are given the chance to attend a four-week practical course in various WDR divisions and two weeks' training in journalistic theory. Most of the young journalists that have gone through the "WDR-grenzenlos" program have stayed with the broadcaster. http://www.grenzenlos2007.de/

Box 6.5   Increasing awareness in the media workplace

In December 2007 WDR (Germany) organized a "Diversity Day" with the aim of promoting the culture of acceptance of cultural diversity within the broadcaster, aimed at the employees and management in the corporation. WDR has a program for all its 4,400 employees, called "mobility and flexibility." It includes the opportunity for everybody to choose a completely new department within the company where they can work for four weeks and gather new experiences, for example in one of their multicultural programs.

Trade unions of journalists, professional organizations, and joint actions by these organizations can be instrumental in improving the reporting of diversity and improving the position of minorities in the labour force as well as in raising awareness and improving quality standards on media diversity.

Organizations of journalists should have as a major consideration the equal representation of minorities in the workforce. Consideration must be given not only to the number of people from minorities hired but to ensure their equal distribution within the organizational hierarchy.

women work hard enough and follow directions, they too can become white men" (Coleman *et al.*, 1986, cited in Wilson, 2000: 97). This has led some media employers to take measures to increase awareness of diversity in the workplace, with a view to eventually creating newsrooms that are sensitive and mindful of issues concerning cultural diversity. Examples of such measures and best practices are in box 6.5.

Beyond the issue of awareness, the culturally diverse media workforce face pressures of another kind. These concern what Simon Cottle (2000), following Kobena Mercer (1994), refers to as the burden of representation, and Clinton Wilson (2000) as a paradox. Media workers from an ethnic or culturally diverse background are primarily thought to be representatives of their group, rather than media professionals. On the one hand they are expected to uphold the values and practices of the media organization where they work, and on the other they are expected to work only or primarily in areas that touch upon matters of cultural diversity, where they are seen as expressing the "black" or other minority viewpoint. In addition, culturally diverse audiences expect minority journalists to address their own needs and concerns, thereby placing increasing pressure on those media workers with a minority background. Wilson argues that, whenever black journalists meet, they discuss this paradox, by pondering the question: "Am I a journalist who happens to be Black or am I a Black journalist?" (2000: 97). For media professionals more broadly this dilemma may be creatively constraining, as they feel constantly under pressure to speak with a voice representing their cultural background.

Within this context, it is particularly interesting that Simon Cottle's (2000) ethnographic work on the BBC found that the professional ethos of detachment and objectivity characteristic of the corporation resulted in a detachment of minority media workers from community interests. In this sense, adopting such professional values frees minority media workers from the "burden of representation." Such detachment, however, is not conducive to an engagement with cultural diversity, as it ends up in a watered-down version of multiculturalism as equivalence between communities. This kind of multiculturalism overlooks the important questions of inequality in material and symbolic terms. One of Cottle's BBC respondents eloquently summarized the situation: "I just feel sometimes that we cop out and that we water down … we're just not progressive in exploring the issues facing our community" (in Cottle, 2000: 107).

In addition, producers are often afraid to tackle head on the problems of power imbalances within and between communities, preferring instead to ignore or gloss over them: "[W]e've always been very, very careful, especially in our coverage of Muslim/Pakistani affairs, because of the trouble it can lead to. For example, with our editor and our department, we feel we can't cover specific religious events" (quoted in Cottle, 2000: 108). Overall, therefore, minority media producers within established mainstream media organizations face important dilemmas, which are not easily resolved.

While such constraints may often lead to self-censorship, there are unfortunately more direct constraints placed on minority media workers. These may take a violent form, as in the persecution of ethnic minority journalists. In August 2008, Amnesty International reported that Iran had begun a campaign of intimidation and persecution of journalists from a non-Persian ethnic background in an attempt to keep any ethnic issues off the agenda of the next presidential election. Amnesty International quoted the NGO Reporters without Borders, which reported that the prominent Ahwazi Arab journalist Youssef Azizi Bani Torouf had been sentenced to five years in prison for "threatening national security." In an article for Arab-language newspapers, Azizi had condemned the excessive force used by security forces in April 2005 against Arab demonstrators in the province of Khuzestan, which had resulted in about 160 casualties over several days of rioting. More worryingly, this seemed to be part of a growing trend to silence minority journalists in Iran. Reporters without Borders further reported that journalists from Arab, Azeri, Balochi, and Kurdish origins faced systematic discrimination, often paying a terrible price for their activism. Amnesty further reported that, in August 2008, Yaghub Mehrnahad, a twenty-eight-year-old Balochi journalist and cultural activist, had finally been executed following months of torture, in a secret trial and without legal representation (for more information see: http://blogs.amnesty.org.uk/blogs_entry.asp?eid=1842; see also the International Federation of Journalists, at www.ifj.org).

It is difficult to address this kind of violence without some form of engaged activism regarding media freedom. But even in different contexts, when the problem is not that of direct pressure and violence, the lack of concerted, rigorous, and institutionalized action regarding a more equitable situation for minority media workers in effect ends up compromising the production of mediated cultural diversity. A movement towards accomplishing fair and equitable conditions for minority media workers would involve setting up communities of practice within media organizations, beginning with the training and education of media professionals. The idea of media professionals as a community of practice was suggested by Downing and Husband (2005), who understand it as a means of articulating the institutional dynamics found within media organizations with the subjective aspects – the identities, attitudes, and opinions of media workers. The media workforce as a community of practice implies that media workers are socialized within a certain organizational context, but they bring their own identities and views, which prioritize certain elements over others. While this concept has an important analytical value in understanding the media production process in non-reductive terms, it has important implications for intervention as well. Specifically, it offers the possibility of constant training and learning from each other in the workforce as a means of countering both institutional and subjective biases.

Downing and Husband propose that such an educational or training component within the media as a community of practice take the form of the acquisition of two types of competence: intercultural communicative competence and cultural communicative competence. *Intercultural communicative competence* refers to the communicative skill that allows people to effectively interact with other cultures; this requires flexibility and reflexivity in understanding how both one's own and other cultures operate (Downing and Husband, 2005). Acquiring such an intercultural communicative competence requires that media workers adopt "a critically reflexive understanding of the belief structures and feelings they bring into their relationship with ethnic diversity" (p. 188). Secondly, however, media workers need to acquire specific knowledge about the cultures that they encounter and interact with. This is referred to as *cultural communicative competence*. Cultural communicative competence allows media workers to gain a deep insight into the cultures with which they interact – intercultural competence may then be seen as the necessary prerequisite for this type of more detailed and specific knowledge about other cultures.

These two skills or competencies are generic skills that should, in theory, be relevant to all communities of practice, all types of professionals working in fields such as health, education, and so on. But media workers specifically, argue Downing and Husband, need to acquire an intercultural *media* competence, which refers to the ways in which media workers need to problematize and reflect upon established professional practices and routines – what Stuart Hall has called the "encoding" process – at least insofar as these touch upon issues of cultural diversity. All three are necessary elements for the development of a production context that, at least at the level of individual media professionals, is sensitive to matters of cultural diversity. Moreover, by spreading, as it were, the burden of representation across media practitioners regardless of their background and across media institutions, minority media professionals may then focus more on the creative side of their profession, rather than always having to represent their ethnic background, always having to face the "tyranny" of their culture – to paraphrase Liesbet van Zoonen's (1991) well-known notion of the problems faced by women media workers. In other words, since all media workers become equally responsible for understanding and representing fairly cultural diversity, then media workers from minority backgrounds are not the only ones having to represent their culture.

Table 6.1 Media production of cultural diversity

	Structural level	*Organizational level*	*Individual level*
Constraints and contexts	• Market pressures • Globalization • Concentration of ownership • Neoliberalism	• Media logic (Altheide and Snow) • The media field (Bourdieu) • Mediatization (Schulz)	• Small numbers of ethnic minority media workers • "Burden of representation" • Persecution and violence
Possible outcomes and practices	• Lack of pluralism • Commodification of diversity	• Cultural diversity transformed by media logic • Uniformity of media output concerning diversity • Relay function bridging time and space	• Silenced, invisible, or "watered down" cultural diversity • Lobbying for more equality in the media workplace • Identification of best practices • Setting up of "communities of practice"

6.5 Conclusions

The table above provides a summary of the main points and perspectives covering the relationship between media production and cultural diversity. However, the main question here is how to understand this relationship in terms of a theory of mediation. A theory of mediation, as we saw in Chapter 5, is a processual theory focusing on the dialectical relationship between media and society; this relationship necessarily goes through the process of media production. In terms of cultural diversity, then, to a certain extent we can say that, when it enters the mediation circuit, it is transformed or perhaps produced in a certain way. This requires that it goes through all the constraining and enabling factors that we identified, and which are summarized in table 6.1.

Following a theory of mediation, we may therefore say that cultural diversity is produced in a context that operates under conditions of advanced globalized capitalism, and has to compete for media visibility in an environment often lacking in regulations that might protect it. It is further produced in organizations that operate on the basis of a distinct logic that may then impose itself upon cultural diversity: the production of cultural diversity will take place on the media's own terms and under their conditions of visibility. Individual media producers operate within these contexts and have therefore little input on how cultural diversity is produced. Moreover, the small numbers of workers from ethnic or cultural backgrounds make such an input even more unlikely. The everyday burdens and constant demand that they represent or speak on behalf of their ethnic or cultural group make media work especially challenging for those media workers. Finally, the very real threat of violence and persecution present in some contexts points to the need for activism and constant vigilance in order to protect media workers and safeguard their right to work. However, positive interventions may reverse these trends. Best practices in employment in the media include encouragement, mentoring, and training schemes, as well as the setting-up of media communities of practice. While this chapter focuses on the role of media production in terms of mainstream media, minority or diasporic media might perhaps provide a different context for the production of cultural diversity. This will be discussed in the next chapter.

7
Minority and Diasporic Media
Controversies and Contributions

7.1 Why Study Minority Media?

The main idea behind minority media is that ethnic and cultural groups do not find adequate representation and voice in mainstream media, thereby requiring their own media to address this void. Thus, some cultural and ethnic groups may find that their informational and entertainment needs are not met by mainstream, majority media, and decide to set up their own media, reflecting their own concerns, and offering them a space free from the cultural hegemony of mainstream media. This space might be seen as a kind of public sphere, within which members of distinct ethno-cultural groups can exchange views and opinions, often in their own language. On a more negative note, the exclusion of minority media workers from mainstream media may have contributed to the decision to set up minority media, in which such media workers could contribute. To some extent, therefore, the existence of minority media reflects the exclusion of minorities from the mainstream media, and to some extent it reflects the need for minorities to have their own mediated space.

This is, however, a deceptively simple account. There are several conceptual issues involved in thinking about minority media, not least the terminology employed: why minority and not diasporic, transnational, or community media? We therefore need first to clarify the main assumptions, concepts, and notions underlying minority media. As a second step, we need to locate the contribution of such media: what do they hope to accomplish? What is their role in the context of multicultural societies? What do we actually know about minority media? What types of diasporic media exist, and what are their differences? Finally, what is the form and substance of the politics associated with diasporic media? This chapter will address all these questions.

7.2 Issues of Terminology

In the earlier discussion of contexts of production it became clear that cultural diversity is either ignored or else caught up in processes of commodification. The contexts of media production, at the structural, organizational, and individual levels, are such that they inevitably lead to a problematic relationship between the media and cultural diversity. But this dissatisfaction with mainstream media has been in some sense productive: it gave rise to a group of media that understand themselves as serving exclusively their own communities. In certain historical and social contexts this was the inevitable result of outright exclusion. For instance, Clint Wilson (2000) argues that the black press in the USA "grew and flourished under the impetus of racial injustice and social degradation suffered by African Americans" (p. 85). In other contexts, the creation of minority community media has been the result of more recent migratory movements – consider, for instance, *Dziennik Polski*, the London-based Polish newspaper founded in 1940 as a result of the Polish migration that followed the invasion of Poland by Nazi Germany. In both cases, the underlying idea was that these communities required their own media. However, the increasingly complex migratory movements in the context initially of post-colonialism and later of globalization led to a rather confused state of affairs. The problem lies, firstly, in how to theorize the "diasporic" or "minority" aspect of these types of media, and, secondly, in how to understand the social and political role of minority media. We will discuss the politics of minority media in later sections, but first we need to examine the terms used in thinking about these types of media.

One of the most crucial problems and issues facing minority media regards the very community or minority itself. As we saw in earlier chapters, important critiques of the notion of ethnic identity point to continued problems in pinning down an ethnic community. If, on the one hand, we assume that there is an ethnic community such as, for instance, a Kurdish community in France, then we assume a kind of more or less stable core within this community, which can then be expressed or represented in the community media. On the other hand, however, it may well be that this community is too diverse to be adequately represented by its media. In addition, it may be involved in contentious politics, in which case, its media may well be serving the political interests of a certain faction of the community. Similarly, if we discuss, for instance, Muslim media in the UK, we assume again that they somehow represent the whole of the Muslim community, or that they write from a "Muslim" point of view. These assumptions may be problematic in that the community is too diverse and divided across ethnic, regional, class, gender, and generational lines to be represented as a whole. Thus, in the same way theorists interrogate the role of power in mainstream media, we have to think about questions of power in minority media: who has or assumes the right to speak and represent, and on whose behalf? In short, thinking about minority media requires that we engage with the question of power, within both minority communities and "their" media and mainstream and minority media.

A first step towards this is to refine the terms we are using. The most common terms include "minority media," "community media," and "diasporic media". These may be taken to correspond to successive ways of theorizing in the broader area of post-colonial studies. Moreover, they prioritize different aspects in the relationship between cultural diversity and the media. Of the three, the most widely used term seems to be "minority media." To speak of minority media requires that we think of a small, minority community in the context of a larger community, often thought as the "host" community, which in turn has its own, mainstream, media. This relationship, then, is understood in a minority-majority context, which appears to assume a somewhat defensive perspective of protecting minorities emphasizing struggle, and a quest for survival. Thus, most of the chapters in Riggins' (1992) edited volume *Ethnic Minority Media* address the issue of cultural survival of ethnic minority cultures, particularly indigenous cultures, which find themselves under pressure by dominant cultures.

On the other hand, the term "community media" focuses within communities themselves, emphasizing aspects of democratic participation and voice; community media are thought to express local concerns and to aim to enhance quality of life broadly speaking (Jankowski, 2002). While research in community media has included ethnic community media, it has primarily focused on localized communities in neighborhoods or districts and their concerns. Moreover, the term has also been used to refer to alternative media, that is, non-commercial media, which seek to make a contribution to issues of general concern and to enhance debate outside the pressures of the market and the state (Atton, 2002; Couldry and Curran, 2003). Thus, while emphasizing access and engagement with public issues, community media are not necessarily concerned with the specificity of communities that understand themselves as culturally different.

Finally, the term "diasporic media" has emerged out of discussions of diasporas within post-colonial studies. Specifically, Stuart Hall (1990), dissatisfied with the tendency to essentialize identities, suggests that we see identity as dynamic, always in the process of becoming; he refers to this type of identity as relating to commonality of experiences rather than commonality of being. Thus, people are not African-American or British-Chinese because they share a similar core or essential identity, but because they have had similar experiences. Hall then refers to the diasporic experience as a shorthand for this kind of identity. The concept of diaspora was then taken on by Paul Gilroy (1993; 1997), who developed it further along the lines of dynamism and historical contingency. The term "diaspora" moves beyond understandings of bounded communities and nation-states to capture an existence at the intersection of different cultures: Gilroy builds upon the work of W. E. B. Dubois on double consciousness to capture this idea of complex being, of having more than one identity at the same time. Gilroy's work is concerned with cultural production at the interstices between places, and also across national spaces. This kind of intellectual work, he argues, exemplified by thinkers such as Dubois and Frederick Douglass, leads to a new perspective that is neither wholly "Black or African" nor "European/Western" but denotes a new understanding characteristic of these experiences, to which Gilroy refers to as the "Black Atlantic." Although Gilroy is primarily concerned with African communities, his emphasis on the transnational dimension resonates with the experience of many other diasporic groups, who experience a similar kind of in-betweenness and who live between and across nations. Moreover, the focus on diasporic consciousness appears to capture the changing conditions of the nation-state under the pressure of globalization. Although the term has not been without its problems (see Anthias, 1998), it has generated an interesting body of work, while it signals a conscious attempt to address questions of essentialism when thinking about ethno-cultural identities. The term "diasporic media," then, prioritizes elements of continuous development, of being in between places, of similarity of experience, but not necessarily of nostalgia for a homeland. These characteristics of diasporas, which are often referred to as deterritorialized communities, are both enabled and amplified by diasporic media. Concern with space and location is central in many studies on diasporic media (e.g. Georgiou, 2005a). On the other hand, diasporic media may appear too "benign" a term, failing to capture the power imbalances that exist between and within different groups in certain spaces, still designated as nation-states, characterized by territorial control and sovereignty. From this point of view, minority media may be a more appropriate term for strategic purposes, in order to highlight such power differentials. We can perhaps agree that both terms – minority and diasporic – are useful in their own way. With this in mind, the terms will be used interchangeably.

7.3 Theorizing the Role(s) of Diasporic Media

Even if we agree on the terminological debates, the question that still needs to be addressed concerns the role of minority or diasporic media in multi-cultural societies. In the first place, this role is seen as an internally oriented one: minority media function as a means for preserving the community's cultural specificity (see Dayan, 1998). However, this may lead to several problems. The main problem can be stated in the following terms. In democratic societies, the most widespread normative role of the media is to provide a public sphere where issues can be freely discussed and agreed upon and to circulate fair and accurate information enabling people to form an informed opinion about issues of common concern (Habermas, 1989). For this to be accomplished, we require a more or less united public sphere that provides open access to all regardless of their identity (see Habermas, 1992). If this is the normative role of the media, then what is the scope of diasporic media, which are produced by and address only or primarily certain particular communities? If certain groups in society spend their time using different kinds of media, and in different kinds of language, then how can a united public sphere function? Mightn't such a fragmented public sphere ultimately disadvantage minority members, who will then not participate in the national one, but remain encased in their own, smaller, particularistic public sphere? Why and under what circumstances should a democratic society allow for such a fragmentation of its public sphere? At the same time, what is the broader normative framework within which minority or diasporic media operate? Why and under what circumstances should a democratic state actively support the operation of minority media?

   Indeed, such questions call for a discussion of the role of diasporic or minority media. Two main propositions will be examined here: diasporic media as upholding the right to communicate (Husband, 2000; Downing and Husband, 2005); and diasporic media as contributing to the creation of diasporic public sphericules (Gitlin, 1998; Cunningham and Sinclair, 2001).

7.3.1 Minority media and the right to communicate

In thinking about the role and political function of diasporic media within multicultural societies, Downing and Husband (2005; Husband, 2000) begin with an overall acceptance of the normative function of the media as a public sphere. It is worth repeating this formulation as it underpins much of the relevant argument. It is in the work of Jürgen Habermas (1989) that the conceptual and historical background of the public sphere was made clear and its political function emphasized. Habermas defined the public sphere as "a realm of our social life in which something approaching public opinion can be formed. Access is guaranteed to all citizens" (1974: 49). The relationship between the media and the public sphere is clarified by James Curran: the media "distribute the information necessary for citizens to make an informed choice at election time: they facilitate the formation of public opinion by providing an independent forum of debate; and they enable the people to shape the conduct of government by articulating their views. The media are thus the principle institutions of the public sphere" (Curran, 1991: 2). This normative function of the media, however, is compromised by political-economic factors (see Chapter 6). The logics and pressures of media production processes in the context of global capitalism imply that the media may not be able to play their politically crucial role as the public sphere. In connection with ethno-cultural diversity in particular, Downing and Husband point out that, under such circumstances, the media cannot deliver their democratic promise for diversity of information and vigorous debate because minority media are prevented from operating.

For Downing and Husband, then, the function of minority media is in the first instance to contribute to the function of the public sphere by providing more and different information, by pursuing a different kind of debate, and by representing different interests and identities. If plural and diverse media attest to the health and vitality of a democratic society, then they must allow for the existence and operation of minority media, which in turn guarantee such plurality and diversity of positions and identities. But given the political-economic pressures of neoliberal capitalism, it is unlikely that minority media survive. What is necessary, therefore, is proactive state legislation to guarantee minority media participation in the public sphere. However, this may require a revision of the mostly liberal context of multicultural societies, which recognize individual but not group rights.

Specifically, the liberal model of universal citizenship encounters several problems when confronted with the reality of multicultural diversity. The most important problem is that it often masks the specific problems faced by minorities and marginalizes their experiences. Moreover, there are special cases of ethno-cultural minorities whose histories and experiences require particular forms of redress. To address these problems, the Canadian theorist Will Kymlicka (1995) has argued for a complex model of citizenship that caters for the specific needs of minority cultures. At the center of his argument is the idea that indigenous groups must enjoy different rights from more recent settlers; specifically, they should have self-governing rights, especially on territories linked to their history. In addition, groups may enjoy special representation rights, which take the form of guaranteed seats in the state institutions. Finally, minority groups may enjoy certain poly-ethnic rights, which typically take the form of subsidies and legal support for certain practices central to the groups' identities. All three types of rights have important implications for the media.

Thus, in order to safeguard the existence and operation of minority media in multiethnic and multicultural societies, Downing and Husband argue that states must ensure that some form of differentiated rights policy applies to these media. Building on the work of Kymlicka, they suggest that, firstly, in terms of self-government rights, provision must be made for such communities to operate their own media, as, for instance, the Innuit in the Canadian context and the Aborigines in Australia. Secondly, representatives of minority groups may be offered guaranteed seats in councils running public broadcasting companies, and more broadly in councils or think tanks drafting media and audiovisual policy. Finally, the state has an obligation to fund

**Box 7.1 Declaration of AMARC on the Right
to Communicate**

1   The Right to Communicate is a universal human right which serves
    and underpins all other human rights and which must be preserved and
    extended in the context of rapidly changing information and communica-
    tion technologies.

2   All members of civil society should have just and equitable access to all
    communications media.

3   Respect for pluralism, cultural, language, and gender diversity should be
    reflected through all the media as a fundamental factor in a democratic
    society.

4   The democratic participation of women in communications media should
    be guaranteed at all levels.

5   The rights of indigenous peoples should be respected in their struggles for
    access and participation in communications media.

6   Communications media have a responsibility to help sustain the diversity
    of the world's cultures and languages, which should be supported through
    legislative, administrative, and financial measures.

7   Community media can play an important role in strengthening cultural
    rights, and in particular, the rights of linguistic and cultural minorities,
    indigenous peoples, migrants, and refugees by providing access to the
    means of communication.

8   Access to the means of communication must be supported by education
    and training to assist a critical understanding of the media and to enable
    people to develop their media and communication skills.

9   The market economy is not the only model for the shaping the communi-
    cations infrastructure. People must be seen as producers and contributors
    of information and not be defined solely as "consumers."

10 The continual expansion of transnational corporations characterized,
    among other things, by media conglomerates and concentration of own-
    ership increasingly threatens plurality, including the existence of indepen-
    dent and community broadcasters.

11 New digital broadcast systems are leading to re-planning existing frequency
    allocation and new approaches to regulation which risk further marginal-
    ization of communication services run by and for citizens, communities,
    and social organizations.

12 While convergence between telecommunications, computing, and broad-
    casting is increasing the number of potential users, the telecommunica-
    tions development gap supports the division of the world into those who
    have and those who do not have access to electronic information.

Source: AMARC (World Association of Community Radio Broadcasters), available
at: http://www.freestone.com/kpfa/milandeclaration.html.

minority media production companies. This latter is clearly a controversial proposition, but one which Downing and Husband are ready to defend. Why should taxpayers be burdened with subsidizing minority media? Well, according to Downing and Husband, it is for the wider public benefit that minority voices are included and amplified, and this is precisely what media production companies are doing. But beyond this, and perhaps more fundamentally, financing and enabling the operation of minority media is an obligation of the state, on the basis of the "right to communicate" (see, *inter alia*, Hamelink, 1993; Husband, 2000; Keane, 1991, 1998).

This "right to communicate," suggested in 1969 by a French civil servant, Jean D'Arcy, was subsequently accepted as a fundamental human right in several resolutions by Unesco and other organizations (see: http://www.righttocommunicate.org/). For instance, AMARC – the World Association of Community Radio Broadcasters –adopted a detailed resolution plan in 1998, which has proved influential in shaping the discourse on the right to communicate. Box 7.1 gives details of this resolution, adopted in Milan in 1998. If we therefore accept the right to communicate as one of the fundamental human rights, then the state must support the operation of minority media, without which the right to communicate for minority groups might be compromised. In these terms, the function of minority media is on the one hand to contribute to the vitality of the broader public sphere by ensuring that many voices are heard, while on the other to provide a necessary condition for minorities to exercise their right to communicate.

7.3.2 Diasporic public sphericules

Understanding communication as a fundamental right has very important implications, as it supports the creation of independent media, run by communities themselves. On the other hand, however, it does not consider the operation of the wider public sphere. In other words, as the media proliferate, audiences can only watch, read, and hear a fraction of what is around. The result then is that the public sphere becomes fragmented into smaller and isolated public sphericules (Gitlin, 1998) or micro public spheres (Dahlgren, 1995; Dayan, 1998).

The implications of such fragmentation are not clear. Daniel Dayan (1998) argues that the problem is that these micro public spheres are not immune from the workings of the larger one. Thus, rather than producing diversity, in fact we may find that minority media operate as mirror images of the larger public sphere and its mainstream media; this means that they are as likely to be influenced by the market as the other media, and that they are as likely to adopt the media values and production logics of mainstream media. The result might then be that, instead of diversity, we have more uniformity, despite the existence and operation of minority media. This, in turn, may have important implications for the community as a whole. Its internal structure and power dynamics may shift as a result of the new modes of legitimation imposed by the community's media (Dayan, 1998). For example, it may be that the visibility gained by certain community members in the community's media may now become one of the means for gaining more power. Such a development would certainly be predicted by Bourdieu (1998), according to whom visibility becomes the principle of legitimation within the media field.

Moreover, instead of preserving the community's cultural integrity, the operation of minority media may end up as a vehicle for its assimilation. Hamid Naficy's (1993) work on Iranian television production in California shows the contradictions in operation in minority media: although they operate in opposition to the mainstream media and the host culture, their very operation as media units promotes the acculturation of both their producers and their audiences, and the adoption of mainstream social values, such as consumerism. From this point of view, the fragmentation of the public sphere through minority media does not really take place, as the latter in fact form part of the broader public sphere in assuming its core values, and in suffering from similar types of encroachment by the market and commercialization.

A parallel argument, found in an essay by Todd Gitlin (1998), holds that, in contrast, it seems that minority media and the advent of new technologies has already fragmented the public sphere to the extent that it does not exist any longer as a unitary one. For Gitlin, the public sphere seems to have "shattered into a scatter of globules, like mercury" (1998: 173). This has led to, or was the outcome of, the proliferation of publics: in other words, the various groups encountered in plural societies are each associated with their own public sphere. There is no overall public in the singular, and no common public sphere within which all members of this public meet across their social and ideological differences in order to establish a common agenda. Gitlin clearly regrets this development, which he sees as an outcome of the broader "individuation" of society, alongside Robert Putnam's (1995) argument of the loss of social capital. For Gitlin, the political implications of the loss of such a civic culture are negative: in fragmenting and segmenting the public sphere political efficacy is lost, while the agenda is dominated by particularistic interests. At the same time, Gitlin dismisses arguments that a singular public sphere is unnecessary as long as deliberation takes place within these sphericules. These would hold, he argues, only insofar as equal resources were guaranteed to all. While Gitlin does not refer specifically to minority media and multiculturalism, some of his arguments echo the concerns about multiculturalism we discussed in Chapter 3: loss of commonality, a common purpose and an undivided social and cultural life.

This emphasis on a united, common and singular public sphere is criticized by Cunningham and Sinclair (2001), who point out its basis in modernist assumptions and nostalgia. In their empirically based work, they found elements of the public sphere in the microcosm of these ethno-cultural public sphericules. For Cunningham and Sinclair the contribution of these diasporic public sphericules constituted by diasporic media and their consumption lies in the ways in which these media play an educational role. Drawing on John Hartley's (1999) influential work *Uses of Television*, they argue that such media provide a permanent and general education to minority members, who then learn the manners, attitudes, and assumptions necessary for participating in the community.

Elaborating further, Cunnigham (2001) argues that diasporic media forms constitute a new form of community and belonging which moves beyond the nation-state understanding of citizenship. This is because they operate in spaces in between nations and nationally based cultural and political formations. They therefore have a unique cultural and political significance and contribution to the lives of minorities. This contribution is firstly based on a kind of negotiation or balancing act between the "host" culture and the culture of "origin", in between elements of the community itself; and, in the case of exilic cultures, between a fetishized and romanticized homeland and the realities of life in exile. Secondly, diasporic media enable the constitution of ethno-cultural micro civil societies, because they intersect with specific state apparatuses; in other words, they enable communities to function as civil societies in the sense of being able to exist separately from state policy and juridical power. They create a space where they can exist autonomously as it were, and they are subsequently re-created by and in this space. In addition, Cunningham (2001) points out that diasporic media constitute communities as such in two ways: firstly as an audience, in the sense that the media address a very specific type of community; and secondly, the community is constituted through the media in the sense that it only comes together for the consumption of these media and may subsequently disperse.

While Cunningham's arguments appear compelling, they mostly focus on the cultural significance of minority media. No doubt their role in enabling the community to come together is crucial, both for its maintenance and its general well-being. But the question of the political significance of diasporic media is still open. If the singular public sphere is indeed being replaced by smaller diasporic sphericules, then what form does politics take in this diffused model of the public sphere? And beyond the question of the form of politics, what is the substance of diasporic media politics? What are the arguments about and how do they serve communities? But this line of questioning assumes that diasporic media form a unitary category – this is an unwarranted assumption: diasporic media may take several forms, and can therefore lend themselves to different politics. Before examining the politics of diasporic media we need first to identify the types of minority or diasporic media.

7.4 Diasporic Media: a Typology

A lot has been written about diasporic media and their classification with different authors suggesting different parameters and relevant dimensions (Georgiou, 2005a). Indeed the task is a formidable one that is complicated further by the histories, policies, and practices in different countries, as well as by the increasing mobility and global flows of people and media. The European project EMTEL (2001–4), coordinated by Roger Silverstone, provided a thorough and detailed picture of the state of minority media in several European countries. For this chapter, however, the focus is on providing a broader and more abstract framework within which to fit the various media. This can be subsequently adjusted and adapted to the specific local requirements.

Taking the risk of simplifying a complex reality, the typology we suggest here is based on previous work and theories we discussed earlier, and specifically on the perspective of mediation. Following upon a mediation perspective, relevant criteria must include at least the three processes involved in mediated communication: production, representation, and consumption. These three will form the axes along which we will classify minority media. The production axis examines two main aspects of the production process: one concerning the economic mode of production, based on the source of financing for different media; and the second concerning the space wherein the media production actually takes place (based on Georgiou, 2005). The representation axis in this context can refer to the forms assumed by diasporic media that subsequently circumscribe their output. Finally, the reception part refers

Table 7.1 A typology of diasporic media

Production I: economics	*Production II: spaces*	*Examples of media forms*	*Types of audiences*
State subsidized or funded through voluntary contributions	Local: produced in a city or province	Radio programs, e.g. Multi-Kulti radio in Berlin	Diasporic/ transnational
Subscription or pay per copy	National or "ethnic": produced and circulated in the "host" nation	Newspapers and magazines, e.g. the *Voice* in the UK; Iranian television in Los Angeles (Naficy, 2003);	Ethnic and/or exilic; transnational audiences
Commercial, supported by advertising income	Transnational: produced in the "home" nation and consumed across the world	Satellite television, e.g. Aksoy and Robins, 2003; Bollywood films	Ethnic and/or diasporic/ transnational

to the audiences circumscribed or constructed by the various media; based on Naficy (2003), this is determined by the audiences' relationship to their home and host countries. Table 7.1 attempts to classify these different diasporic media types.

The source of finance is an important variable for understanding and classifying minority media. As we saw in earlier chapters, the political-economic context of media production is crucial for understanding both the media output and the conditions of its production. Thus, minority media, whose audiences are by definition minorities and therefore small in numbers compared to mainstream media, need to be able to secure some source of finance. In some contexts they resort to commercial sources, seeking to finance their operation through advertising and charging per copy. For instance, *The Voice* and *Q-News*, two UK-based publications for the black and Muslim communities respectively are financed through advertising and charging per copy. This means that these media operate in the same competitive environment as mainstream media. From this point of view, they are as susceptible as mainstream media to the demands of the market. Moreover, the costs of publishing or broadcasting can be prohibitive, leading to some extreme examples. Naficy (1993) cites a case in which an Iranian television station in Los Angeles in 1987 had to broadcast forty minutes of advertisements for every hour of broadcast in order to be able to survive. Similarly, Molnar and Meadows (2001; Meadows and Molnar, 2002) report that, due to financial constraints, the indigenous Australian television station Imparja Television ended up broadcasting standard commercial fare for almost 90 percent of the time, severely compromising its ability to broadcast the voice of Australian Aborigines. On a more positive note, minority media can be important vehicles for the development of "ethnic markets" through advertising services and products by and to community members. Examples here include Muslim media, such as *Q News* and the website Salaam (www.salaam.co.uk) in the UK. At the same time, they circumscribe specific audience segments, which may be of interest to certain advertisers. In this sense they are able to deliver a "narrowcasting" service, which in turn, contributes to their survival. This seems to be the case in Spain, where the proliferation of publications aimed at the Latin American communities is a sign of these communities' increased significance for Spanish advertisers (Retis, 2007). Nevertheless, this heavy reliance on advertising income implies that the primary function of these media is a commercial one, side-stepping the important role of minority media for advocacy and support of minority issues. This is one of the reasons underlying Husband's (2000; Downing and Husband, 2005) recommendation that minority media be subsidized by the state.

State subsidies provide minority media with the possibility of escaping the commercial pressures and hyper-competitive realities of media publishing and broadcasting. Indeed, Georgiou (2005a) found that the number of minority media in countries that had some form of relevant public funding was much higher. On the other hand, however, public funding imposes its own pressures on the operation of minority media. Meadows and Molnar (2002), in the context of Australia, refer to several examples of good practice both by mainstream media such as ABC and SBS and by independent producers in the field of indigenous broadcasting. However, exclusive reliance on government funds depends on the fickle and volatile aspects of relevant public policy, thereby making these broadcasters vulnerable. In addition, complicated and time-consuming bureaucracy, as well as vested interests in indigenous broadcasting, mean that a lot of effort and energy is wasted on filling in applications and lobbying. Meadows and Molnar conclude that Aborigines' access to communication was and continues to be a constant struggle. In other cases, as Naficy (2003) has shown, public funding comes with political strings attached. Naficy cites the example of Korean television in Los Angeles, which receives funding from South Korea, often resulting in promotional programs.

Another form of funding for diasporic media comes in the form of subscriptions. These may be for magazines and newspapers, but more often they are for the provision of specialized broadcasts through cable or satellite. These tend to be media broadcasts produced and consumed in different parts of the world. A common example is the production of Turkish television in Turkey, which is subsequently consumed both locally and transnationally, through satellite broadcasts (Aksoy and Robins, 2003). These media are not entirely dependent on subscriptions, as they are also often funded through advertising and other means, such as state subsidies. Nevertheless, the example of Al Jazeera TV, which is produced in Qatar and broadcast globally, shows that some of these diasporic media are funded mostly by subscriptions, while also looking for advertising income as well. Broadly speaking, however, we can expect the production values and practices of these media to be influenced by the ways in which they are funded.

The second dimension in production refers to the space in which it takes place. This is an important aspect, as it can play a part in determining the kind of output that will be produced. Thus, locally produced media, which are produced by minority or diasporic communities in the location they currently find themselves in, tend to focus on matters of immediate and direct concern for these minorities. For example, the newspapers *Albania Press* and *Tribuna*, published by the Albanian minority living in Athens in Greece, are primarily concerned with issues affecting the lives of this community and only secondarily with issues affecting their homeland and host country or indeed more global issues. Radio MultiKulti in Berlin, which is part of the German public broadcasting service, is another example of local production. Targeting primarily the city's migrant population, it broadcasts in eighteen languages as well as in German with the goal of providing access to information for Berlin's immigrant communities (see Vertovec, 2000; Morawska, 2008).

Nationally produced minority media are also produced and circulate in the "host" country but cover issues concerning community life more broadly and often assumr a political voice, seeking to politically mobilize the community. *The Voice*, published by the black British community, is such an example. The French Muslim magazine *Hawwa*, which is edited by a female team, constitutes another example of such a nationally produced medium (Rigoni, 2005). Finally, transnational media are typically consumed in a number of countries, mostly through new technologies, such as satellite and cable television and the internet. Examples here include Al Jazeera, Bollywood films, and internet sites such as Islam Online (www.islamonline.net). The point here is to think of the location of production as influencing the themes and issues, as well as the viewpoint and "spin," of the stories covered.

An important distinction, finally, concerns the types of audiences constructed by and addressed through these media. Naficy (2003) distinguishes between ethnic, exilic, and transnational audiences. Within a theory of mediation audiences are understood as both constructed by the media that addressed them and as themselves shaping the media through their viewing and consumption habits. This relationship is important if we are to understand the specific audiences of minority media: audiences therefore are not reified entities existing as audiences outside their relationship with the media, while, on the other hand, they are not wholly dependent on the media, but can themselves influence and shape outputs. This relationship will be clarified in subsequent chapters, but in discussing the three categories of diasporic media audience, Naficy argues that these are permeable and overlapping, yet characterized by unique features that deserve further discussion. Although, Naficy's distinction primarily applies to the production of diasporic television, which he describes as a genre, we can adapt it here in order to capture the specificities of the audience of diasporic media.

Thus, an ethnic audience refers to the audiences that come together by local or national diasporic media operated by established minority communities, such as the African-American community in the US, or the indigenous communities in Canada and Australia. Given that these media specifically address the local or broader concerns of these communities, the audience category that they circumscribe consists primarily of people who wish to inform themselves and debate and discuss their experiences as members of particular cultures designated as minorities within larger cultures. Transnational or diasporic audiences form a different and larger category that exists beyond borders; they are brought together as audiences through their consumption of media products usually imported by their "home" country. Spanish-speaking audiences in the US consuming Mexican telenovelas through satellite television are an example of such transnational audiences. Other examples include Turkish audiences consuming Turkish satellite television in Germany and elsewhere, Korean audiences consuming South Korean television programs in the US, and South Asian audiences consuming Bollywood films across the world. These audiences are not concerned with localized issues or issues regarding their experiences as members of a particular community within a "host" country. Rather, they are part of a generalized audience existing across national borders which shares a certain common cultural framework.

Finally, exilic audiences are smaller and tend to be more involved in their homeland politics; the status of these audiences is transitional or provisional (Naficy, 2003), as they are often refugees from their countries. Iranian and Middle Eastern media products often circumscribe exilic audiences, who are brought together in all their diversity through their consumption of such media. Examples here include *Roj-TV*, the Kurdish satellite television, and the website Palestine Remembered (www.palestineremembered.com). For Naficy, exilic media, typically produced by small independent producers in their own language, tend to foreground issues of authenticity, identity, and legitimacy. As such, we can expect them to be more politicized than the packaged entertainment products of large transnational media conglomerates. On the other hand, the politics of diasporic media is rather more complex than that. This will be discussed next.

7.5 The Politics of Diasporic Media

In thinking about the politics of diasporic media it may be helpful to distinguish between form and substance. The form of diasporic media politics refers to the ways in which this politics is conducted: the "how," of the processes, and the broader outcomes in terms of issues such as political participation, political integration, and the like. The substance of diasporic media politics refers to the actual political messages and positions assumed by these media. This distinction is important in understanding the politics of diasporic media because it separates the role of these media in politically engaging minorities from the specific political directions assumed by some of these media. As we shall see, while the political direction may not always be "progressive" – not always concerned with issues of social justice and equality – the broader political role of diasporic media is important in enabling minority members to acquire the necessary competencies in order to have a political presence. This role is crucial in multicultural democracies, as they are based on inclusion and participation.

To begin with the question of formal politics, the twin concerns of multicultural politics include, as we have seen in earlier chapters, the diptychs recognition–equality, universality–particularity, and essentialism–fluidity of identity. To reiterate, the diptych recognition–equality refers to the need both to recognize the existence, integrity, and specificity of certain ethno-cultural identities, and to move towards a more equitable distribution of wealth and power, which will include these communities and address their needs. The diptych universality–particularity highlights the need to address particular needs of communities while upholding a universal – i.e. common and applicable to all – set of values, such as citizenship based on a "color blind" kind of equality. Finally, the diptych essentialism–fluidity of identity refers to the requirement that cultural identities are characterized by a certain "core" or by some degree of stability so that they can be recognized as distinct identities, while also accepting that they are dynamic, fluid, and permeable identities.

It is at all three levels that we can locate the contribution of diasporic media in formal terms. Thus, minority media often provide a visibility necessary for struggles of recognition. If mainstream media ignore or marginalize minority voices, diasporic and minority media provides such a voice, which is crucial in struggles for recognition. But if we are to see minority media involved in struggles for recognition and visibility, then they must operate in a space that connects them to majority cultures. In other words, and here we find one of the problems regarding diasporic public sphericules, to be recognized requires that others, in this case majority cultures, perceive and become aware of minority cultures and their demands and issues. If minority media are a means of promoting visibility, they must become involved in findings ways that connect them to the wider public sphere.

An interesting example is found in Isabelle Rigoni's (2002) work on Turkish and Kurdish media in Europe. Rigoni refers to the short-lived example of *Perşembe*, which was a weekly supplement of the German daily newspaper *Tageszeitung*. It was written in German and Turkish and was the only Turkish newspaper produced in Germany. *Perşembe* lasted for only one year, from September 2000 to August 2001, and dealt with issues concerning the Turkish minority in Germany, its relations with the host country, and specifically with questions of integration and citizenship. Importantly, as Rigoni points out, the newspaper served as a reminder to mainstream German society that it is a country of immigration and that young people of immigrant origin want full social, political, and economic integration. In this sense, minority media provide a means by which to seek recognition and to demand equality in material and symbolic terms – but crucially this can only be accomplished if there are connecting lines and synergies between minority media and the broader public sphere.

At the same time, the existence of minority media contributes to both the reproduction and the transcendence of the universalism–particularism diptych. To operate as minority and thus as particularistic media these media forms can exist within a universal framework that allows the concurrent existence of other particularistic media (Georgiou, 2005b). Moreover, some diasporic media fully endorse and replicate values and processes associated with the universalistic mainstream. Georgiou refers to Al Jazeera as an example of this reproduction of universalistic values. In this sense, they reproduce the distinction between the universal and the particular. On the other hand, however, minority media "translate" the universal into the language of the particular, often quite literally. Georgiou (2005b) refers to London Greek Radio, which broadcasts a program on social security benefits in Greek. The program encourages listeners to phone in with their problems, which are addressed by the presenter. In this manner, the universalistic framework of benefit entitlement is translated into, and thus rendered compatible with, the particular needs of this community. In this manner, the dichotomous understanding of universal versus particular is transcended – minority media act literally as mediators between the particular and the universal. From this point of view, minority media can help accommodate the requirements of ethno-cultural minorities for particularistic distinctiveness within the universalistic framework of citizenship.

Finally, the diptych of essentialism and fluidity of identity, which is the source of much tension among communities, is inevitably encountered in minority media. The tendency of minority media to "interpellate" – summon or construct – a particular audience points to their ever-present essentializing features. Addressing, for instance, the Somali community in Italy or the Moroccan community in Spain raises the question of the identity of these communities. The minority media set boundaries between communities and reproduce dominant and often problematic aspects and views of these communities. Moreover, the question of power is never far behind: who defines and who is allowed to address a given community? Are all the community's diverse elements included in these appellations? Yet the need to conduct a minority politics requires that such generalizations are made: if minority media are to participate in the politics of recognition of their identity, they must first claim a common identity. But in doing so, they overlook their internal diversity. While there is a sense of inevitability in this conundrum, understanding minority media as involved in a process of mediation provides an insight into this constant tension between essentialism and diversity. Thus, accepting that the minority media are themselves subject to criticism, rejection, and negotiation by their audiences points to the ways in which they are able to perform a balancing act between essentialism and fluidity. They may address and summon a certain kind of community only to find no one willing to respond, or a critical response that shifts priorities elsewhere, thereby pointing to the dynamism of cultural identities. But for this to happen, the channels of communication between minority media and their audiences must be at all times open. This makes the internet the example *par excellence* of this productive tension, since its interactive character belies attempts to control and essentialize identities (Siapera, 2005).

If we are, however, to consider the actual contribution of diasporic media to politics in more substantive terms, things become more ambiguous. Cunningham (2001) has pointed out that minority media are sites for intense negotiations between the tendency to safeguard cultural distinctiveness and the tendency to assimilate to, or at least accommodate, the demands of, the host society. The results of such negotiations can often be politically reactionary. Naficy's study of Iranian television in Los Angeles showed how the need of Iranian exiles to retain their identity while also surviving in exile led to a curious mixture of reactionary politics and extreme commercialization. Specifically, Naficy's study in the late 1980s showed that Iranian television in Los Angeles was produced by Shah-supporting Iranians who found themselves in exile following the Islamic revolution of 1979. Consequently, their political position was vocally against the Islamic Republic. At the same time, the lack of funding led to the need to accept advertising income, resulting in an output of anti-Islamic Republic political messages interspersed with advertisements. A similarly ambiguous politics has been pursued by the Cuban American minority in Miami. In addition, Rigoni (2002) reports that the Turkish state has attempted to control Turkish communities living in Europe both in political and cultural terms. Rigoni argued that through continued references to "homeland nostalgia (*vatan hasretleri*)" Turkish satellite television attempts to portray a unified community acting in the interests of Turkey (p. 3).

On the other hand, more "progressive" or liberal minority media have often found themselves in the receiving end of threats and open criticism. Lohmeier (2007) reports a series of interventions by the Cuban American National Foundation against the *Miami Herald* and its Spanish-language counterpart *El Nuevo Herald*, through ads on buses, blogs, and letters to the editors. Dissatisfied with what it perceived as a liberal bias, the Cuban American National Foundation sought to influence these media and direct them to an editorial perspective more in line with their anti-Castro politics. Rigoni in her study of Turkish media in Europe describes an interesting incident regarding the French radio program *Arc-en-Ciel*, run by a younger generation of French-Turkish immigrants. In the wake of the French Parliament's vote on the Armenian genocide passed in early 2001, the program's presenters called for an open debate on the issue and a fraternal dialogue with Armenians. Controversially, Turkey does not accept that there was a genocide against Armenians in 1915, refusing to come to terms with what the program presenters referred to as "a dark and tragic

Table 7.2 Minority media: a summary of the main issues

Terminologies, functions, and theories	*Types of media*	*Politics*
Terms:	A typology based on:	Forms of politics a platform for the quest for recognition

• minority media
  • Emphasis on numbers, and power differentials
• community media
  • Emphasis on internal cohesion
• diasporic media
  • Emphasis on dynamism and "in-betweeness"
	• production economics
	  • financing source
	• production space
	  • local
	  • national
	  • transnational
	• media forms
	  • transnational media products, e.g. satellite TV, films and internet
	  • national media products, e.g. newspapers and magazines
	  • local media products, e.g. radio broadcasts
		• a bridge between universalism and particularism
		• a loop connecting essentialist and flu constructions of identity
		
		Contents/direction of politics
		
		• unpredictable and ambiguous – could be reactionary or progressive

Minority/diasporic media:
 	
• provide the right to communicate
• formulate diasporic public sphericules, which allow for complex negotiation and identity construction
	• Audiences
	  • ethnic
	  • transnational or diasporic
	  • exilic
		Political efficacy
		
		• Agenda setting within minorities
		• Directly influencing public sphere through connecting lines
		• Indirectly influencing politics through preparing minority members for political participation

page of our common history" (in Rigoni, 2002: 13). Within days the show's presenters were accused by Turkish nationalist media of anti-Turkish propaganda, and were accosted in the streets by "angry listeners" demanding a retraction. Such examples clearly show the struggles between essentialized and more dynamic identities within communities; on the other hand, they also show that minority media are not always coterminous with progressive politics, and that they are not always involved in quests for equality and social justice in their host countries. In contrast, they are often at the centre of homeland politics, often reproducing political polarizations present in the communities' countries of origin.

A final issue to foreground concerns the political efficacy of minority media. The question here concerns the extent to which minority media can actually influence and improve the political situation of their communities. Because of their "narrowcasting" aspect, minority media very rarely form a critical mass able to influence the political agenda in their host country (Cunningham, 2001). On the one hand this shows the political marginalization of minorities, and the inability of minority media to interact or connect with the broader public sphere. This points to the need to think of minority media politics in terms different to those of mainstream media. Their political role cannot be one of directly influencing national political debate and taking it towards certain directions – they cannot in other words act as agenda-setting media for the national political agenda, although they may do so for their own communities. Ghanem and Wanta (2001) report that Spanish-language media in the USA have an agenda-setting effect for the Hispanic community. However, they point out that this may be the result of the limited media choice that Spanish speakers have in the USA. Thus, not able to consume English-language media, parts of this community end up somewhat isolated from the broader national public sphere.

Rather than thinking of such communities as further disenfranchised by their media, we should locate the political contribution of minority media precisely in their ability to operate in a parallel and to a degree alternative public sphere in which minority members participate on an equal footing. This subsequently trains and prepares them for participation in the broader public sphere. But this rests on two provisos: firstly, as we saw above, that there are lines connecting minority media and the broader public sphere; and secondly, that the broader public sphere allows for a plurality of voices. Minority media is therefore politically efficacious in an indirect manner, in that it prepares minority members for political participation (see Cunningham, 2001; Siapera, 2005), and in a direct manner, through interlinking with the broader public sphere.

7.6 Conclusions

This chapter examined several aspects of minority media. Table 7.2 summarizes the main points. Minority and/or diasporic and/or transnational media reflect a series of debates and controversies. Social, cultural, and political life is influenced by the existence and operation of such media. Notwithstanding the contentious politics in which they are sometimes involved, the works reviewed in the chapter unequivocally support the existence of these media. Whether seen as part of the inalienable human right to communicate or as a necessary factor for the function of multicultural democracies, minority media are here to stay.

Finally, from a perspective of mediation we need to point out that a focus on minority media requires a focus on their processes of production, representations, and reception. Just like mainstream media, diasporic media are subject to political-economic pressures, representational logics, and audience usages. Some of these will be discussed in subsequent chapters.

8
Theories of Representation

8.1 The Work of Representation

Representation is found at the heart of mediation: indeed, without representation neither production nor consumption would have any meaning. Representation is, on the one hand, the outcome of the media production process, and as such it has to be understood within its contexts of production. On the other hand, however, representation cannot exist outside the contexts of its reception. Representations will remain suspended until people see, hear, or otherwise perceive them, until they interpret them in their own ways, until they consume them and subsequently employ them in other contexts. But this interdependence between the processes of production and consumption of mediated representations should not obscure the work of representation as such. But what exactly do we mean by (mass-mediated) representation, and how exactly is it involved in the process of mediation? And, closer to this book's concerns, what are the implications of mediated representations for cultural diversity? This chapter will sketch a response to such questions through a review of an extensive body of literature that has approached the question of representation from different perspectives, and located it at different levels.

Some of the earliest work in this area was socio-psychological, concerned with the ways in which individuals process information from the world around them, thereby considering representation as part of what links individuals to society. The emphasis of this body of work is on information processing, and the cognitive dimensions of representation; as such it is often concerned with errors or biases in perception. Racist or otherwise prejudiced views reflect, within this cognitive model, such errors of perception. This emphasis on distortion is further amplified in theories that view representation as reflecting ideological processes at work. In other words, the cognitive bias identified by socio-psychological approaches cannot be explained by referring to the individual him- or herself. Rather, we must look to society at large, and identify the systematic distortions that give rise to racist and prejudiced representations of difference. This assumption of ideological distortions is common to a number of very influential perspectives, including those of framing (Goffman, 1974; Entman, 1993) and discourse analysis (van Dijk, 1991). The main argument is that representation is constructed in and through discourse – discourse is here understood as language not only as an abstract system, but as language use, as communication, both interpersonal and mediated. The anti-racist agenda of this perspective is clear from the outset. From the point of view of anti-racism, therefore, what needs to be done is to identify these linguistic and/or discursive structures that are linked to racism, and through this identification to eventually eliminate them.

But this emphasis on distortion and ideology raises the question: is there anything outside ideology? Is there any possibility of having access to "reality" in a direct and truthful manner, outside stereotypes, frames, or discourses? Well, no, would be the short answer offered by the French theorist Michel Foucault. There cannot be anything outside ideology because reality and truth are mediated by discourse. We can only have access to the world around us through language and discourse. Ideology is nothing more than the production of a set of specific discourses, which then acquire the status of unassailable truth. But even other ensembles of discourse do not qualify as undistorted reality either: they are merely alternative versions of reality, sometimes, but certainly not always, involving less oppressive aspects. For this reason, Foucault was concerned not with identifying "distortions," but rather the conceptual antecedents of particularly forceful discourses (Foucault, 1966/2002). From an analytical point of view, to understand mediated representations of cultural difference, we need to find out their conceptual antecedents, their "conditions of possibility," and to sketch out their implications, with the goal of contributing to the construction of less problematic representations.

However, the function of representation is not one of simple reproduction of problematic, unfair, and outright racist images and discourses. Rather, it has to be seen as a condensed form of the symbolic value of cultural difference, circulating through the many channels of communication available. But it is precisely this constant circulation of representation that renders it unstable. The more it finds itself diffused and spread across different channels and/or media and across different contexts, the more the meaning and value of representation shifts and changes. The performativity and iterability of representation are the two main elements by which representation operates in a dynamic and ever-shifting manner (Derrida, 1988; Butler, 1997).

This chapter will expand on these arguments, and sketch their implications for understanding the process of mediated representation. The aim of the discussion is to show the different assumptions underlying the work of representation, which inevitably lead to different responses to the question of racist and prejudiced forms of representation in the media.

8.2 Stereotyping: the Cognitive Aspects of Representation

> *I am a Jew.*
> *Hath not a Jew eyes? Hath not a Jew hands, organs,*
> *dimensions, senses, affections, passions; fed with*
> *the same food, hurt with the same weapons, subject*
> *to the same diseases, heal'd by the same means,*
> *warm'd and cool'd by the same winter and summer,*

as a Christian is? If you prick us, do we not bleed?
If you tickle us, do we not laugh? If you
poison us, shall we not die?

(*The Merchant of Venice*, III, i, 58–66)

Shakespeare's *The Merchant of Venice* is in many ways revealing of the work of the ethnic stereotype. Firstly, the Jewish character Shylock is meant to embody all the characteristics of his heritage – he is a stand-in for the whole culture. The frequent references to him as a "Jew" throughout the play instead of using his name illustrate this point clearly. Secondly, in the portrayal of Shylock as a vindictive moneylender, the other characters are able to preserve their dignity and justify their actions. Thirdly, the only redemption for the stereotypical Jew is to renounce his Jewishness: "The Hebrew will turn Christian: he grows kind," says Antonio (I, iii, 180). Finally, and this is where the quote above is most revealing, the hurt and injury of stereotyping: people are not treated in terms of their individuality or humanness, but in terms of a generalized, and in this case extremely negative, image. But Shylock's speech above raises another crucial point: who is really this man Shylock? Is he the "Jew" or the human being? Is he a vindictive, money-grabbing usurer or a tragic and betrayed father? It is perhaps to Shakespeare's credit that there are no immediate answers in his text. More broadly, however, the underlying issue here concerns the links between stereotypes and reality. This section will touch upon these themes, provenance, ubiquity, functions, and outcomes of stereotyping, as well as the relationship between stereotyping and reality.

In 1922, Walter Lippmann, in an attempt to explain how democracy should work, and why so often it doesn't, referred to the "pictures in our heads," the mental images on the basis of which we apprehend and act upon the world. And for the most part, these pictures in our minds are generalized abstractions, simplified versions passed to us through our culture. And because they are repeated across time, because they are so pervasive, they have acquired a rigid structure and are resistant to change. The term stereotype, stemming from the printing process, where it referred to the reproduction of print through the use of metal moulds, was subsequently coined by Lippmann to denote the repetitive and rigid attributes of these mental images. Lippmann attributes stereotypes to "culture" in the sense of socialization, but in a revealing passage he makes an explicit link between stereotypes as "pictures in our heads" with images more widely available, and specifically with those in the cinema. If an Athenian wanted images of the gods, he says, he would go to the temples, if a Florentine wanted to imagine the saints, he would go to the church to see the frescoes. In the modern world, however, "the word picture, the narrative, the illustrative narrative, and finally the moving picture" have taken over the role of providing pictures for our imagination (Lippmann, 1922/2004: 50). When we read something, he argues, our memory and imagination fill in the blanks and generate certain images, corresponding to what we read. "But on the screen the whole process of observing, describing, reporting, and then imagining, has been accomplished for you" (Lippmann, 1922/2004 – cf. McLuhan in Chapter 5, who held the exact opposite view). For Lippmann, although traditional means of dissemination of stereotypes are still present, the mass-mediated images are far more influential in propagating stereotypes, because they already provide images that we can then store in our memories, and conjure up whenever necessary.

Although the role of the media in the production and dissemination of stereotypes is important, socio-psychological research has shifted the focus towards the functions served by stereotyping. The most well-known work in this area was conducted by Henri Tajfel (1981). Tajfel argued that stereotypes serve five important functions both at the level of the individual and at the level of the group. At the level of the individual, these functions are cognitive and psychological: the former refers to the simplification and systematization of the environment, and the latter to the motivational aspects of preserving the status quo and other important values. At the group level, functions include the explanation of the world and the justification of action, as well as the maintenance of positive intergroup distinctiveness – the idea that one's group is better than others. Indeed, Lippmann had already identified the cognitive simplification and efficiency associated with stereotyping, as well its value in preserving social values: "The systems of stereotypes may be the core of our personal tradition, the defenses of our position in society" (Lippmann, 1922/2004: 52). But Tajfel rightly argued that most research in stereotypes focused primarily, if not exclusively, on the individual cognitive functions. Tajfel (1981) made two important suggestions: first, that research in the group functions of stereotypes might provide a better insight than studies of merely cataloguing stereotypes. Second, that research should try to provide links between the individual and group levels, starting with the former, and detailing its effects on the latter.

Tajfel's points were addressed to early research on stereotyping that was limited to the study of the content of stereotypes. The earliest such study was conducted by Katz and Braly (1933), who asked 100 Princeton students to find adjectives to describe a range of nationalities: they came up with a list which included descriptions such as "quick-tempered" for Italians, "ignorant" for blacks, and "cruel" for Turks. Such characterizations, or contents of stereotypes, argued Tajfel, can only be meaningful in terms of the groups' involved histories, traditions, values, interests, and so on. We must therefore understand the broader socio-cultural context in which stereotyping occurs in order to get a better idea of the role of stereotypes in social life. Secondly, in terms of the links between the group and the individual, it is crucial to show that group membership is an important source of individual meanings and values and vice versa: that individual values, preferences, and interests feed back into the group (Turner, 1984). Hence, stereotypes provide groups and persons with an important means of understanding themselves and others – in other words, they form part of people's identities.

Viewed from this perspective, the outcome of stereotyping appears equivocal. Stereotypes may be a source of values, pride and positive distinctiveness, but also a source of stress, violence, and negative self-image. Indeed, Gordon Allport, in his influential 1954 book *The Nature of Prejudice*, noted: "One's reputation, whether false or true, cannot be hammered, hammered, hammered into one's head, without doing something to one's character" (p. 142). Allport's comment relies on a concept suggested by the sociologist Robert Merton: the self-fulfilling prophecy. This refers to "a false definition of the situation evoking a new behavior which makes the original false conception come 'true'" (1948: 195). But Allport expanded this notion, and included a range of behaviors associated with the targets of prejudiced and negative stereotypes. He noted that constant confrontation with negative stereotypes may cause people to become obsessed with their self-image. This may lead to a rejection of one's own group – an endorsement of the negative stereotype to the extent that one despises one's own group. In addition, negatively stereotyped persons might become stressed and suffer from anxiety, expecting to face prejudice and discrimination in various aspects of their lives. But affected groups may decide to fight back, through the development of counter-stereotypes, or through mobilizing negative stereotypes against other groups, which ultimately leads to polarization and social fragmentation. Allport, however, notes more fruitful avenues, such as the possibility of militancy: the ongoing attempt to redress negative stereotypes. In short, there are several problems associated with negative stereotypes, particularly those that affect certain cultural groups. But even stereotypes that are not necessarily negative might prove to be problematic in that they distort or otherwise misrepresent reality.

Indeed, the question of reality is never far away from the discussion of stereotypes. For the most part, stereotypes are considered to be falsehoods. Allport defines them as exaggerated beliefs, and hence always inaccurate. Lippmann is equally unequivocal: "Real space, real time, real numbers, real connections, real weights are lost. The perspective and the background and dimensions of action are clipped and frozen in the stereotype" (1922/2004: 156). In other words, stereotypes may be in some ways useful, but they are not facts. Moreover, in their rigidity, they impede the quest for factual and accurate information. The persistence of this question, however, led researchers to try and find out the precise relationship between reality and stereotype. This led to the kernel-of-truth hypothesis and debate, in which it was argued that, because of their cognitive elements, stereotypes must contain a measure of truth (Vinacke, 1949 in Oakes *et al.*, 1994: 22). The argument involved here is that, if groups came into contact with each other, then their stereotypes would more accurately reflect each other's attributes. Thus, in a study by Triandis and Vassiliou (1967), Americans who came into increased contact with Greeks developed a more favorable self-stereotype and less favorable stereotype of Greeks, who were then seen as "unsystematic, lazy and theoretical" (Triandis and Vassiliou, 1967: 320, in Oakes *et al.*, 1994). For these researchers, the first-hand contact meant that the stereotype had some basis on reality. But such research did not heed Lippmann's insight that the ubiquity and inescapability of stereotyping affects perception at all levels.

The question of reality, however, is a persistent one. In more recent socio-psychological literature, a line is drawn between what is psychologically valid – the process of cognitive categorization that leads to stereotypes – and what is historically valid (Oakes *et al.*, 1994). And stereotyping, it is argued, may fulfil important cognitive and psychological functions, but it is still subject to the historical, political, and ideological processes that give meaning to our lives (Oakes *et al.*, 1994). This perspective reconciles stereotyping as a cognitive process with the clear observation that stereotypes tend to be highly prejudicial, without necessarily resorting to a functionalist explanation of the necessity of (negative) stereotyping. In other words, even if stereotyping is found to be an adaptive response to a complex environment, inaction vis-à-vis clearly racist and negative stereotypes still cannot be justified, as their contents reflect problematic relationships between groups. The question of reality is therefore one of constructing better, more appropriate, less prejudicial "pictures in our heads." But this perspective, an extension of social-identity theory (Tajfel and Turner, 1986) known as the self-categorization theory (Turner, 1985; Oakes *et al.*, 1994), made another important contribution. It showed that, rather than being rigid, stereotypes must change and evolve all the time: if not, their validity as an adaptive response would be seriously compromised. Changes in stereotypes must therefore reflect the unfolding of history, or, as Tajfel maintained, the changing relationships between social groups, their struggles, oppressions, and negotiation of self-interest.

In everyday talk, however, stereotypes are still associated with negative and rigid images about certain groups. In thinking the connections between stereotypes and representations, therefore, although both refer to the same phenomenon of imagining or constructing pictures, both "in our heads" and in communication with others, stereotypes are typically considered to be a particular class of representation, namely, a negative and rigid representation of a social group. From this point of view, the question of representation is more subtle than that of stereotype, although they both raise the issue of who gets to write the social history that becomes embedded in stereotypes and representations, whose perspective is primarily represented – in short they raise the question of ideology. This will be explored further in the following section.

8.3 Framing and Discourse: a First Link to Ideology

Govt: Kostunica's statements have negative impact on Serb integration Mimoza Kusari [Kosovo Government spokeswoman] said … "Kostunica's statement isn't surprising, because he is a proven ultranationalist … [T]he Government is fully committed to integrating all communities. But we would've been more successful with the Serb community if it were not for such statements by Belgrade." (*Koha*, Kosovan daily newspaper, March 4, 2004, in UN Mission in Kosovo Media Monitoring)

The way in which problems are talked about has profound implications on the possible solutions emerging. The above excerpt is taken from a Kosovan newspaper in March 2004, and illustrates some of the issues involved: firstly, the problem is defined as "Serb integration" in Kosovo – this clearly sets up the Serbian population as posing a problem. Earlier in the article, the Serbian solution to the problem is described as "cantonization," alluding to the Swiss political system of autonomous but federally linked areas. While this may appear positive, the exact phrasing is "cantonization or division," which lends an overall negative aspect to the solution. Who is to blame for this? The ultranationalist Serbian Prime Minister. And what is the outcome here? That Serbian integration remains a problem. This example shows what is often at stake in representation: the way reality is relayed profoundly shapes the reality to come. As we saw in the above section and its insistence in the cognitive necessity of abstraction and categorization, reality is apprehended through representational strategies. This, in turn, implies that the social historical circumstances that shape reality may be represented in ways that may sustain or conversely undermine the positions of certain social groups. The social historical reality, in other words, becomes subject to ideological processes which mask the operation of power by presenting the views of a social group as unassailable truth. And, of course, the more powerful and dominant a social group, the less likely it is for its views to be questioned. This section will cover the issue of the ideologically charged representations of cultural difference, beginning with a discussion of ideology, and then examining two parallel approaches to ideological representations: frame and discourse analysis.

Frame Analysis is the title of a well-known book by the sociologist Erving Goffman (1974), in which he introduces and uses the term as a means of analyzing everyday social life. Goffman, who was a microsociologist, focusing on the minutiae of everyday life as experienced by the people involved, was primarily interested in finding out how social life is organized. Goffman (1974: 10) defines frames as the basic "principles of organization that govern events," and frame analysis seeks to examine and map these principles. People behave, interact, and communicate in a social context depending on how they define the situation they find themselves in. This definition of the situation is guided by various frames available to us as part of our social vocabulary. The ultimate goal is to understand social life: interaction is possible because of sharing such frames, and, conversely, social life makes sense only because we have created such common frameworks of reference. Goffman's work provides a useful conceptual and quasi-methodological apparatus for the study of everyday life, including talk, in terms of the frames, or principles, that structure it.

Goffman's work, and his focus on the formal aspects of social interaction, has proved very fruitful in media and communication research, as it provides an opportunity to look at the media output in a more structured way. Thus, when we are confronted with media images, these do not capture the world in its complex entirety, but rather *frame* it in specific ways to make it more readily communicable to audiences. In mapping the specific frames, the first thing to note is that the process of framing inevitably involves selection: from all the possible "definitions of situation" that can apply, one is chosen as the most appropriate. Entman (1993) in his attempt to sketch a research agenda on framing provides the following definition: "To frame is to *select some aspects of a perceived reality and make them more salient in a communicating text, in such a way as to promote a particular problem definition, causal interpretation, moral evaluation, and/or treatment recommendation* for the item described (Entman, 1993: 52, italics in the original). Media representations from this point of view contain specific frames that guide interpretation and understanding. The main idea underlying theories of framing is that there is a finite number of discourses that organize reality around us, and that each of these leads to a different interpretation and action. For example, Gamson (1992) in his analysis of the US media coverage of Arab–Israeli relations identified five different frames, each offering different problems definitions, causes, and solutions – see table 8.1. Of these frames the ones that enjoyed extensive media coverage in the US were the Strategic Interest and Feuding Neighbors frames.

In these terms, framing appears to provide further insights in the cognitive aspects of representation. Although differing from stereotyping, framing still involves certain themes, ideas, and tropes organized in specific ways, and stored in people's heads. Framing in the media can therefore be seen as another way of talking about media effects – the assumption is that people are likely to endorse the problem definition and solution. Indeed, Snow *et al.* (1986) posited that frame alignment, i.e. the gradual agreement with the frames encountered, was a necessary prerequisite for action, while Gamson's (1992) own work was geared towards explaining the conditions for collective action. Framing as a form of representation is considered important only insofar as it leads to certain actions among those who perceive these representations. As with stereotypes, in framing, the work of representation appears to be a cognitive one, leading to certain cognitive maps or frames, which then guide action. Framing studies

Table 8.1   Arab–Israeli frames – based on Gamson (1992)

Frame	Issue definition	Outcome – action
Strategic interest	Region strategically significant, part of a "global chess game"	No action is possible – "realpolitik" – the US must get what it needs from the region
Feuding neighbors	Vicious cycle of attack and retaliation	Innocent victims die – ultimately the fault lies with both sides
Arab intransigence	Arab extremists feed the conflict	Israeli victims – Arabs must be stopped
Israeli expansionism	Western-supported Zionist aggression oppresses indigenous people	Arab victims – Israeli aggression must be stopped
Dual liberation	Both sides have valid points, the right to safety and self-determination	Compromise

have attempted to show the role of the media in promoting certain frames over others – primarily in terms of frequency and salience of frames – implying the operation of ideological elements. Yet others emphasize the mutual and dynamic interaction between frames, which inform each other, creating new opportunities, but also restricting others. Focusing on these differences, D'Angelo (2002) distinguishes three paradigms of framing research, each prioritizing a different aspect and explanation of the role of the framing process. *Cognitivist* framing highlights the cognitive aspects of framing, looking for correspondences between media frames and mental schemata; *constructionist* perspectives look for the constructive ways in which framing leads to new solutions, which though may sidestep or prevent alternative ones from emerging; *critical* approaches to framing look for the ideological aspects of framing, the exclusions and dominations it effects.

While D'Angelo argues against the subsumption of all three under a single umbrella theory of framing, it is possible to see them as complementary rather than mutually exclusive, in that they can be seen as operating at different levels, the cognitive, socio-cultural, and political respectively. In other words, a frame can be seen as having a cognitive component, found in people's minds, a socio-cultural one that includes the various socio-cultural exchanges that have given rise to it, and finally a political one in the sense of lending itself to a particular hierarchy and power distribution. A "racial" frame, in this sense, might include a cognitive schema of "race," a socio-cultural component, stemming from the particular value and substantive contents associated with "race" in a given culture, and a political aspect, which then justifies the location of "race" in power hierarchies. But this is where the problems start: framing tries to do too much with the result that these levels become either conflated or overlooked, particularly when the focus is on one rather than the others. Framing often results in considerable theoretical confusion, particularly when it comes to ideology and its role. This is more of a problem for the study of media frames, which focus on salience and frequency, extrapolating power and influence on the basis of these. At the same time, studies of media frames are typically concerned with identifying the frames, rather than linking them to existing discourses of power, and/or drawing links connecting them to other socio-cultural discourses. In other words, what typically occurs in media framing studies is that they extrapolate from the cognitive to the ideological, while mostly ignoring the socio-cultural level. What is necessary here is a way in which we can link the cognitive with the ideological and the socio-cultural, in order to provide a more complete and systematic approach to representation. This is precisely what discourse analysis purports to do.

Although there are many strands of discourse analysis, one of the most influential ones in media and communication is the socio-cognitive discourse analysis associated with the work of Teun van Dijk and others (1988, 1991, 1993; Fairclough, 1995; Hodge and Kress,1988). This approach is widely known as Critical Discourse Analysis (CDA). Van Dijk looked specifically at racism and sought to identify and explain the socio-linguistic structures through which the media reproduce it. For van Dijk discourse is understood as socially situated text and talk, and he locates it at the interface between the cognitive and socio-political levels. In other words, discourse is the means by which ideologies and belief systems find their way in people's consciousness. Clearly, the scope for media involvement is great: as the purveyors of discourses *par excellence*, the media become a privileged space for the reproduction of ideology. The goal of Critical Discourse Analysis is to investigate how discourses and socio-cultural practices are "ideologically shaped by relations of power and struggles over power; and to explore how the opacity of these relationships between discourse and society is itself a factor securing power" (Fairclough, 1995: 132–3). The analyst's task is therefore to expose to the light these ideologically charged discourses, and through this to challenge existing power arrangements. Media representations of cultural difference in these terms are directly contributing to the maintenance of the current power hierarchy among different groups in society, and CDA seeks to expose these unfair power arrangements.

Notwithstanding the invaluable contribution of CDA in understanding media representations, its emphasis on hidden ideological messages spread through the media raises several questions. The most pressing question is whether there is anything outside ideology. In CDA terms, ideology is a set of core or fundamental beliefs shared by members of social groups (van Dijk, 2004). But from this point of view, it is very difficult to discern what is ideology and what isn't. For van Dijk, the cut-off point is the extent to which the beliefs are widespread and held by more than one group or community – then they are upgraded to "knowledge." However, knowledge itself is often seen not as neutral and value-free, but rather as an indication of power, and specifically the power to name and control (Foucault, 1980). Van Dijk recognizes that knowledge itself might be based on ideology – thus he says the ideology of human rights has now become knowledge – but finds it more pressing for CDA to concern itself with the latter. Yet the question persists, particularly for media representations of cultural diversity: how can we distinguish between knowledge and ideology, and how can we identify a representation as ideological? Moreover, CDA has traditionally focused on news and current affairs, but media representation of cultural difference in fiction and entertainment genres complicates matters even more, as the "us/them" distinction operates at different and more complex levels. A possible reason for this confusion is the emphasis of CDA on the socio-cognitive level, and on the discursive reproduction of ideological beliefs such as racism. This has resulted to a relative neglect of the socio-historical level, and the processes by which ideas become consolidated as "knowledge." Indeed, because of its focus on news and the here-and-now discursive reproduction of problematic representations, CDA gives the impression that the media somehow deliberately and intentionally conspire against cultural difference. The socio-historical and cultural background within which the media operate is not taken into consideration, thereby weakening CDA's denunciations of media racism. Indeed, if racism and the problematization of difference are the culmination of a long historical and cultural process, then media racism merely represents cultural reality. An analysis at the level of CDA must therefore be complemented by a more in-depth analysis that will contextualize the media in a historical and cultural context. This is the type of analysis associated with Michel Foucault, and specifically for cultural difference, with theorists such as Edward Said.

8.4 Semiosis, Discourse, and Representation: an Historical Analysis

I am at the barber's and a copy of Paris-Match *is offered to me. On the cover, a young Negro in a French uniform is saluting, with his eyes uplifted, probably fixed on a fold of the tricolour. All this is the meaning of the picture. But, whether naively or not, I see very well what it signifies to me: that France is a great Empire, that all her sons, without any colour discrimination, faithfully serve under her flag, and that there is no better answer to the detractors of an alleged colonialism than the zeal shown by this Negro in serving his so-called oppressors.* (Barthes, 1973: 112)

In this excerpt from his famous essay, Roland Barthes clearly shows the levels in operation in a single image. Firstly, we come across the overt, apparent meaning of the image: a young black boy saluting the French flag. But underlying this image, there is a more complex meaning, which is caught up in history and culture. For a French reader of the 1950s (the magazine cover was from 1955) the meaning is clear: in the midst of wars for emancipation in various colonies, this cover presents an image of a united French Republic regardless of color and background. This representation therefore implicates cultural meanings that are historically located and readily available to members of specific cultural communities. Perhaps for readers today, this picture evokes more the terrible fate of child soldiers in Africa than the "French Empire." But the point remains: to understand media representations today, we must be aware of the cultural, historical, and political background within which we encounter these representations. A second point concerns specifically representations of cultural diversity. Far from being marginal or incidental, these representations are co-constitutive of history and culture. These points will be elaborated further in this section, which will discuss structural semiology and Foucauldian and poststructuralist approaches.

As with Critical Discourse Analysis, semiology begins with language. But unlike discourse analysis, which focuses on linguistic structures, semiology focuses on the distance or interplay between words and meanings. Drawing upon the work of the linguist Ferdinand de Saussure (1916/2006) on the one hand and structuralism on the other, the semiologist Roland Barthes (1973, 1977) attempted to find the structure of forms of communication including narrative and image. Semiology was defined as the study of systems of signification (Barthes, 1964). In semiology, meaning emerges only as a result of a complex cultural and historical accumulation of signs. A semiological analysis should then be able to trace the beginnings of signs, and their original meanings, as well as the originary signs on the basis of which all meaning emerged. But semiological analysis is not only interested in signs in a general sense; it is a critical study of signs, aimed to show how a specific culture, that of the ruling class, becomes naturalized as a universal culture. This Marxist understanding of the ideological role of signs – which is clear in Barthes' analysis of the Paris-Match image – shows the functionality of systems of representation. Their presence always conveys something above and beyond what is immediately perceived. This is the level of myth, which serves the function of making things appear natural, unquestionable truths. Semiology's task is to denaturalize this relationship, to show the arbitrary links between signs and meanings.

For cultural diversity, this has important implications. Denying the naturalist and biological assumptions underlying difference, particularly when this is mapped onto signs such as "race" and ethnicity, semiology allows a more nuanced and culturally oriented understanding of how difference is actively produced through the mobilization of signs. Media representations of cultural difference can therefore be understood as mobilizing signs, which are in turn linked to certain myths about difference. Ultimately, within structural semiology, these can be traced to certain constitutive signs. Here the work of the anthropologist Claude Lévi-Strauss is instructive. Lévi-Strauss (1963, 1970) argued that "mythologies," i.e. the systems of signification central to any culture, are based on a series of binary oppositions, which operate through transposition: thus the binary nature/society corresponds to other sets of oppositions, such as raw/cooked, primitive/civilized, and so on. Representations can be meaningful only insofar as they mobilize these binaries, and these binaries in turn draw upon myths, as well as reinforce and naturalize them through constant repetition.

The main point here is that media representations cannot but follow and reproduce the socio-cultural world around us. They have to be intelligible, and therefore must mobilize signs in ways familiar to us through our participation in culture. Ultimately, for Lévi-Strauss, all societies, all systems of signification can be reduced to a set of building binary oppositions that have been used to create all meaning. From the point of view of a more equitable society, intervention may be necessary in showing that this relationship between the binaries is not a necessary or natural, but rather an arbitrary one. It is here perhaps that structural semiology encounters the most problems: firstly, the structural analysis might privilege a cultural understanding of representation, but at the same time it tends to dehistoricize meaning by reducing it to ever-present binaries. Secondly, Barthesian semiology, notwithstanding, its emphasis on the mythological/ideological function of signs and representations locates meaning in language rather than in the forces that shape language. This is a criticism against semiology launched by Michel Foucault, whose emphasis was more on the workings of power as constitutive of language and signs. Indeed, absent from the semiological perspective on representation is a broader theorizing of how and why specific meanings (e.g. primitivism) became attached to specific signs (e.g. blackness).

Foucault understands discourse as a system of knowledge that determines what something is, what can and cannot be said about it, and how to deal with it. In his various works Foucault (e.g. 1966, 1972, 1980) refers to the concept of discourse or discursive formation to capture the antecedents and conditions of possibility, as well as the contents, of the knowledge we have about the world. A discursive formation does not so much represent its objects as construct them as specific kinds of objects, and determines how they are viewed, spoken of, classified, and retrieved, and so on. Representation in language, the mass media, in academic books, and so on, is therefore itself a product of discourse – discourse precedes and prefigures any cognitive and linguistic aspects of representation. In other words, media representations may have cognitive, linguistic, visual, etc. components, but these have already been determined by the discursive formations in operation. This approach clearly allows for a historically nuanced understanding of representations of cultural difference. But, crucially, Foucault's work highlights and emphasizes the role of ideology not as distortion but as the mobilization of power and dominance. It is through power that discourses become consolidated, while at the same time, certain discourses privilege certain concepts, objects, and subjects, thereby enabling them to dominate. Discourses therefore always betray the operation of power. Power, in turn, does not reside in individuals, regardless of how "powerful" they seem to be. Rather, it is found in the operations of the various discourses which enable and justify domination and governance, and which construct subjects as leaders, masters, and experts, or conversely as followers, subordinates, and ignorant (Foucault, 1977: 1982).

These conceptual points are poignantly illustrated in Edward Said's *Orientalism* (1979). Said's main argument is that representations, or rather *discourses*, of the Orient found in the scientific publications of Europe, in its literary output, its political speeches, and its popular culture, are constitutive not only of an Orient that is in every respect the Other of Europe, but also of Europe itself. The Orient, the socio-cultural and geographical configuration at the East of Europe, is "Orientalized," in the sense of being made into a particular entity. From as early as the classic Greek era, the Orient is produced as first and foremost incapable of representing itself; the Orient is only able to make itself known not directly, say through dialogue with Europe/the West, but through the work of those Europeans who have travelled there, have studied the East, and can therefore represent it for their fellow countrymen and women. The Orient's inability to speak or represent itself is repeated and elaborated in the discourses of the colonial officials of the nineteenth century. In their work, Said finds the justification for this: the Orient's speech is inarticulate, lacks lucidity and logic, and is full of contradictions and untruths. Lord Cromer, Egypt's colonial ruler between 1882 and 1907, put it succinctly: "Want of accuracy, which easily degenerates into untruthfulness, is in fact the main characteristic of the Oriental mind. The European is a close reasoner ... The mind of the Oriental, on the other hand, like his picturesque streets, is eminently wanting in symmetry. His reasoning is of the most slipshod description" (Cromer, in Said, 1979: 38). More broadly, the contents of Orientalism construct an Orient much along the lines of the binary oppositions detailed above; as Said puts it: "The Oriental is irrational, depraved (fallen), childlike, 'different'; thus the European is rational, virtuous, mature, 'normal'" (p. 40). But Said went further than the identification of the contents of the Orientalist discourse, to specify the processes by which it came about, and the functions it served.

The process-oriented account of Orientalist discourse focuses on the conditions under which the Orient became an object of inquiry and study. And here Said finds colonialism as the underlying condition of possibility for Orientalism, thereby firmly historicizing and politicizing it. It is in the discourses of the politicians, philosophers, scientists, artists, travellers, and journalists of the European colonial powers that Orientalism comes alive as an object for governance/administration, and frequent discipline and punishment, as an object of study and scrutiny, as an object for conceptualization and aesthetic apprehension, and as an object to be illustrated and reported upon. All these elements of the discourse are in direct contact, informing, influencing, and reinforcing each other. At the end, their combined efforts result in Orientalism, which is a tightly knit set of discourses with internal correspondences and connections, characterized by a continuity in which the Orient is always subordinate and inferior to Europe. These discourses are couched in the themes and tropes specific to the various perspectives (science, politics, art, etc.) that contributed to it, and always reflecting the power and domination of the West over the Orient.

The functions served by Orientalism are twofold: firstly, to control and contain the Other, and secondly, to justify its continued domination. As we saw above, the representation of the Oriental Other, i.e. the fact that the Orient is always represented through the voice of Europe, points to its inability to speak or represent itself in an articulate and direct manner. The resulting representation serves to paint a picture of the Other as exotic but comprehensible, as different, but manageable or knowable. Representation is in this sense *containment* of the Other: by representing him/her, the threat posed by an unknown and distant Other is diminished, because s/he is now known. This is a crucial argument, particularly coupled with the observation that the Other never represents itself, but is always represented. This containment is, in turn, linked to the continued necessity to control and master the Other; in Said's terms, Orientalism justifies the ongoing domination of the East by the West. In his 2003 preface to *Orientalism*, Said draws a direct line of continuity between the early Orientalists of the nineteenth century and the current area experts and advisers to Western governments in matters pertaining to the Middle East. His point is that these discourses have important material consequences: if the Orient is deemed incapable of governing itself, then the West must assume its historical responsibility of "helping" it, militarily and otherwise.

Said's work has forcefully illustrated the power of discourse and representation, and their very material consequences. It further provided a much-needed historical background and context, within which such discourses have developed and evolved across time. It does not come as a surprise that Said's work has generated both acclaim and critique. The controversy surrounding *Orientalism* revolved mainly around the extent to which Orientalism was indeed a more or less unified discursive formation that constructed Oriental subjects as inferior to Western ones, or whether this was a political argument made by Said on the basis of selectively focusing on some works but ignoring others (Lewis, 1982; Said, 1982). While the controversy continues, fuelled by the post-9/11 climate, there is another aspect in Said's work that is more relevant for our discussion of media representations: the active role played by the Other in disputing, challenging, or otherwise discrediting Orientalist assumptions. A consequence of Said's focus on Orientalism as a totalizing discourse was that the "Orientalized" Others are seen as completely devoid of any agency at all. Moreover, whatever actions they take are interpreted as reactions to and against Orientalism. By stripping the Other from any agency, Said's work inadvertently repeats the Orientalist assumptions on the inability of the Other to act or represent herself. A related problem concerns the extent to which *Orientalism*, with its insistence on a continued "Orientalization" from ancient Greece to the present day, ends up essentializing both Europe and the "Orient" – any discontinuities, ruptures, contradictions, resignifications, and power struggles within and between these "entities" are overlooked, thereby assuming an almost monolithic version of the West and the East.

In this respect, Said did not take into account another, crucial, aspect of Foucault's work on power: that power not only constrains but also enables, it not only subjugates but also produces and empowers. Indeed, for Foucault power works on two premises: "that 'the other' (the one over whom power is exercised) be thoroughly recognized and maintained to the very end as a person who acts; and that, faced with a relationship of power, a whole field of responses, reactions, results, and possible inventions may open up" (1982: 220). These creative and resisting elements were hardly taken into account by Said. To be fair, he did attempt to consider the cultures of resistance that evolved in colonized countries in his subsequent work *Culture and Imperialism* (1994). There Said spoke of cultures emerging contrapuntally, as in a kind of dialogue within and between themselves (see Silverstone, 2006). However, for now, we must insist that *Orientalism* overlooked the ways in which power is productive and creative, as well as dominating and repressing. Notwithstanding the contribution of Said's work in understanding the way in which discourse and representation are implicated in relations of power and domination, the above problems cast serious doubts on it. The next section will sketch out an alternative approach, building on the above but considering representation in more dynamic terms.

8.5 The Performative Force of Representation

The question of the role of the Other in representation is something that continues to vex discussions of representation. The problem is that, if we insist that the Other has agency and does contribute to representation, then we may end up overlooking the role of ideological and political domination exerted by representation. On the other hand, if we assume that the Other has no power or agency at all, then we fall back to a position of further victimizing him or her. As we have seen in chapter 5, media theory moved from understanding the role of the mass media as exercising total domination towards one where they exerted hegemony (Gramsci, 1971). When hegemony is applied to the question of representation it becomes a dynamic field of action and struggle. The main idea behind hegemony is that power is (also) the result of consent, hence it must always justify itself, open itself up to criticism, and eventually change or adapt to new challenges. In these terms, both dominant and subordinate groups, ideas, and concepts must continuously reinvent themselves if they are to retain dominance and/or be able to challenge existing hierarchies. Representation can therefore play a crucial role in this struggle, as it comprises the field of appearances, the space where arguments are heard, images are constructed and circulated, events are presented, and narratives, stories, and discourses are told and retold (see Silverstone, 2006). Representation can be seen not only or primarily as cognitive, discursive, linguistic, or ideological but also as a field or space wherein difference is performed. The choice of the words "performance" and "appearance" is significant. Although they may be taken to point to drama or theatre, and hence to make-believe rather than reality, their use here is meant to indicate the importance of appearance and performance as bringing objects and subjects to the fore, making them *visible* and thus "real." This is why and how representation matters: because of its ability to establish, control, or alter relations of visibility, and their respective claims to power. Because of this explicit politicization of representation – the fact that its main concern becomes the control, management, or contestation of relations of visibility – we can talk of a politics of representation (see Hall, 1997). These arguments will be explored through a discussion of Judith Butler's work on performativity.

Judith Butler's *Excitable Speech* (1997) is in the first instance a book against censorship, and particularly against the kind of censorship that is motivated by "good" or "progressive" goals, such as gender and racial harmony. Butler wants to dispute the need to legislate against hate and injurious speech, and hence against racist and sexist representations. In doing so, her arguments reveal firstly a theory of discourse and representation and secondly a politics of subversion and resistance. Butler's theory of discourse and representation is an extension of Foucault's concept of power as a productive force, combined with Jacques Derrida's reading of John Austin's theory of speech acts.

John Austin, a philosopher of language based in Oxford, developed an approach to language that focuses not so much on the intrinsic meanings of the words but on their use by people. His view was that people *do* things with words – indeed his book is entitled *How to Do Things with Words* (1962). He refers to utterances that not only state something but perform it or make it happen; he calls these performative statements or *speech acts*. He then distinguishes between three levels of speech act: locutionary, illocutionary, and perlocutionary. A locutionary act is any meaningful and grammatical sentence; an illocutionary act is performed *in* saying something, e.g. in asking, promising, stating and so on; a perlocutionary act is performed *by* saying something, i.e. it has an effect beyond the actual meaning of the words. A statement such as "I now pronounce you husband and wife" is locutionary insofar as it is grammatically correct and it makes sense; it is illocutionary in making a pronouncement; and perlocutionary in that it has far-reaching legal, social, psychological etc. consequences, as it has bound two people together in marriage.

Derrida, in an important and influential essay titled *Signature Event Context* (1972/1988), extended and modified Austin's theory of language in three significant ways. First, he moved from the spoken to the written word as the paradigm for language and meaning. Derrida's main point here is that, although in thinking about language we typically understand spoken language with writing as a second best, a mere representation of the spoken word, in fact written language assumes paradigmatic priority. Since the advent of the mark, of writing, argues Derrida, the relationship of the spoken to the written word has changed: speech was thought to convey meaning directly and almost transparently, making clear the intentions of the speaker. Writing, however, must work in the absence of the author: we write something because we cannot be present to speak it. Writing therefore denotes absence, it must work without the presence of the author, it must be intelligible and understood, even if the author is not present to explain it. This for Derrida means that writing must be *iterable*, repeatable across contexts and in the continued absence of the author. The possibility of iteration and citation is for Derrida the very condition for language to mean, and moreover to perform. This is in his view the "illocutionary force" that makes language work. This is why he questioned and removed the speaker's/author's intentions (or illocutionary force) as a determinant of meaning or of the success of the utterance/sentence. Writing or language must mean something beyond or even despite the author's intentions. The key issues for representation emerging from Derrida are, firstly, that language relies on representation, in the sense that language as the invocation and use of signs always involves a *re*presentation or a stand-in for the original thing that cannot be apprehended directly; secondly, that every repetition, citation, reiteration, and representation is simultaneously an-other, different, separate to the first one, to the "original" thing represented. Clearly, for Derrida, representation is the very condition of difference.

Butler takes over from Austin and Derrida, expanding on the concepts of iterability and performative force (i.e. what makes the performative "work"), and rethinking the role of possible failures of performatives. Iterability, or the in-built ability of language to mean through repetition, implies that a word must operate beyond any given context, and therefore break with the context(s) in which it originally occurred. But this inherent break with context implies that anyone can use the word, which in turn may lose its performative force. Words are used in a manner consistent with the norms of language. But since contexts in which they are used are different, the same words in different contexts may lead to misunderstandings, failure, or incredulity. Consider an example: a judge proclaims someone as "different"; a student in a cafeteria points a finger at someone else, telling them "you are different"; an advertisement tells viewers that they are "different." This is not merely an illustration of polysemy (multiple meanings): for something to be able to convey meaning across contexts, it must be bound to a meaning. What this shows is that the word's "break" with its original context and the consciousness or intention that created its original meaning implies that, every time it is used, it will create a new context. In every instance, the word/utterance performs something different, altered from the "original" use-meaning of the word. It should be noted, however, that the performative force created by these utterances in these contexts is not equal: a verdict, an insult, and a compliment respectively differ in their force to condemn, hurt, deceive, and so forth.

But what determines this force? In other words, what determines the success or failure of the performative? Pierre Bourdieu (1993a), who criticizes Derrida for intellectual formalism, would argue that the success of the performative depends on the social power enjoyed by the speakers (see also Butler, 1997:142–51). But, argues Butler, if this were indeed the case, if only powerful people could make performatives work, then we would not be able to explain social change and transformation, along with the possibility of language to generate new meanings, and hence new objects and subjects of thought. If, on the other hand, language precedes power, then how does power and performance (the ability to do/accomplish something) come about? Well, argues Butler, actually Bourdieu (1991; 1993a) has a concept that might help: habitus is a notion developed by Bourdieu to account for the way in which individuals embody the social rules, conventions, and knowledge that enable them to operate within given cultural contexts. Habitus, insofar as it refers to a bodily disposition, (re)enacts these rules and conventions – feels embarrassment, for instance, cries, or gets angry. In doing so, argues Butler, it performs these social rules again and again, it reiterates them in different contexts. Here, though, lies the possibility of failure, of inappropriate behavior, of misunderstandings, and even parody that produces different performances whilst using the same words, the same rules, and the same bodily dispositions. Some of these instances may become subversive, openly questioning the very social rules that produced them and made them signify in the first place. For instance, racial or gendered slurs, as Butler puts it, "live and thrive in and as the flesh of the addressee"; but in the same place, in the body as the "sedimented history of the performative," is also found a possibility of using the very same performatives to oppose this history and inaugurate "a future through a break with that past" (Butler, 1997: 159). In other words, Butler finds in the performatives a force that is at once linguistic, social, and bodily, a force that is at the same time (re)productive and formative, that produces subjects while at the same time giving them the means by which to oppose their production as certain subjects. It is here that Butler locates the politics of the performative.

For representation, these arguments have important ramifications. Firstly, following Austin, representation must be seen as having a performative force, as doing things and bringing things into being. Secondly, following Derrida, representation – to the extent that this involves, indeed rests on, repetition – is the very condition of difference: no representation can ever be true to an "original" but is an ongoing repetition that generates difference. This makes it impossible, or at least fraught with difficulties, to speak of "true" or distorted representations by referring to an original essence. Thirdly, following Bourdieu, we must take into account the possibility of social power and authority, which always accompanies representation, and which makes some representations more "valid" and their performative effects more "real." But both social power and authority depend, following Butler, on the extent to which they are embodied in the habitus of the subjects they have brought into representation. Representation, and the repetition on which it rests, preclude total control, and allow subjects to resist or reform themselves again via representational means. The field or space of representation, therefore, becomes a very important domain in its own right, and to this degree independent of – though inextricably bound to – both production and consumption. If representation is seen as reproducing forms of subjection that might subordinate, offend, and exploit their subjects, then these can only be countered by inaugurating new forms, but again via representational means, by using and repeating the same forms but expanding, resignifying, and in the end reforming them. Ultimately, representation is a weapon in the arsenal of both dominant and subordinate groups.

8.6 Conclusions: Representation and Mediation

A theory of mediation assumes a dialectical (or at least a dynamic and reciprocal) relationship between the media (understood as comprising processes of production, representation, and consumption) and society. It therefore needs a dynamic account of representation, an account that shows clearly the role played by representation in containing, controlling, and dominating cultural difference, but which also allows room for the subversion, questioning, and rejection of representations. In these terms, an account of representation needs to show how it works, how it can be effective both in containing cultural difference and in subverting such efforts. The complexity of the theories discussed in this chapter shows that this is not an easy task. Representation operates at cognitive, linguistic, socio-psychological, social, historical, and political

Table 8.2 Summary of theories of representation

Theory	Key theorists	Key arguments	The work of representation
Stereotyping	Lippman (1922/2004), Tajfel (1981)	Stereotypes are images in our minds, coming from culture, including the media. They are typically negative and rigid representations of social groups	At the group level, stereotypes explain the world and justify action, while at the individual level they help people orient themselves in the world, they provide status and value, or conversely, a negative self-image.
Framing	Goffman (1974) Gamson (1992) Entman (1993)	Frames are the basic building blocks of social organization (Goffman). Framing is based on the selection of certain aspects of a situation over others. The media consistently choose some frames over others.	Frames provide clear maps of a situation or specific "problem definitions" which subsequently guide action.
Critical Discourse Analysis (CDA)	Van Dijk (1988) Fairclough (1995)	Language as the means by which ideology operates. The task of CDA is to identify how discourse operates in ways that give power to some and exclude others. The media construct and circulate such ideological discourses	The work of representation is mainly ideological: it justifies and perpetuates existing power structures.
Semiology	Barthes (1973)	Meaning operates at three levels: the denotational, in which something is described the connotational, which attributes a certain value to the thing represented the mythical, which operates at the level of cultural beliefs and meanings, and which locates the thing represented in existing systems of meaning.	Signs and their meanings structure the world in certain ways, through mobilizing widespread and deeply held cultural beliefs
Discursive formations	Foucault (1966/2002)	Discursive formations refer to systems of knowledge that determine what something is and how to deal with it	Representations as part of wider discursive formations construct reality, enabling and justifying domination
Performatives	Austin (1962) Derrida (1972/1988) Butler (1997)	Representations "perform," i.e. create (new) objects, subjects, and situations. E.g. "I pronounce you husband and wife" or "I name this child …"	Representations "do" things – they enable both identity and difference, and they provide the means and the space both for domination and resistance, because to re-present always implies a certain difference from the original, which in turn contains the possibilities for resistance and change

levels, and in their quest to illustrate exactly how it works, theorists tended to discount the possibility of change and the active subversion of dominant representations.

Thus, cognitive accounts of representation primarily focused on how people's memories need simplified and oft-repeated representations in order to effectively order the world around them. Stereotypes, from this point of view, are functional: they allow people to define and successfully deal with certain situations. But while these accounts might show the deep hold of stereotypical images, they do not discuss their links with power asymmetries, or indeed with the social environment within which they operate. In other words, while perhaps holding a stereotypical image of, say, an Italian-American as a mobster may be useful in understanding relevant cultural references, we also need to know how such representations came about, who profits from their perpetuation, and how they can change. Framing and Critical Discourse Analysis can provide some answers to these questions, because they explicitly link racist discourses to power structures, with a view to challenging and eventually changing them. However, the problem is that such accounts posit a problematic distinction between ideology and truth, between distortion and reality.

Discourse and language have a complex relationship with reality: if we accept Foucault's arguments, discourse constructs, orders, and in this sense determines reality. Representation as discourse must be understood in its entirety as structuring the world around us, determining what is important, where everyone fits, what can be said, and what cannot. Discourse/representation defines, shapes, and controls its objects more forcefully than any kind of prison. Edward Said's work has powerfully shown how the "Orient," a whole region of the world, is effectively dominated, and how this domination is justified through discursive means, through the linguistic, conceptual, and discursive apparatus that sought to apprehend, describe, and define what this region and its people are, what they need, etc. But again here there are problems: if discourse is so total and so effective, how can we account for change?

To view representation as dynamic as well as effective requires an understanding of the very way in which language operates. Language is, following Austin, performative: it does or accomplishes things. As language is the primary or raw material of representation, the latter must be seen as accomplishing things as well. This view enables us to see representation as an autonomously significant process in mediation: in other words, representation is significant per se, because it does things. But this performative aspect of representation is also the one that allows it to change: representation, based on language (and images), must be able to be widely recognized by most people, who can then understand more or less the same thing. At the same time, representations are used and repeated across different and uncontrollable contexts. This use or repetition – which Derrida calls iteration – attaches different meanings to representation, some of which effectively undermine the meanings originally intended.

Understanding representation as performative and iterable provides a means by which we can understand the crucial role this process has in the mediation of cultural difference. Its performativity allows us to understand how representations construct culturally different subjects as inferior and unreasonable, thereby justifying their continued oppression and domination. Its iterability, however, the possibility of being repeated across contexts, destabilizes representation, and frees it from the process of production. Once produced and circulated, representation acquires a life of its own; it follows an unpredictable and often surprising trajectory, beyond the control of either its producers or its users. But here we must also allow for the asymmetrical relations within which representation exists. The unpredictability of representation does not mean that all representations are equal: they are ordered, or structured in a hierarchical manner, which betrays the relations of power and domination which produced them in the first place. In the following two chapters we will discuss different representations, their contents, operations and relations to each other, as well as their role in supporting or undermining current relations of power.

9

Regimes of Representation

9.1 The Multiplicity of Representations

In the previous chapter we examined theoretical approaches to the question of representation, arguing for a synthesis that can accommodate, to some extent, most existing approaches to representation. This theoretical synthesis insisted that the work of representation remain the same across different media, across different cultural settings, and across different times, although representations themselves, as contents, remain elusive, dynamic, unstable, and beyond the control of those who produce them. This and the next chapter present a snapshot of representations of ethnic and cultural difference in the media, with a view to making clear the coexistence of several types of representations. This coexistence, far from being harmonious, in fact betrays the ongoing struggle over representation, over who speaks and how, and over the right not to be misrepresented. This insistence on the concurrent existence of a multitude of representations – we will refer to them as different representational regimes for reasons that will be clear shortly – is a deliberate attempt to question any views of a historical progression from racist to non-racist representations.

To map and understand the concurrent existence of multiple types of representation, we can use the term "regimes of representation." This term is loosely based on Michel Foucault's (1997) concept of "regimes of truth," which denotes the convergence of certain ideas and discourses with certain power structures and mechanisms which then sustain these as "truth." In doing so, such regimes exclude, modify, constrain, marginalize, and otherwise control other ideas and discourses. From this account, we retain the political implications and issues pertaining to the distribution of power in society, the claims to truthfulness and accuracy, and the exclusions imposed by certain regimes of representation. In addition, by using regimes in the plural, it is possible to highlight the hegemonic character of representation: no single representational regime is capable of fully controlling the field of representation. There are always contending voices, images and discourses – in short representations – which struggle against other representational regimes. Yet the term "regime" denotes a certain regularity and systematicity as well as a degree of control and power: representational regimes are not all equal, nor do they enjoy the same degree of power. We must therefore think of representational regimes as operating within a representational hierarchy, in which certain regimes are dominant over others, while still allowing some room for other, often competing, representational regimes. In distinguishing between different regimes, we need to consider the regularity and systematicity associated with such regimes; these point to a certain stability or core within each regime. There are recurring themes and images that immediately suggest that certain representations belong to certain regimes.

This view of representations of cultural difference as constituting different regimes of representation builds upon and considerably expands Stuart Hall's (1997) concept of a "racialized regime of representation." Hall, examining historical representations of race and ethnicity, argues that they "racialize" people, in inscribing certain "racial" characteristics structured on the basis of binary oppositions, and in reducing complex human beings to a set of physical features. Although Hall recognizes that this regime was challenged, he rightly points to its dominance and persistence across time. Nevertheless, representations and their regimes must be dynamic and changeable, while also retaining key features across different contexts. As argued in the theoretical discussion of representations, they always combine two apparently contradictory characteristics: firstly, a core set of features that must be abstract enough so that they are transferable across contexts; and secondly, precisely because of their transferability, an ability to change or accrue different meanings. This means that representational regimes are all subject to change and that their mutability leads to the formulation of new representational regimes; at the same time, new representational regimes may emerge as a response to already existing ones.

In these terms, the racialized regime is but one of the representational regimes in operation in today's media, and it corresponds to what we may also term an outright *racist regime*. Based on an analysis of the literature on representations of cultural difference, it seems that there are at least four more representational regimes in operation. We can term these the *domesticated regime*, which includes representations and representational practices that signal a shift from the brutally racist representations towards a milder, but no less virulent, form of racism, which "accepts" cultural difference only insofar as those seen as different fully and unquestionably adopt the characteristics of the dominant group; the *regime of commodification*, in which representational practices coopt cultural difference to serve commercial and consumer-oriented interests; the *essentializing regime* of representation, which seeks to represent, in all senses of the word, to control, contain, and define cultural difference from within; and, finally, the *alternative regime* of representation, in which representational practices allow for the expression and reconstruction of cultural difference in ways that leave room for all its ambiguities to emerge. This chapter will focus on the first three regimes, while the next chapter will discuss the latter two regimes, which, as we shall see, represent a qualitatively different perspective on representing difference.

9.2 The Racist Regime of Representation

To recognize the operations of a racialized regime of representation, as both Hall (1997) and Malik (2002) do, means to identify the ways in which persons become members of a particular race, and their defining characteristics become those attributed to this race. The next step forward is to evaluate these "racial" characteristics in certain ways that betray the dominant racial hierarchies. As such, the racialized regime of representation is a necessary precursor to what we call here the racist regime of representation. On the other hand, in more recent years, the concept of "race" has expanded to incorporate not only imputed biological characteristics, but cultural ones as well – this is the so-called new racism (Barker, 1981). In the new racism, "culture" becomes as rigid and essentialized as race, with members of particular cultures assuming *en masse* characteristics attributed to their culture. This shift, first identified in the 1980s, marks a significant departure from biology-based racist arguments. Muslim communities living in Western countries often find themselves at the receiving end of this new type of cultural racism, as do asylum seekers/refugees and economic migrants. It is, however, clear that in most of these discriminated groups, "race"/ethnicity and "culture" coincide, so that ethnicities are characterized by their culture, which in turn becomes a shorthand term for race/ethnicity.

Thus, in both types of racism persistently unfair and inaccurate judgments are made, which are then used to justify certain groups' social status, symbolic and material. "Old-fashioned" (pseudo-)biology-based racism still persists alongside cultural racism. "Racialization" in these terms must be widened to encompass any groups subjected to any kind of racist treatment, whether biologically or culturally based. It may be more appropriate to place "race" and "cultural" racism as the two poles of a continuum, and then trace the various representations within this regime across this continuum.

As we shall see in this chapter, racism, instead of abating following the civil rights and other protest movements of the late 1960s, has returned with renewed vigor, and has broadened to include a wide variety of groups while also using a wide variety of justifications. Specifically, this regime constructs alterity primarily as irrational, or not rational enough, and therefore brutal, violent, and sexualized; it is further constructed as generally unable to speak, while, when it does speak, it is seen as demanding but not deserving because of its irrationality: hence, it must be treated primarily through power. On the other hand, alterity is often constructed as natural victimhood – an example here is the well-known Uncle Tom from Harriet Beecher Stowe's novel *Uncle Tom's Cabin* (1852). Here, racialized subjects are sentimentalized, and constructed as servile and "naturally" and willingly inferior, with their fortitude signalling a meekness and submissiveness that requires strong guidance at all times. The "natural victim" side of this regime is often gendered – that is, women. Through these contentions, the racist regime of representation justifies the continued oppression of, and discrimination against, ethno-cultural minorities.

Early studies of racism in the media have clearly shown the brutality of such racist depictions. In his review of relevant research, Stuart Hall (1997) provides several examples of such overt and brutal racism. The research shows widespread racist depictions, ranging from early advertisements to Hollywood films. In his well-known study on Hollywood and race, Donald Bogle (1973/2006: 8) identified a series of dominant racist representations in American films. These include: (i) *Toms*, and (ii) *Mammies*, which construct black men and women respectively as essentially good, but always submissive and servile, never questioning the current state of affairs; (iii) the *Tragic Mulatto*, primarily referring to women of mixed race, sexualized and exoticized, while at the same time "doomed" because of their "racial" blood; (iv) *Coons*, constructing black men and youths as lazy, unreliable liars, "good for nothing more than eating watermelons" (pp. 7–8); and (vi) *Bad Bucks*, constructing black subjects as cruel, violent, over-sexed, savage enemies of the "white race." The first three representations capture the sentimentalized, "victimized" aspects of the racist representational regime, while the latter three encompass the irrational, uncivilized, and outlaw elements. Together, they justify the continuing exclusion and marginalization of racialized subjects.

The racist regime of representation has spread across "races" and "cultures." The same themes come up time and again, whether the racialized subject is black, Asian, Muslim, Indian, or indeed Eastern or South European. The violence and lawlessness of racialized subjects is a common and recurring theme in the media of countries as diverse as Denmark and Greece, while the sexualization and "pitiful'/"tragic" lives of racialized women in particular are often sensationalized, whether these are hijab-wearing women or victims of human trafficking. And this racist regime of representation is mobilized to justify stringent immigration laws and race-based anti-terrorist and anti-crime initiatives, as well as leading to pressure to assimilate, resting on the ongoing negative and prejudicial representation of other cultures.

Mustafa Hussain (2000, 2007) and Hervik and Berg (2007) have found a consistent pattern of racist representations in Danish media, concerning generally immigrants to Denmark, and more specifically Muslims. The "racialization" of Muslims revolves around rigid, dogmatic, and simplified ideas of what constitutes Muslim culture, and attributes the negative characteristics associated with this culture to every single Muslim person. "Culture" in this sense becomes a biological category in its rigidity and general applicability. Hussain (2007) and Hervik and Berg (2007) focus specifically on the cartoon controversy, which started when, in September 2005, the Danish daily *Jyllands-Posten* published a series of derogatory cartoons of the Prophet Mohammed, including one portraying him as a terrorist. The depiction of Mohammed is considered blasphemous in Islam, and the cartoons sparked worldwide protests, which saw often violent street protests. But, in both reports cited above, the authors identify an ongoing tendency towards negative reporting against Muslim immigrants in Denmark and Islam more broadly.

In an earlier article, Hussain (2000) analyzed the Danish news coverage of ethnic minority issues and found that there was an overwhelming number of negative articles, specifically identifying Muslims as a "problem" minority, and associating them with violence, crime, and general "backwardness," particularly in their supposed treatment of women. But the cartoon controversy gave rise to an explicitly racist discourse in the news media, in which all Muslims were tarred with the same brush. Hervik and Berg (2007) translate a typical editorial:

> It is simply an abuse of language to expect that Danish Christians, Jews or pagans have to show respect towards a religion which [sic] practice goes against that of human rights. (*Ekstra Bladet*, editorial, March 1, 2006, cited in Hussain, 2007: 4)

And in another editorial, Islam is compared to Christianity and Christian values:

> Islam is the opposite of Christianity … We must understand that some Muslims also in this country have a fundamentally different way of thinking than us and some of them simply will not accept our way of life and our democratic values. (*Berlingske Tidende*, editorial, February 5, 2006, cited in Hussain, 2007: 5)

This construction of Islamic faith and culture as a rigid system, unchanged through time and place, is characteristic of the racist regime of representation. Islam's apparent rigidity and immutability replace the role of biological "race," while still retaining the same essentializing relationship between race/culture and members. Thus, insofar as persons are truly Muslim, they are dogmatic, "fundamentally different," enemies of "our" democratic values, and hence posing a threat for "us." The slide here between Christianity and democracy is unmistakable, as is the division between "them" and "us" across lines of culture and faith. Coupled with pictures of flag burning and street protests, the "racialized" Muslim subject emerges as violent, irrational, unable and unwilling to rationally discuss with others. Moreover, as Hussain (2007) notes, ordinary Muslim voices were conspicuously absent from the Danish coverage. This absence further adds to the representation of "racialized" Muslims as unable or unwilling to speak.

The construction of Muslims as a threat to civilization parallels in many ways an early racist representation of Asians (mainly Japanese and Chinese) in American and European media and popular fiction in the early twentieth century. "Yellow peril" was a phrase that originated in the American popular media, referring to the epidemic of yellow fever, an infectious disease, but also alluding to the perceived threat posed by Asian states or their people – then imported as cheap laborers, or "coolies" – for the "civilized" nations of the West (Shim, 1998). The political fears of the West regarding the expansion of the influence of China and Japan were echoed in the popular fiction of the time, which created evil Asian characters, set to conquer the world, such as Fu Manchu, created by Sax Rohmer in 1912 (Clegg, 1994). In the years preceding the Second World War, the term was often used to refer to Japanese expansionism, and reached its peak after the attack in Pearl Harbor in 1941. In more recent years, similar, but not quite so blatant, representations have resurfaced in connection with Japan's and China's increasing economic prowess and influence. The yellow peril reappears as the "Asian invasion" (see Shim, 1998), repeating well-known clichés and racist stereotypes. The aspects of the representation are familiar: irrationality, violence, and cruelty, alongside criminality. Films such as *Black Rain* (Scott, 1989) and *Rising Sun* (Kaufman, 1993) capture an anti-Japanese sentiment, engendered by Japan's economic success. Japanese characters in these films are overwhelmingly constructed as violent, cruel, and barbaric, while in more recent films such as *Lost in Translation* (Sofia Coppola, 2003) they are constructed as an alien culture, lacking the ability to communicate in a manner comprehensible to Westerners.

While "racialized" Islam and Asia are considered to be "Others" to the West, the racist regime of representation expands beyond specific races and cultures to encompass alterity in all its forms. Thus, in the so-called new Europe, the EU of twenty-seven member states, Eastern European immigrants are often "racialized" in the media, through racist representations constructing them as irrational, criminal, violent, and cruel, and placing them at the margins of civilization. In an article on the German media coverage of Eastern Europe, Ingrid Hudabiunigg (2004) refers to "Polnische Wirtschaft," a term used widely in German media, literally meaning Polish economics, but metaphorically used to refer to lack of planning and chaos. More specifically, Hudabiunigg argues that Polish people are constructed as irrational, through references to an almost primitive Catholicism associated with Karol Wojtyla, Pope John Paul II, who was seen as representing the Polish nation as a whole:

> [Pope John Paul II] did not always succeed in making the connection between his deep religious beliefs and convictions and a more rationally based faith. On the other hand many German Catholics were unable to set aside their intellectual reservations and to follow the religious devotion coming from the Vatican. (*Frankfurter Allgemeine Zeitung*, in Hudabiunigg, 2004: 373).

Irrationality and barbarism are common themes in the racist regime of representation, which spans different religious and cultural backgrounds. In a report from 1998, the non-governmental organization Greek Helsinki Monitor, which monitors minority human rights in Greece and in the broader Balkan region, gives details of the Greek press coverage of Turkey – a coverage that captures precisely the aspects of irrationality and barbarism:

> Even though Kemal [Mustafa Kemal Ataturk] tried to change them, to Europeanize them, the Turks remain deeply Turkish! Not that as individuals they lack any virtues. However, as an organized state, they are presented as despotic, autocratic, ruthless, arrogant and anti-democratic … The West and Turkey are two different worlds. (Editorial in *Apogeumatini*, October 7, 1997, in Rougheri, 1998: 17)

A similar incompatibility is reported in connection with Romania in the German media. For Hudabiunigg, Romania is one of the countries constructed as incompatible with Western life. Her analysis found that, when discussing Romania, and more broadly the Balkans, the German media mix in myths about spirits, demons, heathen deities, and the like, producing a picture of a primitive, backward, and ultimately lost region. With references to "Dracula's mob from the Carpathians" and "The Demons of the Balkans" (in *Die Zeit*, May 1999, and *Die Welt*, May 10, 2001 quoted in Hudabiunigg, 2004: 381–2), the German media construct the Balkans as an inherently and inevitably violent region:

> Driven by an inevitable force, the demons of the Balkans seem to haunt one country after the other. None of them is spared a bloody fate, it seems, and the West's hands are bound. (*Die Welt*, May 30, 2001, in Hudabiunigg, 2004: 382).

The next step in this racialization is to show the violence in which these subjects are supposedly steeped, as shown in these reports from Greek media:

> At least 25 more women – apart from those who were raped by four Albanian criminals the day before yesterday, have been raped by foreigners since the beginning of the year. (*Eleftheros Typos*, October 9, 1997, in Rougheri, 1998: 8)

> Albanians kill us, they rob us, they rape women in the middle of the street, while some "liberals" continue to talk about racism. (*Adesmeftos Typos*, October 11, 1997, in Rougheri, 1998: 11)

This pattern of equating (Eastern European) immigrants with criminality, particularly and significantly with violence against women, continues unabated. Ten years on from the above newspaper reports, the Italian media reported the rape and murder of an Italian woman by a Romanian immigrant in a very similar vein, describing in sensational terms the brutal attack in the hands of a twenty-four-year-old Romanian immigrant belonging to the Roma minority. The report broadened out from the actual crime to discuss Romanian immigration to Italy in general and subsequently proceeded to call for the arrest and expulsion of all Romanian immigrants, thereby criminalizing and blaming the whole community.

The point here is not in any way to excuse any crimes committed, but rather to show how subjects become racialized, in the sense of acquiring the negative characteristics attributed to their community. But what is also significant in this coverage is the emphasis on crime against women. The gender aspect of the racist regime of representation is significant, as its justificatory work is different to the one discussed above.

Specifically, the aspects of the racist regime of representation that focus on violence, crime, irrationality, and barbarity justify the political, social, and cultural exclusion of racialized subjects because they construct them as incompatible with the values of dominant, non-racialized subjects. The other side of the coin is the construction of racialized subjects, primarily women, as tragic victims. This is a sentimentalized representation that, on the one hand, reinforces the construction of racialized subjects as violent and barbaric and, on the other, removes agency and autonomy from gendered, racialized subjects. This articulation of gendered discourses with the racist regime of representation therefore works to justify the political, social, and cultural exclusion of ethno-culturally different women because they lack agency, autonomy, and free will, and hence are constructed as unable to represent themselves autonomously and participate in political processes as equal citizens.

The most common representations here include the so-called honor killings, and the headscarf (hijab) or whole-body cover (niqab) used by Muslim women, two practices that have become linked together as typical Muslim cultural practices. Another commonplace gendered and racist representation is that of trafficked women, particularly Eastern European women, but often also East Asian women. In all these, women are constructed as passive, voiceless victims, while at the same time they are sexualized, and invested with almost mystical (and mythical) sexual powers, which further remove them from the rational, civilized, and (sexually) controlled Western/European or more broadly dominant cultural group.

One of the most visible signs of Islam and the Orient, the veil has come to symbolize Islam's "oppression" of women, but also, more generally, to signal the "backwardness" of Islam as opposed to the progressiveness of the West. Veiling and unveiling is seen as a central dynamic in Western racist or Orientalist thinking, whereby the veil represents the oppressed, mystical, backward, and, more recently, radicalized, Islam, while unveiling implies "liberation," Westernization, moderation, modernization, and so on. It is a common news media trope to feature veiled women as a symbol of Islam more broadly. But this metonymic relationship is not innocent. Rather, it encapsulates and reinforces the binary opposition between Islam as backward, oppressive, and tyrannical, and the West as liberated, progressive, and democratic. In political terms, the justificatory work that the veil has been mobilized to do includes legitimation of Western intervention and rule in overseas territories. Leila Ahmed (1992) and Lila Abu-Lughod (2002) have both argued that, by constructing Muslim women in need of liberation and "saving," the West in fact masks its colonialist interventions as human rights projects.

In recent years, media images of veiled women in Afghanistan have been similarly mobilized in the media in order to justify Western intervention. Specifically, Klaus and

Kassel (2005), looking at German media, and Stabile and Kumar (2005), looking at US media, both reach similar conclusions: that the media overage of veiled women in Afghanistan was essentially hypocritical, and its main purpose was to justify the war in Afghanistan. Using Critical Discourse Analysis, Klaus and Kassel, report that both *Der Spiegel* and *Focus*, the two German news magazines they studied, repeated a "gender logic" which constructed veiled women as passive victims, and celebrated their unveiling as liberation, without really delving into their actual conditions of life. Mobilizing unveiling as evidence of liberation and progress, the magazines justified and supported Western military intervention as a war of liberation and women's rights. This emphasis on the unveiling of Afghan women, which constructs them as vulnerable and suffering at the hands of their brutal men folk, simultaneously constructs Western military forces as saviors and liberators. Stabile's and Kumar's findings confirm the news media focus on veiling/unveiling, corresponding to fundamentalist Islam/enlightened West, at the expense of deeper analysis of entrenched patriarchal dynamics both in Afghanistan and in other parts of the world. The celebratory tone of most of the articles analyzed by Stabile and Kumar belied the continuous difficulties faced by Afghani women in their daily struggle to survive in a war-torn country. The dominant metaphor was that of light: photographs of women shedding their burqas were captioned "Hello Sunshine" (*Time* magazine, November 26, 2001, in Stabile and Kumar, 2005: 773), while *Newsweek* used headlines such as "Now I See the Sunlight" and photo captions such as "finally in the light" (*Newsweek*, November 26, 2001, in ibid.). The implication is clear: the military intervention brought these women from the darkness into the light, from the brutal Dark Ages of Muslim fundamentalism to the enlightenment and liberation of the West.

This type of coverage clearly constructs veiled women as passive victims, who can only be rescued by Western men, overlooking their own struggles for liberation, and their attempts to articulate their own voices. In this manner, such representations disenfranchise women more effectively than any veil: their political role and participation is reduced to photo opportunities, which are quickly forgotten as the media lens moves on. But what remains is the representation of women hidden behind their veils, passively waiting and expecting the West to intervene and save them. Both Stabile and Kumar and Klaus and Kassel, alongside other authors, such as Myra Macdonald (2006), highlight the hypocrisy and racism of this representation, which chooses to ignore feminist struggles across the world in favor of constructing non-Western(ized) women almost exclusively as victims. At the same time, it attributes feminist achievements to some vague notion of "Western civilization," which generously handed rights to women, choosing to ignore the struggles of women who fought and continue to fight in order to acquire and consolidate equal rights.

While the veil has in recent years lost some of its sexual allure (see Macdonald, 2006), other groups of women are constructed as sexual victims. Specifically, Eastern European and East Asian women are constructed as victimized by trafficking and prostitution, in representations that at the same time construct their men folk as brutal, immoral, and exploitative, and the women in need of (Western) protection, while also possessing mystical feminine and sexual powers. The sexualized femininity of this representation mainly refers to submissiveness, a trait long associated with exoticized women. The image of "China Dolls" and "Geishas," submissive women willing to do anything for a man, is widespread through Hollywood movies and popular fiction.

Films such as *M. Butterfly* (Cronenberg, 1993), *Miss Saigon* (Schonberg and Boublil, 1989), and *The World of Suzie Wong* (Mason, 1957) all contribute to this construction of submissive and sexually available exotic feminity. For Ford and Singh Chanda (2002: 11) the greatest appeal of such a construction is that it represents "non-threatening, male-glorifying 'essential' women who fulfil desires and pacify male anxieties." At the same time, the Western male is constructed as a hero and a savior. As Marchetti (1993: 109) argues, the Western male "functions as a white knight who rescues the non white heroine from the excesses of her own culture."

Similarly, Eastern European women are constructed as submissive, passive, and exploited, awaiting their (Western) saviors. It is no coincidence that Western media products position both East Asian and Eastern European women as prostitutes or concubines, often returned to a virtuous life by their Western saviors. Otherwise, they are represented as mail-order brides, equally available to Western men, who are willing to save them from poverty. Films such as *Birthday Girl* (Butterworth, 2001), *Lilya 4-ever* (Moodysson, 2002), British and Swedish productions respectively, portray Eastern women as mail-order brides and trafficked prostitutes, while Eastern European prostitutes have had many an appearance (usually as corpses) in the *Law and Order* and *CSI* franchises. In his analysis of *Lilya 4-ever*, Kristensen (2007) argues that she is constructed as the essential European "Other," a victimized woman-child, whose clear victimization served, in the Swedish context, to support the introduction of a law banning the purchase but not the selling of sex. But in doing so, and notwithstanding its alignment with feminist objectives, the film used "the Russian Other in commenting on a transnational European reality, where the post-Socialist subject is seen as the victim of a poverty that strips the subject of agency" (Kristensen, 2007: 10). The point here is not to deny the exploitation of vulnerable women through trafficking, but rather to show how it is primarily *certain* women who are exploited, who are constructed as lacking agency and power, and who have no say in their own lives. And once more, the Western savior, in this case the legal and institutional apparatus of the West, is the liberator of the passive and victimized women. If, on the other hand, women attempt to act and take their lives into their own hands, they are constructed as "Dragon Ladies," manipulative, untrustworthy, two-timing, and dangerous females, as for instance Nicole Kidman's character in *Birthday Girl* (Butterworth, 2001), or Cynthia, the Filipina mail order bride in *The Adventures of Priscilla, Queen of the Desert* (Elliott, 1994).

Despite its spread and dominance, the racist regime is by no means the only one in operation. Other regimes negotiate, modify, reject, and actively counter the racist regime of representation with varying degrees of success.

9.3 The Domesticated Regime of Representation

Contrary to the outright rejection of difference encountered in the racist regime of representation, the domesticated regime seeks to "tame" and contain difference within confines deemed safe and acceptable. The regime of domestication can be understood as one of assimilation or subsumption of difference, which is therefore considered irrelevant. Ultimately, this regime negates difference through domestication, through making it "our" own, everyday, and banal, or else tempers it through mixing or hybridization.

However, contrary to the sometimes positive understanding of hybridization as a means of celebrating difference (e.g. Nederveen Pieterse, 2004), the regime of domestication accepts hybridity only insofar as it still displays the characteristics of the dominant race/culture. Hybridization within this regime is the ultimate means of subsuming difference, which in this manner is homogenized and ultimately destroyed.

The main themes within this regime include, firstly the stripping of difference of any threatening qualities by highlighting its folkloric dimensions; secondly, an emphasis on sameness to the detriment of any actual engagement with difference; thirdly, a kind of hybridity, a mixture of races/cultures/ethnicities, which insists on the ultimate subordination of difference. The justificatory work of this regime differs from the racist regime of representation, which justified domination and oppression. Through insisting on sameness and similarities, and through exorcizing any potential threats from difference, the regime of domestication in the end homogenizes and negates difference. This has two consequences: firstly, difference is ignored and marginalized, and persistent inequalities, symbolic and material, are overlooked; secondly, difference is destroyed, ultimately leading to an intolerance of any positions defending deep and substantial diversity. Crucially, this regime must not be thought as antithetical to the racist regime of representation, which appears to reify and sustain difference; rather, they both act together and must be seen as the two sides of the same coin. If difference cannot be controlled and dominated through the racist regime, then it is contained and refused through the regime of domestication. Both regimes are equally unable to tolerate difference. This coexistence of the two complementary regimes is clearly illustrated in the presence of domesticated difference in the same media that denounce difference as irrational and incapable of rehabilitation.

It is mainly indigenousness and traditional elements within cultural difference that fall prey to representations that render them folkloric. Through folklore, difference is made quaint and picturesque and is not taken seriously as difference. Folkloric difference is reduced to external elements or symbols of culture, such as dress, food, religious festivals, and cultural artefacts, which appear to celebrate difference, while at the same time ignoring its demands for equal recognition. Moreover, the folklorization of difference in this regime has the effect of ossifying culture, looking at it as a relic of the past, charming but ultimately irrelevant in the modern world. An example of such folklorization is found in the otherwise complex popular drama series *Ugly Betty* (ABC, 2006–). Often seen wearing a poncho, Betty is stereotypically constructed as a Latina. In some episodes of the series, Betty is seen eating tacos, burritos, and other Hispanic food, often leading her non-Latino colleagues at work to complain about food smells. Betty's father is often portrayed in the kitchen cooking traditional Mexican food. In all these portrayals, difference is reduced to external signifiers/symbols, which, while ostensibly speaking of authenticity and tradition, at a closer look reveal a refusal to take difference and its demands for recognition seriously.

As with the racist regime of representation, folkloric representations are widely spread across the world. For instance, in the popular Indonesian television show *Extravaganza* (Trans TV, 2007), Chinese people are portrayed in a folkloric way, wearing traditional costumes, having long moustaches, and dancing traditional dances such as the Lion Dance. Similarly, *The Muppet Show* did a feature on Greece, featuring bouzouki music, plate smashing, and traditional dancing. Fokloric portrayals are common in media products, as they present an easy and recognizable means of ethnic identification and recognition. There are also instances where we can see how this type of folklorization can be a source of comedy. The problem, however, lies not in poking fun at other cultures, but in locking them forever into their traditional and folkloric signs and symbols.

Other examples of folklorization include the news coverage of religious/cultural festivals, including celebrations of Hanukkah, Ramadan, Diwali, Chinese New Year, and so on, or "ethnic" fashion shoots, in which impossibly tall and beautiful white women stand next to cute natives in exotic locations. Such coverage, although in general terms positive, when coupled with the absence of a broader diversity of representations of cultural difference, and with the presence of racist ones, as examined in the previous section, leads to a clear reduction of difference to folklore, and silences demands for recognition through a shallow and short-lived attention to superficial signs.

While folkloric representations domesticate difference through focusing on superficial and stereotypical aspects of cultural difference, another theme within the same regime is that of insisting on similarities and the essential sameness of people. The problem here is not that people are not the same, but rather that sameness is rendered a condition for acceptance. In other words, through insisting on the essential similarity of human beings, the regime of domestication in fact poses a dichotomy: diverse cultures will only be accepted if they are similar to our culture. And here lies another problem: similarity is evaluated on the basis of criteria drawn from dominant cultures. Difference is therefore not accepted as such, but rather refused and negated through focusing on similarities. The notion of similarity or sameness must be somewhat clarified: this does not refer to commonalities emerging out of common engagement, interaction, and the building of a shared and common world; rather, it refers to the reduction of the complexity of difference to certain key aspects, thought to be similar, alike, or approximating those of dominant cultures. Through emphasizing similarities with the dominant culture, therefore, the theme of sameness within the regime of domestication effectively neutralizes the threat posed by difference.

One of the clearest examples of the theme of sameness is the portrayal of unveiled and "modern" Muslim women, or more broadly the stereotype of the "good Muslim" (Mamdani, 2004). Mamdani reports that in the pages of the *New York Times* one finds clear accounts of who are the "good Muslims": they "are modern, secular, and Westernized" (p. 24). In other words, within this theme, Muslims, or Others, can only be accepted if they become similar to the Western secular model. As a clear counterpart to the racist representation of veiled Muslim women, the unveiled, Westernized Muslim women that are often praised in the Western media reveal the operation of the theme of sameness. It is often the case that Muslim women in public life cannot be accepted unless they appear the "same" as Western secular women. For instance, the French politician and former Justice Minister Rachida Dati, who was, until her resignation in 2009, the highest-ranking person of North African descent in France, is a thoroughly modern and Westernized woman. The media's broader acceptance of Dati revolves around her image as a "liberated" and fashion-conscious woman. In December 2007, the French magazine *Paris-Match* featured a cover and article on Rachida Dati headlined "The face of a changing France." Dati's fashionable poses and beauty were certainly admired – although there were dissenting voices, criticizing the frivolity of such pictures – and she was broadly seen as emblematic of ethnic minority success in modern France. However, success is conflated with becoming Western/French, and with erasing any overt markers of difference. The "changing face of France," which appears to be very similar to the "old face of France," implies that France is willing to accept difference, but only insofar as it accepts Frenchness and negates itself.

A final aspect of the domestication of difference concerns the theme of hybridity. Although many scholars have endorsed hybridity as a way of side-stepping the problems of essentialism and the reification of difference (e.g. Nederveen Pieterse, 2004), within the regime of domestication hybridity functions as a way of neutralizing the threat posed by difference. This neutralization takes place through the focus on, and celebration of, hybridity understood as alterity tempered with sameness: a mélange in which the two parts remain unequal, as difference must be subsumed under sameness, and its radical or threatening characteristics erased. Hybridity within this regime of representation therefore operates first through reproducing difference as a threat, then subsequently modifying it through a mixture with sameness. In these terms, hybridity is not the dialectic of alterity and identity, but rather the domination of the former by, and through pollinating it with, the latter. On the other hand, emphasis on hybridity highlights the impossibility of purity and the porousness or fluidity of borders. Several theorists have persuasively argued that mélange, the continuous mixing of cultures and identities, is in fact the very condition of cultural identities, and the only guarantee for their survival (see among others Bhabha, 1995; Hall, 1996; Papastergiadis, 2005). From this point of view, hybridity must be seen as equivocal: it contains aspects of conformity to dominant identities, while also carrying the seeds for the latter's destruction.

Images of hybridity in at least the mainstream media are inevitably characterized by this ambiguity, which they therefore try to contain and control. Hence, more often than not, hybridity in mainstream media and culture ends up inscribing cultural identities in the existing hegemony of culture and power. In these terms, representations of mixed cultures and "races" in popular culture end up erasing difference by on the one hand downplaying it in favor of the hybrid, while on the other ignoring the conditions that reproduce hierarchies of difference in the first place. Thus, popular culture figures such as Halle Berry, Jennifer Lopez, Beyoncé Knowles, Shakira, Alicia Keys, and others are celebrated as successfully combining elements of both black/Latino/Middle Eastern and white cultures, operating in multiple languages and codes, and apparently able to shift between "racial" and cultural registers. However, the conditions of production of "racial" and cultural hierarchies and classifications remain present and unchallenged. In other words, as Irizarry (2007) argues, hybridity reproduces dominant ideas even if it ostensibly purports to question them, while it also contributes to the establishment of a clear hierarchy where ("pure") dominant cultures are at the top, followed by the hybrid cultures, while the ("pure") dominated cultures remain at the bottom. It establishes a kind of compulsory hybridization as a means of moving up the hierarchy, in practice doing nothing for the recognition and acceptance of "pure" difference. It is for this reason that hybridity under the current conditions of media production and consumption is placed within the regime of domestication: through mixing and injecting sameness into difference, hybridity ends up removing and ultimately ignoring the challenges placed by the Other. In this manner, alterity is domesticated, accepted, and even celebrated, but only under the condition of compulsory mixing.

9.4 The Regime of Commodification

In the representational regimes discussed earlier, representations of cultural difference explicitly rejected and subjugated cultural difference, subjected it to ridicule, or otherwise tamed, contained and controlled it. The regime of commodification, however, operates on a different premise: that of the accepting cultural difference and alterity but subsequently subsuming them to another logic: that of the market. This is what we may term commodification of identity. Specifically, this refers to ways in which identities (both of "self" and "other") are made into "things," exchanged, bought, and sold, thereby losing their complexity and humanity. The political economist and historical sociologist Karl Polanyi was the first to observe the process of commodification, understood as the supremacy of the market across all fields, and linked to the rise of the self-regulating market model, or laissez-faire capitalism. In his book *The Great Transformation* (1944/2001) Polanyi spells the worst implications of this, including the dominance of the market logic over nature itself, and over understandings of social justice embedded in the moral backbone of all societies. As he put it in one of the most famous passages, "To allow the market mechanism to be sole director of the fate of human beings and their natural environment, indeed even of the amount and use of purchasing power, would result in the demolition of society" (p. 73).

In recent years we can add identity – who human beings *are* – as another dimension of human life that becomes subject to the market. Polanyi himself implied that human beings were affected by the degree to which their labor was valued or used by the market, but commodification of identity goes one step further or perhaps deeper: identities themselves are valued only to the extent that they are marketable or of use to the market and its demand for profit. Thus, the commodification process, which begins with an initial levelling of all identities, as they have to become detached from existing hierarchies, proceeds with a reordering, this time on the basis of profit generation. The more profit an identity can generate the higher it is valued. Conversely, the less profit an identity can generate the more invisible and marginalized it becomes.

As a regime of representation commodification therefore prioritizes these elements of different identities that can be successfully marketed or branded and ignores the rest. And, crucially, it ignores persistent inequalities and power differentials in favor of a superficial levelling or equivalence of all identities: we are (or can be) all equally beautiful, sexy, powerful, successful, each in their own way. Although this appears to be a positive development, and to an extent it is, particularly when compared to the racist regime of representation, caution needs to be exercised: the initial democratization of identities ends up acknowledging only these identities, and within them only these elements, that lend themselves to the economic imperative of monetary gain – everything else is negated or ignored. Representations that can be classified as belonging to this regime tend to operate by focusing on aspects of style, appearance, and looks, by creating certain associations between specific identities and styles, and through commodifying cultural identities. In all instances, the function of this regime is ultimately to capitalize on difference: if it finds it cannot, then difference and alterity are at best ignored and at worst destroyed.

This regime is more clearly encountered in images of consumer culture and advertising. Perhaps the most evident example of this commodification of identity through focusing on style and appearance is to found in the "United Colors of Benetton" campaigns. Tinic (1997) reports that Benetton's first foray in the world of global advertising was the 1984 campaign "All the Colors of the World," which depicted people of various ethnicities having fun together, wearing Benetton clothes. By 1985, the brand "United Colors of Benetton" was born; the brand name became less and less visible in the adverts, although the style was by then already closely associated with Benetton.

The Benetton ads worked by juxtaposing models of different ethnicity in close proximity, touching or embracing each other. They were also very colorful, playing with the dual applicability of the notion of difference in colors to both ethnicities and clothes. As Tinic (1997) has argued, the problem with these representations is that they decontextualized social issues from their original surroundings and recontextualized them within a framework of product or brand promotion. This is why these representations only remained at the superficial level of style and appearance, and, in doing so, they failed to address the wider problematic of difference and the ways in which it is mapped on inequality, both symbolic and material. Additionally, by using young and beautiful models, these representations in fact created new divisions and obscured or marginalized the significance of being "other." More broadly speaking, the regime of commodification's insistence on the superficial elements of style and appearance contribute to the marginalization of the more profound aspects of difference. The contexts in which difference and alterity are discriminated against, oppressed, or exploited are removed, with the result that no serious understanding and analysis of the issues involved can take place. Thus, notwithstanding Benetton's stated motivation of raising awareness about social issues, the end result is to further hinder debate on such issues by obscuring the complexities involved.

Similarly, the regime of commodification operates through associating a particular style and/or characteristics with a particular identity. This rests on the wide diffusion of cultural/ethnic stereotypes, but playfully reinvents them as brands. This element is close to the aspect of folklorization discussed under the regime of domestication. But while the goal of the latter regime is to remove the threat posed by difference, the aim of the regime of commodification is to promote or sell specific ethnic identities. Examples of this branding are found in abundance in tourist advertising and promotion, as well as in certain popular cultural or "ethnic" products, such as ethnic restaurants. This aspect of the regime operates through using and amplifying existing themes, signs, or symbols linked to certain identities.

Girardelli (2004) examines the way in which Italian identity is commodified and sold in chain restaurants in the USA. Girardelli reports that this occurs through the mobilization of specific myths associated with Italian identities, such as expressivity, the importance of family, the slow-paced lifestyle, closeness to nature, etc. Girardelli focused on a US restaurant chain called Fazoli's, which, notwithstanding its trade in "authentic Italian food," is in fact Japanese in both its financial capital and its management chain. Girardelli reports that in 2001 the chain run an advertising campaign titled "Everyone is Italian," which featured people from different ethnic backgrounds performing stereotypically "Italian" (and Italian-American) behaviors and expressions, such as gesticulating intensely, using phrases such as "bada-bing, bada-boom," and singing opera tunes. This focus on superficial and stereotypical aspects of Italian identity is subsequently used in order to brand Fazoli's and market their "Italian" food. Clearly, the attributes associated with "Italianicity," to use Barthes' (1977) term, are only the most positive and well-known aspects, and they do not include any controversial features. If they do, these are used in a humorous and playful way (e.g. the "bada-bing" expression widely disseminated through Mafia-related TV shows) and removed from their original context and meaning. The result is that ethnic identities are reduced to their most superficial and non-controversial elements in order to become safely associated with specific brands.

A third aspect involves the transformation of identity into a commodity to be consumed. In an important article, bell hooks (1992) describes the processes by which black and other racial identities are commodified and consumed. For her, this consumption – "eating the Other" – operates as a metaphor for the association of sexual pleasure and desire with the Other. This consumption or possession of the Other results in an appropriation of Otherness and its ostensible "life-giving" aspects, the newness and excitement it is associated with. It is therefore cultural appropriation of diversity that is involved in consuming the other as a commodified identity. Often this consumption takes the apparent form of an encounter, but, as hooks points out, this encounter is never one between equals, but always one embedded in existing frameworks of domination. Unless explicitly acknowledged and confronted, such frameworks will involve the consumption or appropriation, possession, and ultimately the continuous exploitation of one identity by another. An example of the unequal character of consuming identities is to be found once again in consumer culture. The rise of ethnic dolls, and specifically ethnic "Barbie" dolls, is a case in point. Ostensibly developed to cater to a changing world, more attuned to cultural diversity, the production and consumption of such dolls may be seen as a metaphor for the production and consumption of difference, which ends up repeating the same cycle of domination and exploitation. This is because it does not really problematize, question, or discuss aspects of difference and identity, but merely focuses on, and reproduces, superficial markers of difference. As pointed out by Ducille (1994), all dolls are made by the same mould, and are very similar if not identical, with the differences between them located in their colors or dye jobs, and in the subtle changes of some features, such as the stereotypically slanted eyes in the Asian Barbies. In most cases, therefore, difference is marked by variety in dress and other external markers.

These similarities between the dolls are, as Ducille (1994) argued, due to commercial considerations: long straight hair is more marketable, as young girls like to play with it; all bodies must have the same dimensions, so that clothes and other accessories can fit them. In an interesting twist, Benetton has created a clothing line especially for Barbie. The presumption here is that all these dolls, and the identities they represent, are equal, equally beautiful, equally attractive, equally desirable. By implication, the cultures they represent are presumed to be equivalent to each other. From this point of view, the regime of commodification appears a more equitable or even democratic one, since it appears to equate and attribute the same value to all identities. However, there are two problems involved here. The first concerns the presumption of equality: to insist that all identities are equal in the face of palpable inequalities observed in everyday life is to obscure the issue of inequality and the way it is mapped onto cultural difference. Unless problems are acknowledged, they cannot be resolved. Similarly, if inequality, both symbolic and material, is not acknowledged and recognized as such, then it cannot be properly addressed. Thus, although the regime of commodification appears to level all identities, a more careful examination reveals that it is complicit in the continuous exploitation of cultural diversity. A second issue here is that these commodified representations are not "real" and they do not in any way accurately capture cultural diversity. Rather, this regime creates a superficial and often idealized and stylized version of difference, whose only purpose is to be consumed as a novel product. Any aspect of difference that is judged as inappropriate for consumption – as for instance a larger body with thicker thighs, smaller breasts, different hair, etc. – is dismissed. In the first instance, as with the earlier regimes, this may be seen as part of the ongoing misrepresentation of cultural difference. However, at the same time, it raises important questions regarding authenticity and the right to represent oneself. These themes and regimes will be discussed in the next chapter.

9.5 Conclusions

This chapter discussed three regimes of representation: the racist regime, the regime of domestication of difference and the regime of commodification of difference. The concept of a "regime" is used because it forcefully constructs subjects along certain lines, which then have important material and symbolic consequences. In the racist regime, these lines include the "racialization" of subjects, i.e. the attribution of people's characteristics, behaviors, customs, and so on, to their membership of an almost immutable category, such as a "race." In addition, "racialization" implies a constant comparison between "races" and cultures, which introduces a "them" and an "us," in which "they" always come out as worse than "us". The dominant themes of this regime include irrationality, violence, and brutality attributed to racialized subjects; at the same time, racialized subjects under this regime are constructed as weak victims. Both aspects construct subjects as unable to reason, speak, and govern themselves, while conversely co-constructing the non-racialized subjects, the "us" identity, as rational and reasonable, articulate, moral, and so on.

An important argument here is that the racist regime of representation concerns both "race" and "culture." Thus, the term "racialization" also applies to those subjects belonging to certain cultures, who are also constructed as irrational, violent, cruel, and weak victims. Culture has therefore become another shorthand for "race," which has ostensibly got rid of the discredited biological elements associated with "race," but has retained all the brutality of racism. Our review here has shown that no culture is immune from "racialization": black, Muslim, Albanian, Romanian, Polish, Turkish, Chinese, as well as gendered subjects: black, Muslim, Eastern European, and Chinese women are all subjected to this regime, which constructs them as irrational brutes or weak and sexualized victims, thereby removing agency and the ability to act in a reasoned manner. It is crucial that the gender dimension is not overlooked in analyses of the racist regime of representation, as the co-articulation of race–culture–ethnicity with gender reveals previously hidden areas of oppression and marginalization.

The regime of domestication appears benign, but is in fact equally pernicious. This regime moves to negate difference through domestication, through making difference everyday and banal. The regime of domestication operates through representations that construct difference as harmless folklore and through insisting on sameness to the

Table 9.1 Regimes of representation

Regimes of representation	Key themes	Main outcomes
Sets of words and images, ideas and views, arguments and opinions that systematically construct difference in certain ways	The ways in which these regimes operate and the means by which we can identify them	What does each regime accomplish?
Racist regime: constructs people as members of specific "races" whose core biological or cultural characteristics are stable and unable to change	Difference is seen as irrational, brutal, or violent, often sexualized, or conversely as a victim and in need of being rescued. Unable to speak and reason, it has to be governed by the rational "races" or "cultures"	Justifies domination and oppression, naturalizes inequalities, and perpetuates injustices
Domesticated difference regime: understands difference in superficial terms, constructing it as safe and unthreatening	Emphasis on folkloric aspects, on these elements that denote sameness, and on mixtures or hybrids	Homogenizes and ultimately negates difference, resulting in overlooking persistent inequalities. It also breeds intolerance towards deep and substantive diversity
The regime of commodification of difference: accepts difference only to subsume it to the logic of the market. All identities are values, each in their own way, but only insofar as they can be marketed and generate profit	Emphasis on style and appearance, the creation of links between identities and styles-commodities, turning ethnic stereotypes into "brands," to be consumed by all	Levels all identities and reorders them on the basis of profitability. It literally capitalizes on difference. If not overlooking inequalities then creating new ones

detriment of difference. It further operates through the theme of hybridization or mixing, but in a way which ultimately rejects outright difference and accepts it only insofar as it mimics or acquires the attributes associated with the dominant culture or ethnicity. This regime ultimately justifies the rejection of difference, by limiting it to superficial elements, or by focusing on sameness, or else by mixing and hybridizing it.

Finally, the regime of commodification emerges as a more "democratic" regime, in that it treats all identities in an equal manner. The regime appears to even out any aspects of inequality in considering all identities equivalent as commodities. It operates, firstly, by decontextualizing any social aspects from their original environment and placing them in a context of product or brand promotion; and secondly, by associating cultural identities with certain products, removing their more controversial elements, again for promotional purposes. In the end, by commodifying and consuming cultural identities as products, this regime imposes a surface and shallow equality and equivalence that ends up masking and obscuring the ongoing exploitation, misrepresentation, and domination of certain identities by others.

All these regimes appear to be pernicious for cultural difference, and all appear to co-exist in different media, and in different countries. We came across an astonishing commonality of these regimes across countries, across media, and across time – certainly a depressing finding, in contrast to much of the optimism that followed the 1960s civil rights movements. The upshot of the operation of all these regimes is that continued oppression and exploitation are justified, while the associated political marginalization ensures that no active steps are taken to redress the material and symbolic injustices suffered by people marked as different. But this does not mean that these regimes remain unchallenged – this would imply that cultural difference indeed lacks agency. In the next chapter we will discuss the ways in which other regimes have developed as a response to the insidious and harmful regimes of racist, domesticated and commodifying representations of difference.

10

Self-Representations of Cultural Diversity

10.1 Representational Dilemmas

The previous chapter discussed the ways in which cultural difference is represented by others, and particularly by those understood as dominant or majority groups. The concept of regime was used to indicate the systematic treatment of difference in certain ways. Throughout this discussion we outlined the means by which difference is oppressed, marginalized, controlled, and subdued, and concluded that neither of these regimes could do any justice to the complexity of cultural difference. To an extent this might be attributable to the fact that these regimes are developed and used by majority or dominant cultures, which may be afraid of, or otherwise misunderstand, cultural difference. But now another question emerges: how might cultural difference represent itself? Although the easy answer is to claim that any self-representation is bound to be more accurate and fair than other types of representation, several questions arise. If we endorse the view that only self-representations are accurate, aren't we refusing the very possibility of understanding cultural difference as difference? In other words, insisting that only community members can represent themselves implies that only sameness or identity can be understood and not difference. And, additionally, communities are complex entities, which are internally diverse: who, within the community, has the right to represent the whole group and to claim accuracy? This reveals that questions of power are involved in self-representations as well. Thus, the thorny issue of representation and the right to represent are not easily resolvable by resorting to the issue of who is doing the representing as a proxy for the accuracy or fairness of the representation. From this point of view, the kind of self-representation involved in producing and delivering cultural and media products involves more than the actual contents themselves: it implicates the representation or image associated with the producers or artists themselves at least as much as their actual output. The representational "battlefield" becomes therefore wider and broader, as representational contents implicate the identities of their producers and performers.

If we accept the involvement of power, then the concept of regime, which explicitly incorporates the dimension of power, can be usefully applied here in order to show the ways in which self-representations are implicated in the construction of certain versions of truth. In this chapter, two such regimes will be discussed: the essentialist and the alternative regimes. While the former almost always emerges from within the community – or at least certain parts of the community – the latter regime might be the product of either communities themselves or non-community members, while both regimes might also be thought of as part of an ongoing dialogue between identity and difference. The essentialist regime, as we shall see shortly, operates by removing internal diversity and by imposing a particular version of history and authentic community identity. In so doing, it may end up marginalizing difference within the community and ignoring the dynamism involved in constructing identities. The alternative regime, on the other hand, operates through resisting closure and through inviting discussion, questioning, and critique. In some ways, the alternative regime may be thought as forever posing the question "who are we?", in which this "we" is variable and changes all the time.

An assessment of these regimes might appear straightforward: the essentialist regime is exclusionary, and hence must be criticized and negatively appraised, while the alternative regime is open and inclusive, and hence can be accepted as the most fair way of representation. However, as we shall see the following discussion, the essentialist regime contains some important political possibilities that cannot be ignored, while conversely, the alternative regime might involve some political losses, which must equally be taken into account.

10.2 The Essentialist Regime of Representation

This regime posits that the right to represent belongs only to "self," only to those belonging to the identity represented, and that accurate representations must authentically capture the "essence" of the identity portrayed. This is a polemical perspective, often developed as a response to the racist regime of representation, that seeks to redress the misrepresentations and insults associated with the racist regime. In doing so, however, it appears to impose its own version of an unchanged essence of identity, which is no less rigid than that of the racist regime. Moreover, in insisting in an essential core identity, the essentialist regime ends up policing and controlling processes of representation, denying the inherent dynamism of identity and, even worse, excluding and marginalizing those who disagree or who somehow deviate from this imagined core identity. In many ways, therefore, this regime, while operating as the counterpart of the racist regime of representation, culminates in the exclusion, marginalization, and oppression of internal difference, a process as hurtful and unacceptable as the one perpetrated by the racist regime. This, we must insist, occurs notwithstanding the more "benign" motives of those who seek to represent an essential, core, and authentic identity as a response to the misrepresentation and misrecognition encountered.

The essentialist regime of representation operates via three themes: firstly, the theme of continuity, the uninterrupted manifestation of identity across time and place. Here, the regime mobilizes historicity – historical concepts and notions – and implicates time in the formation of identity. Through this mobilization of historical aspects, this theme seeks to establish a past history and background to identity that marks it as different to, and often better than, other identities. At the same time, this representation of a commonly shared historical past presents an alternative picture to that of the racist regime, which cuts off culturally diverse identities from their past, or interprets their historical past as irrelevant and backward. From this point of view, the essentialist regime's insistence on historicity seeks to rehabilitate the lost past, but in claiming an unbroken historical continuity it ends up constructing a rigid and straight line connecting the past to the present in ways that overlook variation, deviation, and, in the end, difference itself. Secondly, the regime works through the construction of an essential core, an unchanged set of commonalities that persist across time and place. In a move that follows the theme of historical continuity, the theme of a stable core refers to certain cultural characteristics that serve as markers of identity. Representations here mobilize well-known images and types, recognizable by all group members, whose stereotypical aspects serve to confirm and reinforce the idea of a stable, core identity. At the same time, the theme of an essential core prescribes belongingness to the group. This part of the essentialist regime operates by positing this essential core as containing the prototypical characteristics that one must have in order to be a group member. Loyalty to these is, according to this regime, necessary for group membership and belongingness. Thirdly, the regime works by making claims of authenticity and authority, by asserting the right to speak on behalf of the community and by claiming to represent it as a whole. In this manner, this part of the regime effectively sets up an "us" and "them" distinction in which "outsiders" have no right to speak for, or even in connection with, the "insider" community, as they are not "authentic" bearers of the community's identity. In so doing, such claims to authority and authenticity set up and police the borders of the community, as well as its internal space, as they grant the right to speak only to those deemed authentic community members.

If we look into these themes is some more detail, the mobilization of historicity within this regime may be directly related to the grotesque representations of the racist regime. Thus, groups who rightly felt their identities were misrepresented in the racist regime seek to redress this by sketching a more complex story, one that involves continuity through time and a past common to all community members. The best examples of this are to be found in film, as this medium's expressive and aesthetic qualities lend themselves better to historiography. Examples here include Emir Kusturica's *Underground* (1995) and, according to Virdi (2003), a good part of Hindi popular films. Similarly, the historical reimagining of Africa in contemporary black culture is also a case in point.

Underground was partly funded by Belgrade Television and won the 1995 Palme d'Or in the Cannes Festival. As evidenced in its subtitle, *Once Upon a Time There Was a Country*, the film was meant as an allegory for the disintegration of Yugoslavia. Specifically, the film represented Yugoslavian history from the Second World War until the collapse of the former federal state into war in the 1990s. Through the eyes of the two protagonists, Marko and Blackie, a Serb and a Montenegrin, and interspersed with documentary footage, the film shows the traumatic and war-ridden history of the region. The film has been at the centre of controversy precisely because of its mobilization of a contentious version of history. Contrasting footage of Croats and Slovenes welcoming Nazis with scenes of devastation in Belgrade, the film appears to suggest that Serbs were alone in bravely fighting an anti-fascist war on behalf of the whole of Yugoslavia, and, moreover, that they continued to act for freedom and unity, even if their efforts were misdirected. Kusturica's interpretation of the wars in former Yugoslavia involved an essentialist understanding of history, in which the region is thrown into turmoil because of primordial passions ruling the Balkan region, embracing but also celebrating the stereotypical image of the inhabitants of the Balkans as brave, passionate, and somehow more real than the decadent West (Žižek, 1997b; Iordanova, 2001). The cyclical wars in which Yugoslavia and the Balkans find themselves are understood as a natural result of the Balkan history and character, foreclosing any possibility for historical change. In this manner, the film operates within the essentialist regime of representation, mobilizing a version of history that places emphasis on the themes of continuity, unity, and destiny, preserving a notion of community identity that remains connected and unchanged through time. In mobilizing an essentialist understanding of history, this regime naturalizes and justifies the community's self-identity.

In a similar fashion, Virdi (2003) argues that popular Hindi films mobilize historical themes and allegories in order to reinforce dominant readings of the Indian nation through the prism of Hindu nationalism. The 1947 simultaneous independence and partition of India and Pakistan is often replayed in films such as *Amar, Akbar, Anthony* (Manmohan Desai, 1997) and *Henna* (Raj and Rhandir Kapoor, 1991), in a manner that imposes an almost canonical understanding of Hindi national identity and its interconnection with other identities in the subcontinent. As Virdi shows, both films ostensibly deal with the eternal themes of love and life, but underlying these we encounter the narrative of the nation. In addition, both films espouse a secular and humanist rhetoric of belongingness to the nation, which, however, is undermined by their plots and denouements: *Amar, Akbar, Anthony* is the story of three brothers who get lost in the confusion following the day of independence, and who are then adopted by a Hindu, Muslim, and Catholic family respectively. In the end, the film shows how they unite in order to fight the villain who was responsible for the family's (and metaphorically the nation's) disintegration. Finally, they get on with their lives, contently marrying women belonging to their own communities. In *Henna*, the protagonist becomes lost in the Jhelum River, which divides India and Pakistan in the region of Kashmir. He subsequently suffers amnesia, from which he recovers just at the moment when he is due to marry his Muslim bride, who then dies helping him to escape. Upon his return to India, he reunites with his Hindu bride. Both films are interpreted by Virdi as adopting, repeating, and re-enacting the divisions and fault lines found in the Indian nation. In so doing, they naturalize them, and justify their existence as an integral part of the nation's identity. In this manner, this use of history that seeks to establish unbroken continuities and to naturalize existing states of affairs operates as part of the essentialist regime of representation.

At the same time, the regime operates through positing a definitive set of characteristics that form the essential core of the group. In *Underground* we saw that, for the Balkans, these include the bravery and macho behavior of Balkan men, their violent but always passionate inclinations, and so on. Other relevant examples here include the genre of Blaxploitation, which flourished in the US in the 1970s. Films by black directors such as Melvin van Peebles' *Sweet Sweetback's Baadaaass Song* and Gordon Parks" *Shaft* (both released in 1971) set the tone for the genre, which revolved around popular cultural stereotypes of black masculinity as highly sexual and prone to violence, with black men working as pimps, hustlers, and small-time crooks, or otherwise at the borders of legitimate work. Such films thematized and to an extent celebrated life in the ghetto, showing at once a stereotypical black culture of small-time crooks and prostitutes and providing an alternative aesthetic and a set of anti-heroes. In a similar vein, Spike Lee's films, such as *School Daze* (1988) and *Do the Right Thing* (1989), appear to promote a very different but equally stereotypical and masculinist portrayal of (American) blackness, centered around notions of work and the work ethic ("you are only worthy if you hold a job"), heterosexual sexuality ("to be black is to be straight"), a revered set of canonized icons (Martin Luther King, Malcolm X, Mohammed Ali), and victimization at the hands of the police (Lubiano, 1997). Another example here is *Latinidad*, or Latina/o identity, and its representation as a set of condensed signifiers that purport to capture the whole group. In films like *Selena* (Nava, 1997) and *Frida* (Taymor, 2002), but also in the famous telenovelas, *Latinidad* revolves around linguistic symbols, such as accented English or Spanish, passionate (heterosexual) affairs, religious symbolism, and brown faces, and significantly, it is located in the domestic sphere, understood as the sphere of intimate, sexual, and familial, relationships (Aparicio, 1999; Molina-Guzman, 2006). Similarly, a core identity of sexual chastity and "innocence," loyalty to family, humility, and devoutness are placed at the centre of Hindu identity as represented in typical Bollywood films. In this manner, within this regime of representation, identity is ultimately reduced to a set of stereotypical and rigid images that then form the essence or core of the group. In so doing, this regime excludes those who do not conform to this core set, while at the same time seeking to unite and place diverse groups under the same umbrella.

Very often, such attempts to circumscribe and police the group's internal and external borders are legitimized through claims of authenticity. Authenticity, in turn, has two components: firstly, to have the right to speak and represent the community; and secondly, to be true to one's identity, one's core self. Both aspects are accomplished by focusing on a specific ethno-cultural identity as the determinant of all attitudes and behaviors, and by accepting and endorsing a set of core values, traditions, and customs associated with this identity. In so doing, this part of the regime legitimizes and reinforces both the claims to a continuous past and the unity of identity. In terms of the right to speak and represent the community a clear and unambiguous preference is given to group members. For instance, only black actors can play "black" parts, only black directors, producers, and writers can speak for the black community, and so on. Although it appears common sense to have group members speaking on behalf of their community, the point here is that the diversity and multiple voices and perspectives of the community become reduced to the view of a few spokespersons, who are then seen as expressing the views of the whole community. Thus, a first strategy for claiming authenticity within this regime is to draw attention to your identity as a community member – authenticity only works if those who claim it are visibly part of the community. A second and related strategy is to insist that your identity as a community member is the true or real identity because of its association with established cultural practices, and therefore you have the right to represent and speak on behalf of the community as a whole, while at the same time criticizing and rejecting any "inauthentic" community members. Authenticity claims, therefore, are not only based on evident group membership, but also on the prototypical character of such membership.

Examples here include cultural products that concern certain groups, such as, for instance, the film *The Joy Luck Club* (Wang, 1993, based on Amy Tan's 1989 novel). *The Joy Luck Club* describes the lives of four Chinese-American families, weaving a narrative told from the perspective of mothers and daughters. Notwithstanding the positive and non-stereotypical ways in which the book and film represented (Chinese) femininity, both the novel and the book attempt a reconstruction of Chinese immigrant communities which in the end appears to impose a single narrative: based on personal trauma, occasionally connected to wider historical events (such as the Japanese invasion of China), the generations of mothers and daughters can only reconcile through the latter's acceptance of their ethno-cultural heritage. In other words, the identity conflicts described in the book are in the end resolved only through the total acceptance of a set of values constructed as common to the community. It is only through accepting and reconciling with their Chinese past and traditions, that the daughters, the next generation, can be truly themselves. In these terms, authenticity in this film is constructed as finding oneself and as being true to oneself; and, in a second move, culturally different identities cannot be authentic or true unless they endorse cultural traditions as an integral part of their identity. The younger generation moves from an initial rejection of Chinese culture to a gradual acceptance of it, and to a deeper understanding of its core values. In this manner, the film contributes to what Stuart Hall has called "a collective true self." Specifically, Hall argues that one way of defining cultural identity is by reference to "the idea of one shared culture, a sort of collective 'one true self,' hiding inside the many other, more superficial or artificially imposed 'selves'"(Hall, 1996: 211). This is precisely the type of "authentic" identity that this regime appears to be constructing.

In narrative terms, authenticity as acceptance of traditional cultural practices develops through setting up a conflict between the new and old cultures, which is then reconciled through a kind of "return to the roots." Thus, in *The Joy Luck Club*, the daughters initially criticize, question, and apparently reject the Chinese culture of their mothers, only to return and reconcile with it later, thereby becoming "true to themselves." This narrative device of a conflict between the old traditions and customs and new cultural practices is also found in "ethnic" sitcoms, such as the Asian American *All American Girl* (ABC, 1994–5) and the British *Tandoori Nights* (Channel 4, 1985–7). Films such as *Bend it Like Beckham* (Chadha, 2002) and *My Big Fat Greek Wedding* (Vardalos and Zwick, 2002) also revolve around a clash between the new cultural identities of the younger generation with old cultural practices and traditions. In all these, the intergenerational conflict represents a culture clash between the different cultures, which in the end is reconciled through the acceptance of the validity of cultural traditions. Authenticity and staying "true to yourself" become, therefore, closely intertwined with traditional ideas, customs, and practices, to the extent that any identity that proceeds through outright rejection of these will inevitably end up being excluded from membership.

Although there is little doubt that rethinking and reconfiguring traditions and customs is of great importance and as such deserves a central place in representations, the emphasis on authenticity as necessarily entailing acceptance and understanding of old traditions may end up excluding those who decide to follow a different route. Inevitably, only those reconciled with the community's customs have the right to speak on behalf of the community, as they are the ones who can claim authenticity. A related issue here is that these past traditions and cultures are themselves too dynamic to form any stable core for authentic identity formation. Thus, such traditions are more often than not stereotypes and not actual living practices. For instance, the notions of Chinese culture as revolving around values such as obedience and subservience, of Greek culture as overly demonstrative, family-oriented, and observant of archaic customs, and of Indian culture as based on arranged marriages, appear to be rather crude versions of the complex reality of these cultures.

An additional issue here is that this emphasis on authenticity contributes to the creation of a separatist, "purist" culture, in which only "authentic," core-group members can represent the community. Perhaps the clearest example of such tendencies towards separatism can be found in other cultural formats, notably, music. Paul Gilroy (1993) has written about the ways in which musical formats associated with blackness, such as jazz, blues, soul, reggae, and hip hop, raise questions of identity and authenticity. Such music formats pose the question of the particularity of black culture, as well as its political role. Gilroy reads claims of authentic black culture, and the associated return to Africa, as attempts to deal with threatening situations such as economic recession and ongoing populist racism. In addition, for Gilroy, the Afrocentrism found in such rhetoric represents a kind of radical utopianism that becomes a potent political tool both for opposing racism and for elaborating new forms of black cultural identity. This, as Gilroy argues, is the kind of myth-building that seeks to invent a novel but equally totalizing black culture that moves beyond memories of the Caribbean or other motherlands, and creates a mythic Africa, as the bedrock of a uniquely black civilization. Gilroy's discussion of authenticity in black music reveals the struggles lying beneath such claims. Such authenticity claims seek to safeguard a community's cultural "purity" from two related threats: firstly, that of cooptation by mainstream or dominant cultures, and secondly, that of assimilation or losing cultural distinctiveness. Gilroy refers to the conflict between the famous jazz musicians Wynton Marsalis and Miles Davis. Marsalis understood jazz as an authentic depository of black cultural values, and therefore argued that it must remain true to its roots and established patterns. Davis, on the other hand, viewed jazz as a dynamic and creative musical form, inviting experimentation, and saw no reason to stick to established patterns. Marsalis was then taken to represent an authentic black jazz, while Davis' experimentation may have made him an important musical innovator, but led him away from expressing an authentic black culture and experience. Similarly, Gilroy discusses Jimi Hendrix's appeal to white pop audiences, which was seen by many as a sign of betrayal of black culture and of Hendrix's lack of racial authenticity.

In more recent years, hip-hop has taken over the black music mantle from jazz and blues and has been placed at the centre of authenticity claims. McLeod (1999) argues that such authenticity claims lie behind the well-known "keeping it real" metaphor, which occurs not only in hip-hop lyrics, but also in the everyday black American vernacular. McLeod analyzes hip-hop lyrics and outlines the ongoing debate within the hip-hop community of artists and listeners about what it means to be "real" or authentic. Delving further into the meanings and uses of this metaphor by the hip-hop community, McLeod finds that it is an explicit call to relate hip-hop to the black experience and culture, which is understood as coming from the streets or the ghetto, as being masculine and straight, as politicized or at least politically relevant, and as resisting attempts to go mainstream. Such claims clearly create a canon and a hierarchy of hip-hop artists, some of whom are understood to be authentic and true to themselves and their culture, and others who are viewed as having "sold out" by not staying true to their inner-city black roots. The point of such authenticity claims is, as both McLeod and hooks (1992) point out, to formulate a response to threats of cooptation and assimilation into the mainstream. Recent developments, including the rise of gangsta rap, the success of white rappers such as Eminem, and the extensive commercialization of rap and R'n'B clearly show the inability of such claims to deal with pressures from dominant (white) and mainstream (commercial) cultures. Nevertheless, the wider debate concerning the possibility of retaining a clear cultural distinctiveness remains at the centre of any discussion of the essentialist regime of representation.

Indeed, it is all too easy to dismiss this regime for seeking to create another totalizing and to this extent oppressive identity. Consider, for instance, rap lyrics such as "I love black thighs, you sisters better realize / The real hair and real eyes get real guys" (Common, "In My Own World," 1994, cited in McLeod, 1999: 141), and "I got my real niggaz in the house / Some real motherfuckin' men" (40 Thevs, "Mad Dogging," 1997, cited in McLeod, 1999: 142). Such lyrics construct a black masculinist identity which is clearly rejecting any possibility for identity experimentation in terms of aesthetics, sexuality, and other practices. And think of the ways in which filmic and televisual representations of cultural diversity construct identities which must necessarily protect and accept their past customs and traditions, or risk rejection and marginalization from the communities themselves. Derogatory terms such as "coconuts," "Oreos," and "bananas" – meaning brown, black, yellow on the outside, white on the inside, respectively used for South Asians, blacks and East Asians who are "acting white" – show the ongoing debates regarding cultural authenticity, and the pressures to conform to a certain cultural prototype. Media and cultural representations within the regime of essentialism tend to reproduce such rigid versions of identity, thereby contributing to the potential marginalization of those who diverge from this path.

On the other hand, however, there are potential benefits from mobilizing a clear and distinct cultural identity, with clear borders and membership criteria. Perhaps the most well-known articulation of the gains involved is found in Spivak's concept of "strategic essentialism" (1996: 214). For Spivak, the problem of essentialism is primarily one of use: when aimed at the "inside" of the community, then it may be involved in oppressing certain parts of the community, in policing its borders, and in presenting certain interests as the interests of the whole community. If, however, it is used strategically, that is with the goal of obtaining certain clear political gains, then it may prove a useful strategy. In particular, Spivak argues that this strategic use of essentialist representations and identities is more useful in the construction of "self-consciousness" for community members, that is, when it is used in order to help community members identify with others within this community, and therefore to organize effectively in protecting and ensuring their interests. Nevertheless, Spivak is very clear that this is only a strategic kind of essentialism which has nothing to say about the actual contents of identity – it must be used only as part of efforts towards "subject-restoration" (1996: 219). In other words, in a context in which the racist and other negative regimes of representation have consistently misrepresented different subjectivities, these must turn towards themselves, seeking to restore their misrepresented and misrecognized identity, thereby becoming subjects as a result of their own efforts to understand themselves, and not as a result of been called – or, as Althusser (1971) would say, "interpellated" – by others or by certain ideological structures. In these terms, the strategic mobilization of essentialist representations, which include a continuity from past to present, a certain set of core values and beliefs, and attempts to police and control the group's boundaries through claims of authenticity, is an effective tool for the construction of politicized identities, and through these for political empowerment.

The political efficacy of essentialist representations is also highlighted by Hannah Arendt, albeit in a different way. Arendt, whose own experiences as a German Jewish woman expelled from Germany during the Nazi years make her particularly aware of the dangers of essentialism, nevertheless argues that it is precisely at times of persecution that one has to claim the persecuted identity as "essential." Arendt (1970) discusses a well-known passage of Gotthold Lessing's (1779) play *Nathan the Wise*. The play deals with the themes of religious tolerance and friendship, but Arendt refers to the passage in which Nathan the Wise counters the command "Step closer, Jew," with the response "I am a man." This response pointing to a common humanity is for Arendt politically wrong: she refers to it as nothing less than "a grotesque and dangerous evasion of reality" (1970: 18). The only appropriate response, according to Arendt, is "I am a Jew." During "dark times," argues Arendt, "in times of defamation and persecution … one can resist only in terms of the identity that is under attack." This is why culturally diverse communities whose identities are misrepresented and misrecognized can and should make use of essentialist representations: in order to confront and fight back against defamatory and racist representations. Otherwise, if identities under attack try to refer to a commonly shared "human identity," then the issue of racism is effectively not addressed. Thus, if Spivak's strategic essentialism is oriented towards the "inside" of the community, Arendt's assumption of what amounts to an essentialist identity is geared towards engagement with the "outside" world, the dominant cultures and their often discriminatory and outright racist behavior. In this case, the response, argues Arendt, cannot merely be "I am a human being, and you ought to treat me as such," but rather "Yes, I am a Jew/black/Muslim, etc. and you must treat me as an equal *because* of who I am." And in order to do so, one must claim such an identity as one's own, a move that requires the construction of a set of core values, traditions, customs, etc. which mark this identity as different.

What we have seen in the above is the equivocal and ambiguous role played by the essentialist regime of representation. On the one hand, it polices boundaries and imposes values and traditions at the expense of the inherent dynamism of identities; on the other hand, it may contribute to the empowerment of disadvantaged or defamed identities, when strategically mobilized. It should be pointed out, however, that it is the *strategic* use of this regime that involves any political gains – any nonstrategic, routine use in everyday contexts is inevitably linked to the negative aspects of this regime: the control, the imposition of values, and the marginalization and silencing of alternative or critical voices.

10.3 The Alternative Regime of Representation

The discussion of the various ways in which representational regimes generate different versions of cultural difference has revealed the ways in which these end up in various misrepresentations with mostly negative outcomes for the bearers of such identities. The question that emerges here, therefore, is whether we can find – or indeed found or instigate – a representational regime that does justice to the complexity of cultural identities, eschews misrepresentation, and shows respect to cultural difference. The theoretical construct of "regime" points to the difficulties in declaring any representation "true" or "accurate," as it necessarily involves the mobilization of certain attributes, images, and discourses at the expense of others. But based on this, perhaps then we can argue that to qualify as "alternative" a representation or set of representations must be radically open to discussions, debates, critiques, and rejections of its images and discourses. In other words, if the previously discussed regimes of representation – racist, domesticated, commodified, and essentialist – all sought, in their own way, to impose one version of truth, constructed one kind of identity, posited one relationship between identity and difference, then the alternative regime can only be alternative if it avoids the imposition of a singular understanding of cultural difference. It is this commitment to plurality, openness, and diversity in all its forms that sets this regime apart. If the other regimes declare: "This is what cultural difference is," the alternative regime poses this as ongoing questions: "What is cultural difference?" "Who might 'we' be?" From this point of view, this regime contributes to the continuous reflection on identity, difference, and diversity.

There are three main themes in the way in which this regime operates: firstly, ambiguity of representation; secondly, the creative ways in which the representation deals with questions of cultural difference; and thirdly, the multiplicity of perspectives and/or identities/images. Through these three techniques, this regime actively interrogates cultural difference, and fights against any closure of what it is or must be. Another relevant aspect here is that, because of the commitment of this regime to openness and diversity, it establishes patterns of communication that transcend, or cross over, the "inside" and "outside" of communities. In other words, if the question around which this regime revolves is "Who are we?", this "we" is neither exclusively minority community members, nor their dominant community counterparts; in addition, this "we" is further problematized through its interlinking with other types of identity, such as class, gender, and age/generation. In these terms, this "we," the very identity of diverse communities, is the object of reflection in this regime of representation.

In mobilizing ambiguous portrayals of identity, the alternative regime of representation actively questions the simplistic morality of good/evil that permeates most representational regimes. By presenting images and discourses that cannot be easily classified as unequivocally positive or negative, this aspect of the alternative regime prevents any easy conclusions from being drawn, and opens up the discussion of morality, expectations, and judgments. To some extent, this is a conscious strategy pursued by independent filmmakers. For instance, the Black Audio Film Collective (1982–98) was an association of black British filmmakers who sought to address the lack of diversity in the films produced at the time and to actively participate in the politics of representation. John Akomfrah, one of the Collective's founding members, clearly outlined this interrogation of a simplistic morality as one of the goals of black filmmaking. Akomfrah argued that one of the goals of such work should be "to assess the importance of representations which went beyond the idea of positive/negative images" (in Bhattacharyya and Gabriel, 1994: 55–6). Indeed, outlining the ambiguous nature of cultural difference constitutes a major technique for showing the inherent and irreducible diversity and complexity found at the heart of any identity. An example of such ambiguity is found in films such as *Bhaji on the Beach* (Chadha, 1993), *East is East* (O'Donnell, 1999), in TV programs such as *Everybody Hates Chris* (2005, CW Network) and the characters of Ali G and Borat Sagdiyev (Channel 4 and HBO, 2000, 2003–4; Baron Cohen 2006). The common denominator in all these works is the lack of a clear-cut morality, which defines some cultural identities as morally superior and hence more valuable and worthy than others. For instance, in *Bhaji on the Beach*, the intergenerational gap created by the tendency of older generations to follow old and even obsolete cultural traditions and the tendency of the younger generations to rebel and reject such traditions are never reconciled, but rather feed into the dialectic of identity and difference. We are never told who is right and who is wrong, but the narrative moves towards formulating an understanding of the complexities of cultural identity, of living with difference, and of managing the challenges of everyday life. Similarly, *East is East*, which portrays a Muslim South Asian patriarch in the UK of the 1970s, who could easily be represented in negative terms, in fact assumes an ambiguous stance towards him. In portraying him as a fallible man, but nevertheless capable of love, tenderness, and understanding, no easy conclusions can be drawn: the film does not allow us to conclude that older men or *paterfamilias* are unequivocally bad, or that younger generations must necessarily reject or conversely accept certain cultural traditions. Rather, both films interrogate cultural identity and life among difference, and ask audiences to do the same.

In a similar manner, TV comedies, such as the highly successful *Everybody Hates Chris* and Sacha Baron Cohen's *Da Ali G Show*, pose questions of cultural identity and living with difference and racism in a lighter but not necessarily easier manner. The centrality of the ghetto and underground life found in the essentialist regime of representation is questioned in *Everybody Hates Chris*, which shows the eponymous hero's life in 1980s Brooklyn. Showing an aspirational family, with dreams of success and social mobility, the sitcom traces the life of Chris, a young black boy, whose character is based on that of the comedian Chris Rock. While it would be easy to show the aspirational family as morally superior in their striving for a better life, the program in fact portrays it in a sympathetic but critical light: the penurious father, who wants an easy life, the strict mother, who projects her ghetto snobbism and often petty aspirations onto her children, and who does not hesitate to threaten or use physical power. This is not a comfortable *Cosby Show* with successful professional parents, always in possession of morally appropriate solutions. Nor are the children involved the typical beautiful, talented, and adorable characters normally encountered in sitcoms. Bullied at school and in the street, faced with overt and covert racism in the predominantly Italian-American school that he attends, Chris has to deal with both the troubles of growing up and the challenges of living in a multicultural society. No easy solutions are provided, no easy denunciation of bullies, racists, and other problematic characters are offered by the show. This lack of explicit moralizing gives it an aura of moral ambiguity: because it does not offer clear villains and heroes, audiences are invited to think independently about the various characters, the situations they find themselves in, and the possible resolutions of the moral problems they encounter.

Such an ambiguity is even more evident in the case of the characters Ali G and Borat Sagdiyev. In the case of Ali G, confronted with a rather bizarre character, we are unable to define him as black, Asian, or even White. He is meant to be a journalist, interviewing various luminaries from a "youth" point of view; his language reflects a youth idiom, resembling Jamaican patois, and his views are clearly those of a rather simple, naive, and uneducated person, often expressing ignorant, misogynistic and similarly problematic views. Yet in this manner, Ali G succeeds in questioning and eliciting problematic responses by some of his interviewees, while also confronting audiences through the expression of such views. Following a similar pattern, Baron Cohen's character Borat Sagdiyev, supposedly a journalist from Kazakhstan, expresses extreme anti-Semitic, racist, and misogynistic views, while at the same time playing with all the racist stereotypes of Eastern European and former Soviet Union countries. Both Ali G and Borat succeed in showing the extent to which such views are entrenched in the "West," and especially in the UK and USA. More to the point, these characters show the general passivity and reluctance of most people to confront and resist such views. But in expressing such views, both characters appear as morally ambiguous: we cannot say that because Ali G is "black" or Borat is from Kazakhstan they are morally good or bad: rather they play with the stereotypes of what is expected of them and in this manner remain open. We are never sure what their actual position really is: is it irony or satire, or are we meant to identify with the ease and simplicity by which hitherto forbidden views are expressed? In confronting us with such prejudices and often overtly racist views, these characters keep open the question of cultural difference and its position in society. The journalist Gary Younge (2000) eloquently summarized this, arguing that key questions, such as "'What are we laughing at?" "Whom are we laughing at?" and "Whom are we laughing with?" are left either unanswered or with contradictory responses. "Is it cos I is black?" was Ali G's popular catchphrase, which in a sense summarizes some of the issues here: who or what is "black," what are the implications of racializing an identity, what is the moral value attributed to a cultural identity and so on. In these terms, the elusiveness of a concrete racial and moral definition for these characters is a central part of the alternative representational regime, and it is precisely this ambiguity that contributes to the ongoing problematization of "racial" and cultural identities and their meaning and position in society.

Another part of this regime concerns the use of creativity, often in the form of camera angles and shots, narrative elements and humor. We have seen in the above how humor creates an ambiguous space, in which we are not told what is appropriate or inappropriate, whom we should like or dislike, but rather are called upon to think about the moral boundaries and limits imposed on certain cultural identities. It is not coincidental, therefore, that all the films and TV programs discussed above mobilize humor in a creative manner. Additionally, they creatively employ visual and narrative tools – for example, *Everybody Hates Chris* is filmed with a single camera, and employs a narrator, Chris Rock, who is meant to be the grown-up version of little Chris. But it is especially the use of humor that is striking here, not least because of its association with unconscious processes. Often, things that are unspeakable or too threatening may be released through humor. Humor was, for Freud (1991), a mechanism of energy release, which provided a useful corrective to mechanisms of repression. However, research has found that often humor and jokes are used in order to justify violence, and to dehumanize targets of joking. Racist, anti-Semitic and similarly problematic jokes have long being used in order to justify ill-treatment of certain groups, to ridicule them, and to dehumanize them so that further violence, does not seem inappropriate (Billig, 2001). This ambivalent character must be kept in mind when discussing humor as part of the alternative regime of representation. In other words, it is not any type of humor that may be thought of as part of this regime, but rather humor aimed consciously at disrupting existing patterns of thoughts and behaviors, and which then contributes to the ongoing questioning of cultural identity and its position in society. It is only humor used as a tool to interrogate entrenched, rigid, and for this reason problematic views of cultural identity that might be seen as part of a set of creative tactics that belong to this regime of representation. Similarly, other tactics, such as camera work and narrative techniques, must equally be assessed as to the extent to which they contribute to the continuous questioning of identity, and to the openness of the boundaries separating different identities.

An example of such use of humor is to be found in the British comic sketch series *Goodness Gracious Me* (BBC2, 1998–2001). Written by Meera Syal and Sanjiv Bhaskar, the series was incredibly popular in the UK, drawing in mainstream audiences as well. Playing on stereotypes of British Asians, and explicitly acknowledging both racism and political correctness, *Goodness Gracious Me* satirized both British attitudes to cultural difference and some of the responses by British Asians themselves (Malik, 2002). Parodying racist attitudes through references to "exotic India," going to an "English" restaurant, as well as popular British Asian stereotypes, such as the ostensibly spiritual but in fact money-grabbing guru, the strict parent, the demanding mother, the Bollywood macho man, and the Asian social climber, the show managed to keep boundaries open and to continuously question the meaning and role of cultural identity and difference. Through satire and parody, audiences are called to laugh at, but also think about and reflect on, entrenched ideas about certain identities and expectations regarding ideas, practices, and behaviors. Crucially, the show does not dictate a given morality or lay any claims as to how things ought to be, but rather creates a space where a discussion on morality, on what is good, right, or wrong, can take place.

In a similar manner, employing parody and satire, *The Simpsons* (Fox, 1989–), with some of its "ethnic" characters, contributes to this discussion and appears committed to openness. In common with Ali G, Borat and *Goodness Gracious Me*, *The Simpsons* articulates an often unspeakable but still festering racism in order to enable us to confront it. In these terms, in articulating such unspeakable views, it succeeds in putting them in our midst, in problematizing them, and in asking us to rethink, reconsider, and reassess the role of cultural difference in our lives and societies. Characters such as Apu, the Indian convenience store owner, complete with a supposedly Indian accent, an unpronounceable long surname, an arranged marriage and several children, and a PhD in computer science, present us with familiar stereotypical images, and through these call upon all of us to rethink our ideas about cultural diversity and its role in society. At the same time, they call specifically upon community members themselves to reassess their own identity, to question established ideas about who they are meant to be and who they are. Seeing such stereotypes, we are led to question their validity, meaning, and use in society, and hence to open up a debate on cultural diversity. In short, through the repetition and parodying of stereotypical images, such representations refuse the closed boundaries and clear moralities of previous representational regimes, and invite all of us to have a conversation about cultural difference.

A crucial requirement for retaining open boundaries between and within communities is to openly address the diversity of views and perspectives. The alternative representational regime can only be truly alternative if it recognizes and acknowledges other points of view. The use of narrative tropes that allow for differing points of view within the same story is one of the clearest ways for supporting such multiplicity of perspectives. Difficult topics, including the topic of violence between different communities, are confronted in this regime through the presentation of different perspectives. Examples include documentaries and documentary-style films such as *Route 181: Fragments of a Journey in Palestine-Israel* (Khleifi and Sivan, 2004) and *Battle for Haditha* (Broomfield, 2007), but also Abbas Kiarostami's *Ten* (2002) among others.

To begin with the latter, although its subject matter is gender in the context of the Islamic Republic of Iran, it allows for a fruitful exploration of a multiperspectival representation of difference. Filmed entirely on a digital camera perched inside a taxi in Tehran, driven by a woman, the film presents ten encounters between the driver and her passengers. These correspond to ten stories, ten viewpoints, ten subjects for discussion, and ten explorations of complex relationships between people. The end of the film returns us to the beginning, in a way reiterating that continuous reflection is necessary in order to understand the world around us. Rather than assuming a unique point of view, a set moral tone, and a clear understanding of how the world and its subjects should live, the film instead embarks on an exploration of the complexities of life, of difference (in this case gender difference), of positioning and understanding one's own self. In this manner, through this open-ended format and multiperspectival representation, it allows for a conversation, an encounter with others that may contribute, if not to a better relationship, then at least to a more insightful understanding of the world.

In a similar, albeit more politicized, fashion, *Route 181* explores the Palestinian conflict from a multitude of perspectives. Filmmakers Michel Khleifi, a Palestinian, and Eyal Sivan, an Israeli, travel from the south to the north of Israel, tracing the borders decided by UN Resolution 181 or the Palestinian Partition Plan (1947). On their journey they encounter several people, young and old, soldiers and civilians, Palestinian and Israeli, whose views and thoughts they record. Subjects are left to talk on their own, to express their positions and to engage in conversation with the filmmakers. Although the political position of the filmmakers is clear – they are against the occupation of Palestine – there is no easy moralizing in the film. Rather, the multiple perspectives allow for an insight into the reasons, justifications, and explanations offered by the various people engaged in the conflict. Israeli settlers explain why they believe they are entitled to the land, while Palestinians and Israeli Arabs relate their experiences of displacement, occupation, and exile. While no clear solutions emerge, this type of multiperspectival representation allows encounters with others, which may not have happened outside the domain of representation and media. It brings together, but not necessarily reconciles, opposing views. In this way it contributes towards a better understanding and respect of difference, diversity, and the Other.

Finally, based on real events, Nick Broomfield's film *Battle for Haditha* deals with a revenge attack by the US army in the Iraqi town of Haditha following an earlier roadside bomb that killed a US soldier. Instead of an easy demonizing of the US soldiers, Broomfield's film offers them a platform to express their views and discuss their experiences and emotions. As well as this, we are shown the views, emotions, and experiences of the Iraqi insurgents who planted the bomb, and, finally, the perspective of the Iraqi families caught in all this violence. No one is singled out as responsible or conversely as a passive victim. In mobilizing these multiple perspectives, the film is not concerned with blaming and attributing responsibility, but with understanding the complexity of conflict. From this point of view, it is a much more fruitful strategy for eventual resolutions and reconciliations. It should be made clear, however, that this multiperspectival trope is not a means of achieving objectivity in the sense of a detached analysis of events. Rather it is a means by which different voices get to be heard without privileging one over others. This does not preclude film-, or program-makers having a viewpoint or political commitments themselves. But, rather than presenting a clear solution, they seek to engage us in a conversation or dialogue about what needs to be done when it comes to conflict, or how best to understand and recognize cultural difference more broadly. As part of the alternative regime of representation, the mode or trope of multiperspectivalism is a way of extending the debate, of questioning borders between identities, and of interrogating set views and rigid understandings of what difference is, and how it is expressed in life.

Although it is easy to accept this regime as the best or fairest way of representing cultural diversity, we must insist once more that this is too simplistic a conclusion. Rather, we must note some of the political losses of this regime. These include its reluctance to posit a positive program for change and the ease by which it repeats, thereby giving some sort of credence to, problematic positions. In addition, although giving voice to all sounds fair enough, we must keep in mind that not all voices are equivalent. More specifically, the alternative regime is concerned with articulating questions and opening up a debate, thereby focusing on the politics of cultural difference as a process that involves debate, critique, and dialogue, but remaining silent as to the actual contents of this politics and the directions which it should follow. In other words, it does not provide us with any specific ideas, proposals, or opinions regarding life under conditions of cultural heterogeneity. In order to begin questioning something, this "something" must be described or represented in some way first. Thus, while this regime is crucial in allowing for openness and dialogue, it is not sufficient on its own for the development of a proper politics of representation. For this,

Table 10.1 Regimes of representation

Regimes of representation	*Key themes*	*Main outcomes*
Essentialized difference regime: constructs people as part of a socio-cultural group whose stable core characteristics are overwhelmingly positive and remain unchanged through time	Establishes a historical continuity of the identity in question. Focuses on the stability of the core elements of the identity despite challenges and the passage of time; launches claims of authenticity and authority	Creates new exclusions, and decides who can represent the group and who has the right to speak; despite this, it is politically efficacious, because it: answers back to the racist regime; can be used strategically to restore pride in one's identity; can mobilize more effectively and demand an end to injustices and inequality
Alternative regime: avoids the construction of a singular understanding of cultural difference. Difference–identity remains an open question	Creates ambiguity and ambivalence vis-à-vis identity and difference; employs creativity in its encounters with difference and identity; mobilizes a multiplicity of perspectives	Contributes to continuous reflection on identity and difference; questions the simplistic morality of good–bad found in other regimes; creates new political possibilities

we require the concurrent operation of all regimes of representation, as it is precisely in the antagonism between these that we can locate such a politics.

10.4 Conclusions

We discussed in this chapter two regimes of representation that engage with the question of cultural diversity from an "inside" point of view. Or, to be more accurate, while the essentialist regime emerges as a representation of the community by (parts of) itself, the alternative regime actively questions the notions of inside and outside. The essentialist regime develops claims of authenticity, a core identity, and a common past and history, which prioritize a certain prototypical identity that subsequently becomes a community's only true identity. The result is that borders between communities become sharply defined and policed, while within communities only certain identities/behaviors are seen acceptable. The alternative regime, on the other hand, insists on openness rather than closure, dialogue on, instead of repetition of, core values, and a questioning, rather than assertion, of identities.

The main argument of this chapter is that both regimes are necessary for cultural diversity. The antagonistic coexistence of these regimes is both a symptom of today's contentious multicultural politics and a necessary condition for the very existence of such a politics. Why? Because if we find identity at the heart of multicultural politics, then we must accept both its tendency for self-assertion and self-preservation, associated with the essentialist regime of representation, and its inescapable dynamism, its multiplicity, internal diversity, and dialogical constitution, encountered in the alternative regime. Since identities must at the same time state their claims and allow for these to be changed, questioned, and debated, these representational regimes provide the means by which both these are possible. But what is necessary too is that these regimes exist in an antagonistic relationship, in a constant to-and-fro, one undermining the other, as it were. Extending this argument further, it may be said that the concurrent operation of all regimes contributes to an ongoing politics of representation, which, in turn, may be considered a crucial part of mediated multiculturalism. This should not be taken as a justification of clearly problematic regimes such as the racist regime or the regime of commodification. Rather, it is meant to emphasize that the existence and power of such regimes must not be hidden, while also recognizing their dynamism and ability to change. Racism can only be countered through open acknowledgement of existing and festering issues and through acknowledgment of the complexity of cultural diversity.

11

Audiences and Cultural Diversity

11.1 What Do People Do with the Media?

Our extensive discussion of representations of cultural difference has revealed a mixed and ambiguous picture. But it has also raised an important question: what is that people actually do with these representations? The implicit – and sometimes explicit – assumption is that people blindly reproduce and believe what they see in the media. In these terms, representation is *the* most important part of the media, because it provides images and ideas which people subsequently adopt: racist representations will lead to racist attitudes and so on. However, this understanding of audiences as uncritically reproducing media ideas is an overly simplistic one, which views audiences primarily as passive and easy to manipulate and which attributes all the power to the moment of representation. But it would be equally problematic to insist that audiences are always active and critical, as that attributes all the power to the moment of reception. Indeed, as the pendulum swings from one pole (passive audiences) to the other (active audience), it is difficult to draw any conclusions. In contrast, understanding reception within a theory of mediation enables us to understand it as part of a wider process, which does not determine but contributes to the overall mediation of issues.

While an important strand of media research prioritizes representation, a parallel focus on the audience has been a constant in the agenda of media studies. However, most of the relevant studies often come up with paradoxical findings that end up questioning the role of the media. Indeed, the audience has constituted an extraordinary present/absent category for many strands of research into the media. Studies have been conducted and policies drafted in the name of audiences, but often without paying much attention to what audiences said or did, as research has focused instead on media output, representations, and texts. On the other hand, when audiences have been the object of study, their behavior has been so elusive and diverse as to actually call into question the extent to which we can even refer to a singular category such as an audience. Research into audiences in the Payne Fund studies of the 1930s to the Uses and Gratifications studies of the 1970s (Blumler and Katz, 1974) attempted to understand audiences, but the result was to fit them in mostly psychological categories.

It was not, therefore, until the late 1980s that an emphasis on audiences led to a paradigm shift within studies of the media. A series of studies of primarily popular media texts sought to "rehabilitate" audiences through proving that they were actively involved in the interpretation of media texts, and that this activity could not be reduced to psychological explanations.

This new paradigm, known as the active audience paradigm, revolved around the idea that audiences were actively interpreting media messages, making sense of them in their own ways, rather than passively accepting them at face value. According to this position, audiences actively construct their own meanings on the basis of media texts and representations, and the range of these meanings is unpredictable. Different audiences understand and interpret media messages in different and often unexpected ways. Personal experiences, socio-cultural backgrounds, and ideological beliefs are some of the factors influencing the interpretative activity of audiences. In its extreme formulation the idea of active audiences ends up removing all significance from media representations, positing it instead as a construction of audiences.

Most notably, John Fiske (1987) refers to the semiotic democracy of audiences, where audiences freely construct their own meanings and interpretations of media messages. Moreover, this interpretative activity acquires political significance, as it is seen as resisting and even subverting the dominant culture. Fiske's semiotic democracy faced extensive criticism, as it equated any kind of interpretation in isolated living rooms to critical political activity. And in our case, accepting this position would mean that racist representations have no power at all, as power rests with people who may extract non-racist readings out of apparently racist texts. This would be – at the very least – bizarre. However, it cannot be assumed that readers of racist texts and representations in fact endorse them.

But what, then, do audiences do with representations of cultural diversity? And what about audiences who are themselves considered members of ethno-cultural minorities? How do they respond to relevant texts? This chapter will sketch a response to these questions, beginning with a discussion of the consumption of mediated cultural diversity, before examining culturally diverse audiences and the role of identity. In a third section, we will look into ways of replying to and communicating with the media as a way of completing the circuit of communication.

11.2 Audience Reception of Mediated Cultural Diversity

To understand and contextualize audience activities, we must begin with a few words on terminology. Terms such as the "reception," "consumption," and "use" of media products circulate widely, but their differences and nuances are not immediately clear. Firstly, audience "reception" implies an empirical inquiry into audience activities. Livingstone (2000) suggests that, after theorists had more or less agreed that texts and meanings are dynamic and divergent, empirical research into audience interpretations and activities became the necessary next step. Relevant studies, therefore, begin with the assumption that audiences are indeed active in their engagement with the media. "Consumption" of media, on the other hand, places the activities of audiences within a continuum or process that begins with production and includes representation; to speak of consumption implies the existence of a (media) product which has been produced under certain circumstances. Media consumption is therefore part of an ongoing process of engagement with the media, and represents one of the defining moments within the communication process – the other two being production and representation. From this point of view, this term is more compatible with a theory of mediation. However, a theory of mediation requires us to see media not only in terms of their outputs-representations, but also in terms of the media objects as such: the television, the computer, the newspaper, and so forth (Silverstone, 1994; Madianou, 2005). To speak of media "use," therefore, places emphasis on the media as objects, and prioritizes research into the spatial and temporal context within which audiences encounter the media. Media use also looks into the kinds of media that people tend to use in different contexts and for different purposes. An analysis of audience reception should ideally look into both aspects: consumption of media texts and use of media objects.

A second clarification concerns the notion of the audience. The audience in the singular implies a rather unitary and homogenous category, but empirical studies have found time and again that audiences are very diverse, and their behavior is notoriously fickle. It is perhaps more appropriate to speak of audiences, but the plural is ambiguous: do audiences exist "out there" as discrete entities or are they inventions of marketing and broadcasting executives? This reflects the idea of audiences as commodities, bought, sold, and exchanged within a capitalist social organization (Smythe, 1981); a parallel issue here concerns institutional attempts to know, measure, and circumscribe audiences (Ang, 1991). And, to further complicate matters, audiences can be further divided into genre audiences and fans, taking pleasure in particular genres (Jenkins, 1992); gendered audiences, with gender determining their encounters with, and pleasure in, the media (Radway, 1984; van Zoonen, 1994); and "ethnic" audiences, whose encounter with the media is seen as reflecting their ethnic identity. The important point here is that the concept of audience and audience-hood is hard to grasp. Where is one to look for these audiences? It is again in Livingstone (1998a; 1998b) that we find a helpful distinction: instead of thinking of audiences as social groups, it might be better to think of them as referring to a set of relationships to the media. In terms of our current remit, this can be translated into: what kinds of relationships do people have with media representations of cultural diversity?

Research here has suggested several kinds of relationship. One of the earliest studies was David Morley's study of the *Nationwide* audience (1980), which found empirical support for Hall's three decoding positions: the dominant, negotiated, and oppositional readings. Liebes and Katz (1993) refer to four decoding positions: real, ideological, ludic, and constructional positions, referring to distinct readings emphasizing the referential, ideological, playful, and aesthetic aspects of media representations. Livingstone and Lunt (1994) refer to a critical viewing relationship, in which audiences assume a distanced, analytical, and evaluative attitude towards the media. In a later article, Livingstone (2000) suggests that audiences' relationships to media products can be understood on the basis of two dimensions: comprehension and interpretation of media messages, which are circumscribed both by the media texts themselves and the socio-cultural background of audiences. The plethora of such discussions and findings make it hard to gauge which of these is more appropriate for understanding the relationship between representations of cultural diversity and audiences. Since, however, the most important aspect here concerns the extent to which audiences are accepting such representations, it seems that the concept of critical viewing may be the most useful. We may reformulate the question therefore as follows: to what extent do readers mobilize critical resources in interpreting (racist) media representations of cultural diversity?

Studies of reception of representations of race among mainstream audiences are surprisingly few. Most studies of media representations assumed that racist representations are more or less accepted by the presumably racist non-black audiences, but this seems to be an unwarranted assumption. It seems that we are faced with a more complex situation in which things, quite literally, are not black and white. Race and "otherness" more generally occupy an ambiguous place in most societies, and the reception of media representations seems to reflect that. In a recent study, Buffington and Fraley (2008) looked into the reception of sports images by a varied audience in the US. They found that the audience's interpretation was largely in agreement with the dominant ideas of the media images of athletes: black athletes were seen as "superior" in terms of physical ability and sporting skills, but lacking in mental skills and leadership. Most readers appeared to agree with these stereotypes, but there was a small percentage of responses that highlighted the stereotypical representation of black athletes, recognizing the contrived aspects of mediated representations. On the other hand, Buffington and Fraley also found extremely stereotypical reactions – e.g. "not many Caucasian males have great talent" and "African-Americans are typically better athletes than whites," (2008: 307) – which differ from the more subtle depiction of race in the sports media. The researchers argue that audiences appear to combine media representations from across the media spectrum, which they use in complementing their interpretations. Thus, audiences would select a black person for physical skills if they looked "like Kobe Bryant" and because they could picture them having a big and flash house such as those shown on MTV's *Cribs* (Buffington and Fraley, 2008).

These findings lend support to the idea of "fit" between pre-existing ideas and media representations, developed by Kitzinger and Miller (1992). In a research project on Aids and Africa, Kitzinger and Miller conducted a series of focus group discussions with British people on the news coverage of the disease. They found that respondents were convinced that media representations of Aids as an "African" disease were correct only because these fitted with their preconceived ideas about the continent. Similar findings are reported by Entman and Rojecki (2001), who report that racist media frames will be accepted primarily by those that already hold similar cognitive schemas; put differently, people will tend to believe in these media representations that coincide with and reinforce their existing beliefs. Such ideas appear compatible with early socio-psychological research, which found that people will tend to (mis) interpret media messages in ways that support their pre-existing ideas and beliefs (Cooper and Jahoda, 1947).

The broader issue here concerns the extent to which these "pre-existing beliefs" coincide with a social or cultural group. Buffington and Fraley could not find such a connection, or a demographic factor connecting the critical or stereotypical audiences. Entman and Rojecki imply that racist media frames were more readily accepted by the "White heartland" but did not actually test this hypothesis, focusing instead on media representations. While Morley (1980) did not study racist representations as such, his work suggested that white middle-class audiences were more likely to accept the dominant readings of media representations. On the other hand, thinking of broad social categories tends to obliterate more subtle differences in interpretation and appropriation of media texts. This quest for a link between media interpretations and socio-cultural groups led some theorists to import the concept of "interpretative community" from literary theory (Fish, 1980).

An interpretative community refers to a group of people who share similar understandings of the world, which they subsequently apply to their encounters with media contents. Although the concept has been used by a number of media researchers (e.g. Radway, 1984; Schroder, 1994), it is considered to be ill defined (Radway, 1987) and too vague to explain for the similarity or divergence of media interpretations. Indeed, one could further criticize this notion for other kinds of ambiguity as well, especially if it is used to causally understand media consumption and interpretation: can we attribute racist readings to the existence of a "racist" interpretative community, or, conversely, attribute critical readings to the existence of an anti-racist interpretative community? This appears to reflect a kind of functionalist fallacy. It is equally likely that such interpretations are the result of membership of certain socio-cultural groups which may influence interpretation, while also the concept adds little to our understanding of the reception of racist media representations in given socio-historical contexts.

Broadly speaking, historical resistance to, and struggles against, racism, have made extremely racist views unacceptable. This implies that most audiences will not accept racist media representations, not least because they will not fit into their pre-existing ideas, shaped in an increasingly anti-racist environment. They are thus more likely to assume negotiated readings, that is, to be critical of some aspects of media representations while accepting others. In terms of our analysis of the different regimes of representation it is likely that most clearly racist representations of the type encountered in early media works such as *Birth of a Nation* will be rejected in favor of more nuanced representations. Audiences are therefore more likely to mobilize their critical abilities to some extent, reflecting shifts in cultural politics and the increased intolerance of prejudice and racism. On the other hand, the degree of critical ability to be applied differs, perhaps because of the viewers; different backgrounds and their individual and socio-cultural circumstances, highlighting in this manner the role played by one's "cultural capital" (Bourdieu, 1986).

11.2.1 Media reception and cultural capital

The term "cultural capital," proposed by Pierre Bourdieu (1986), refers to the knowledge, skills, resources, and experiences available to people as part of their specific heritage as members of a particular generation, gender, family, social group, and social class, and also as part of their personal trajectory in the world. This kind of capital is "embodied," i.e. carried by the person themselves. A parallel form of cultural capital is the "objectified" form, which refers to actual books and other cultural artefacts in one's possession. The main idea involved here is that audiences will respond to media representations in a manner that reflects the cultural capital they possess: formal education, personal experiences and involvement, detailed knowledge of some issues, etc., are all factors expected to shape media reception and influence the degree of critical apprehension of media representations.

Indeed, the concept of cultural capital offers a more nuanced approach to media audiences, as it allows for a diversity of readings, not all of which are subversive or resistant. It further allows us to understand diversity within social groups, which were previously thought as internally homogenous. On the other hand, however, it appears to imply that engagement with the media is somehow determined by one's background; from this point of view, the "power," or at least the role, of the media is disregarded. This approach does not tell us anything about the actual outcome of encountering the media, or the cultural capital acquired or lost in the process. In addition, this approach has not yet been applied to understanding people's responses to media representations, thereby precluding any firm conclusions regarding its empirical applicability. Bennett *et al.* (2006) have used the notion of cultural capital to understand the relationship between use of certain media forms and ethno-cultural belonging, but have not looked at the interpretation of media messages in terms of possession of cultural capital. Thus, although this approach provides helpful insights into the process of media consumption, caution should be exercised: firstly, on theoretical grounds, because it implies that people's reception of the media is predetermined on the basis of their existing cultural capital; secondly, on empirical grounds, because it has not yet been tested in terms of the interpretation of media representations.

11.3 Ethno-Cultural Groups as Audiences

Before embarking on a discussion of ethnic and cultural groups as audiences, we should point to the danger inherent in considering differences and similarities in interpretation as denoting an ethnic or cultural "core" within these groups, and viewing these groups as more homogenous that they actually are. On the other hand, however, the fear of essentializing ethnic groups must not prevent the drawing of some conclusions regarding the relationship between ethnicity and media reception. With this in mind, we can proceed in this discussion. Research studies concerning minority audiences have been numerous, and we can classify them along the following lines: firstly, studies looking at the types of media used by ethnic audiences; secondly, studies looking at ethnic audiences' reception of stereotypical media portrayals. These can be taken to correspond to the division between the consumption of media texts and the use of media objects (see Madianou, 2005). Both reveal aspects of a complex relationship between media and ethnic groups, and show tensions and ambiguities inherent in the mediation of cultural difference.

To begin with, a number of studies reveal interesting patterns of media use by ethnic groups. In the US context, such studies are primarily undertaken by media research companies in order to be able to target certain groups in a more efficient way. Ghanem and Wanta (2001) report an estimate of about $1.2 billion spent annually on Hispanic media outlets in the US, which reflects the media habits of this community and its growing importance for advertisers. This preference for own media use is one of the most consistent findings regarding the media habits of minority groups. Thus, Spain's Asociacion para el Conocimiento de la Poblacion Inmigrante — or the Association for the Understanding of the Immigrant Population – reports that 43.2 percent of their immigrant respondents preferred reading weekly and monthly immigrant-focused publications, as opposed to a preference of 14.9 percent for general national newspapers (ACPI-EMI, 2008). Internet usage tends to be more or less at the same level as with other population groups, but in the UK, ethnic minority households tend to have broadband connection in greater numbers compared with the overall UK population (Ofcom, 2007a). In addition, the prevalence of satellite dishes in immigrant neighborhoods in European cities may be seen as a marker of the stated preference for own media consumption (see, for instance, Ogan, 2001; Madianou, 2005). Generally, the preference for satellite television among immigrant communities is well documented: in the UK, Ofcom reports that 60 percent of ethnic minority households had a cable or satellite TV connection compared to the UK-wide average of 52 percent (Ofcom, 2007a).

Viewing habits and preference for specific media forms are not as consistent. Early US studies on newspaper usage by Hispanics has produced mixed results. Ghanem and Wanta (2001) report that Fielder and Tipton (1986) found that minority populations tend to use newspapers less than whites, but point out that other studies note that the percentage of adult African-American readership mirrors the overall US population (Cranberg and Rodriguez, 1994, in Ghanem and Wanta, 2001). Other patterns reveal a preference for film over television for UK minority groups (Bennett *et al.*, 2006; Ofcom, 2007a) and a slight preference for entertainment rather than news among US Hispanic populations (Greenberg *et al.*, 1983, in Ghanem and Wanta, 2001). Other studies reveal a "hunger for news" among immigrant communities, which is often translated into an increased consumption of news, alongside a preference for more international news than typically found in national news broadcasts and a more critical stance towards national news broadcasts (Christiansen, 2004). Christiansen found this to be the case with Turkish minorities in Denmark, while Gillespie (2000) reported similar consumption patterns among Punjabis in Southall, a London suburb. Finally, Weibull and Wadbring (1998, in Christiansen, 2004) found that ethnic minorities in Sweden tend to consume more news than the indigenous Swedish population.

But the overall picture is a mixed one, with no discernible patterns. This has led researchers to conclude that internal group differences prevent more generalized conclusions, pointing to the need to highlight group heterogeneity (Harindranath, 2000; Bennett *et al.*, 2006). Thus, in a survey study of UK's main ethnic minority groups, Tony Bennett and his colleagues found that age, generation, class, and gender were better predictors of media use than ethnicity. In these terms, we may find this "hunger for news" among first-generation migrants, or among exiles (see Matar, 2006) but not necessarily among other parts of ethnic communities. Similarly, in a study of Chinese-Malaysian audiences, Carstens (2003) found that, although their media consumption denoted a preference for Hong Kong products, there were significant differences in their preferences: young people were more attracted to "Canto-pop," while older Chinese-Malaysians preferred media products that involved Chinese traditions. Carstens notes that Chinese-Malaysian newspapers catered for both, in featuring extensive news and colored photos of singers and actors from Hong Kong, Taiwan, and China, alongside articles on Confucian thought. A similar division was found in terms of gender, with males more attracted to the often violent, cruder, sexier Hong Kong productions and women more likely to enjoy the family and love themes of Taiwanese shows. Carstens also reports a class division, with popular Hong Kong productions appealing more to white-collar workers and average students, while the more sophisticated Mandarin programs were more popular among those with professional or intellectual backgrounds. In these terms, we may conclude, along with Bennett *et al.*, that patterns of media use – but not necessarily of interpretation – reflect more broadly the cultural capital of different community members.

The broader question that emerges here, however, concerns the interpretation of such patterns of media use. The prevalence of satellite dishes in immigrant neighborhoods led some to speak of an "umbilical cord" connecting immigrant groups to their homeland (see Aksoy and Robbins, 2000; Madianou, 2005). This orientation to the "homeland" has led to arguments that minority communities are not well integrated. Especially the consumption of transnational television may be understood as enabling an engagement with "home" politics and culture which at the same time ghettoizes communities who cannot or do not want to engage with their "host" culture. In this sense, the problem here is that, by not consuming the host nation's media, the ethnically diverse communities lose out on the integrative function of these media and end up even more marginalized. At the same time, the feelings of belongingness to their homeland are enhanced by these communities that tend to consume more transnational media. But such arguments, argue Aksoy and Robbins (2000; 2003), are based on a nation-centric understanding of the role of the media and media consumption that does not capture the complexity of a transnational existence. For many of the Turks they interviewed in London, consumption of Turkish television rendered Turkey ordinary and approachable, rather than a mythologized homeland of set customs and tradition. Similarly complex patterns of media consumption are reported by Madianou (2005) among Turkish communities in Greece: they happily move between national and transnational media, using them for different purposes and often being equally critical of both. In a well-known study, Marie Gillespie (1995) found that Punjabi-British audiences moved effortlessly between Indian-produced media and British ones, although they ascribed different meanings to their consumption of these media, and the context of viewing varied. When Hindi films were showing, the whole family tended to watch together, while English television was watched by fewer members of the household.

We can therefore conclude that, although media use by minority groups does involve questions of belongingness and identity, it does not predetermine them: use of transnational television or minority newspapers does not predict or signal one's identity any more than use of mainstream media does. This is even more so since we do not know how these media are interpreted and inserted into people's lives. It is therefore to this that we turn next.

11.3.1 Interpreting media texts

Compared to the wealth of studies on representation there is a relative dearth of studies of reception by groups considered ethnically and/or culturally diverse. Two distinct issues emerge here: one concerns the way in which minority groups interpret media contents in general; and the other, the way in which they receive media representations of themselves. The former is often met with the ever-present accusation of essentialism, while the latter tends to state the rather obvious: minority culture members are unhappy about the stereotypical views of themselves that circulate in the media. Yet there are important insights offered by both these strands, which have contributed to our understanding of the complex process of media engagement by audiences, even if they suffer from some limitations. More recently, important contributions have been made by studies that integrated both approaches, and showed how audiences move from one interpretative position to another as media contents shift from covering general issues to covering issues that directly involve them (Madianou, 2005; Matar, 2006). These studies reveal not only the complexity involved in media consumption but also the close connection between media representations and reception, and the involvement of self and identity. We will discuss all these strands of research next.

One of the first studies of media reception among diverse audiences was *The Export of Meaning* study by Tamar Liebes and Elihu Katz (1993). Although the main goal of the study was to question the top-down assumptions of media imperialism and the so-called Americanization of the media, *The Export of Meaning* showed clearly how different communities engage with media contents in different ways. Specifically, they used the 1980s US soap opera *Dallas* as their text in question, which they then showed to different ethno-cultural groups within Israel: Israeli Arabs, veteran Moroccan settlers and newly arrived Russian ones, as well as members of a kibbutz. Liebes and Katz also selected two sets of non-Israeli groups – American and Japanese audiences – and compared the interpretations of *Dallas* by all these ethno-cultural groups. Their findings suggested different positions for each of these groups: the Arabs and Moroccans isolated the subplots and focused on the linearity of the storylines; the Russians identified overall themes and spoke of the manipulative intent of the show; the Americans and the kibbutzniks retold the story in psychoanalytic terms; while finally the Japanese totally rejected the show, which they viewed as unrealistic. This kind of research shows, on the one hand, the impossibility of a single interpretation of a media text and the variety of readings that it invites, and, on the other hand, the role played by cultural factors in interpreting the media. Thus, the Israeli Arabs and the Americans, for instance, already have a given culture, which determines their engagement with the world and with the media more specifically. It is not difficult to see how this formulation gives rise to accusations of essentialism. Rather than viewing cultures as internally diverse and dynamic, it assumes that they are stable enough to provide their members with a consistent viewpoint from which to interpret the world.

However, cultural background foregrounds or privileges certain interpretations, especially when it involves the self, or themes that are of importance or of particular relevance to the community. Research on the reception of media representations of oneself has focused on the issue of seeing oneself and one's community consistently misrepresented in the media. Indeed, it is this very idea of misrecognition that connects minority groups as audiences to what Charles Taylor (1994) has referred to as the politics of recognition. A common thread in such studies concerns their often frustrated quest for recognition in the media, and, by proxy, for visibility and inclusion in the public sphere. Notwithstanding the issue of internal diversity within communities, some patterns clearly emerge in the reception of media representations by minority communities. These include, firstly, an overall concern with negative stereotyping and racism; and, secondly, a concern with the accuracy and authenticity of the representations. On the other hand, the concern with authenticity reveals the tensions and dynamism within identities.

In general, minority audiences express a concern with stereotypical representations of themselves in the media. This concern is shared by almost all ethno-culturally diverse audiences. Thus, black audiences recognize and reject stereotypical media representations. Karen Ross (2000) reports findings from a research study of ethnic minority audiences in the UK, in which audiences considered that media representations of black characters were stereotypical. Specifically, Ross's respondents first thought that there were only a few minority characters on television overall, and when they were shown they were given bit parts, and portrayed in stereotypical terms. Respondents complained that, for instance, Asian characters always seem to have problems with arranged marriages, and black characters with crime. The complexity and diversity of ethnic minority lives was nowhere to be seen. Similar findings are reported by Poole (2001), whose research has shown that British-Muslim audiences perceive the representation of Islam in the media as stereotypical, focusing primarily on portrayals of violence and terrorism. In the same vein, Jhally and Lewis (1992) discuss the views of black American audiences, who feel that media representations of black Americans are stereotypical and one-dimensional. In Wilson and Sparks' (1999) study of audiences' reception of mediated sports imagery, black audiences comment on stereotypical portrayals of blacks as athletes, who are almost always found in urban centres: "you won't ever see a black person with a book," comments one of Wilson and Sparks' respondents (p. 17). As we have seen in our discussion of media representations, and especially in the racist regime of representation, such feelings and opinions are justifiable.

A crucial finding in relevant research concerns the involvement of race and racism in audience interpretations. Thus, minority audiences will typically interpret media representations of themselves through the prism of race and racism, while in contrast most white audiences will mobilize different interpretative frames. This finding is reported by, among others, Brenda Cooper (1998), who studied the reception of Spike Lee's 1989 film *Do The Right Thing*. Cooper found that the film was interpreted primarily through the frames of race and racism by African-American audiences, while white audiences could not relate to these themes and ended up justifying the racism represented in the film.

Similarly, Rockler (2002) studied the reception of two US-based comic strip cartoons, *Jump Start* and *The Boondocks*, among African-American and European-American audiences. Both strips feature black families, but while *Jump Start* plays down race, *The Boondocks* explicitly tackles racial politics. In addition, it shows the diversity of the black American community, and it engages with themes from black American popular culture, especially rap music and related entertainment. In the current terminology, we could classify the former as part of the domesticated regime and the latter as part of an alternative regime of representation. Rockler reports that, while European-American audiences liked *Jump Start* and applauded its general appeal, they disliked *The Boondocks* and could not relate to it. In contrast, African-American audiences overall disagreed over whether they liked the strip, but agreed that it was a more realistic portrayal of their experiences.

But race is also relevant in other ways. In a well-known study, Jhally and Lewis (1992) found that non-stereotypical portrayals of blacks ended up discounting racism among white audiences. Thus, in their study of *The Cosby Show*, which we can classify as part of the domesticated regime of representation, Jhally and Lewis found that the show was seen by white audiences as evidence of the diminished significance of race in the US context. They refer to this as "enlightened racism," and they argue that in fact these portrayals of race are problematic because they shift the focus from the everyday problems and racism faced by most blacks in the US. In contrast, black audiences found that the show concerned the politics of race. Although black audiences mobilized different and more complex resources for their interpretation of the show, they were overall concerned with race and racism, and the role played by this show in the politics of race. They felt that, although the portrayal of an upper-class black American family was untypical and unrealistic, it was nevertheless worth it, in that it provided an alternative to the negative and often racist representations of blackness.

The Cosby Show, *The Boondocks*, and other complex representations of ethnic diversity raise questions of accuracy and authenticity among ethnic audiences. Media representations are therefore likely to be questioned not only in terms of being positive or negative, but also in terms of their authenticity. Ross (2000) refers to several criticisms of minority characters on British television shows because they lack authenticity. For instance, Ross's respondents criticize the portrayal of the character of Jules Tavernier, a Trinidadian in the soap opera *EastEnders*, who is shown eating beans on toast in the local café. "Where is the Caribbean food, the rice and peas?" wonders one of Ross's respondents (p. 140). Other respondents complain about Muslim characters having Hindu names, or about showing Hindu characters going to the mosque. Similar concerns are voiced by Jhally and Lewis's subjects, who find that *The Cosby Show* lacks authenticity, but, despite this, provides a positive role model for black Americans.

The production of such critical and often oppositional readings led theorists to speak of a black resisting spectatorship (Diawara, 1993). However, two issues complicate such a view: the first is the essentialist assumption of a singular "black" gaze or position of spectatorship; the second concerns the different representational regimes which invite different positions. As we saw in earlier chapters, the question of authenticity is more directly involved in the "essentialist" and "alternative" regimes of representation. Moreover, questions of authenticity reveal hidden tensions in identities and cultures. These include a concern with who has the right to represent, and a concern with what are the most appropriate portrayals in the media. And here audience responses make clear the diversity and dynamism found within ethno-cultural groups. Thus, different generations offer distinct interpretations of authenticity. Both Gillespie (1995) and Ross (2000) found that older generations tended to reject "westernized" representations of ethnic groups as inauthentic and inappropriate. "We are Asian and our culture is very different and those stories go against our culture," comments one of Ross' respondents in connection with the representation of a South Asian couple in the British soap opera *EastEnders* (Ross, 2000: 139). Younger audiences, however, disagree: "I think Gita and Sanjay are quite realistic" (p. 139). Rockler's (2002) black respondents criticized the bland and "color blind" portrayal of race in *Jump Start* but did not agree on whether the more controversial representation of black life in *The Boondocks* was more appropriate. In a study of black audiences of black sitcoms again in the US, Means Coleman (2002) reports that devout Christians among her respondents produced different readings: for instance, one of her respondents preferred the character of Carlton in the sitcom *Fresh Prince of Bel-Air*, whom he found to be a "good boy," although the character is portrayed as "square" and "boring."

Media and cultural products that involve more controversial and ambiguous representations give rise, not surprisingly, to more diverse and often oppositional interpretations. A lot of these involve patriarchal representations of women, encountered in primarily, but not exclusively, the domesticated difference and essentialist regimes, which included representations of victimized women in need of white saviors and sexualized and misogynist representations as in, for instance, gangsta rap. To find that these are resisted by female audiences and cultural critics alike does not come as a surprise (see hooks, 1994). On the other hand, it is equally significant to note that such cultural forms are often consumed and used in contexts outside those of their production, thereby lending them a different meaning. Thus, as bell hooks notes (1994), gangsta rap is not (only) consumed in the ghettoes but is used by white teenagers in the suburbs to articulate their own fears and rage. These white youths do not "become" gangsters or ghetto dwellers through consumption; rather their consumption helps articulate another kind of identity: an angry and frustrated teenager. On the other hand, black or other minority audiences may consume mainstream media products, which they enjoy in ways similar to those employed by mainstream audiences – in such contexts, their identity as members of a certain cultural group is not relevant; rather this media consumption helps articulate a more inclusive identity.

11.4 Media Consumption and Identity

Considering the above, it is clear that the reception of cultural products does not only denote a position vis-à-vis a certain representation or regime of representation, it also *engages* and *articulates* an identity through bridging texts or representations with the contexts of their reception. In other words, the work of audience reception is ultimately a productive one: it *produces* an identity, which can be seen as the result of a complex articulation or binding together of several things. These may include, among others, one's own background, including one's cultural, social, and other forms of capital; the broader socio-cultural and political context; and the media representations and media objects which "interpellate" certain identity positions.

To reformulate the central issue here, media reception is often conceptualized as involving pre-existing positions, which are brought to the surface in a kind of reified manner. Thus, a "black" oppositional position is evoked by, for instance, the racist regime of representation. This view, however, does not do justice to the complexity involved in media reception, to the diversity of identities and the diversity of representations. In rethinking this relationship in more complex terms, we may consider the role of the media representations as not merely inviting positions of interpretation, but also engaging their audiences to (re)think of themselves: who they are and who they want to be, what is of importance to the community, how recognition and justice can be achieved, and so on. Confrontation with negative representational regimes may lead to the salience of issues of injustice and through these to identities articulated with anger and frustration; on the other hand, encountering regimes such as the regime of commodification may contribute to a kind of "mainstreaming" of identity, which lulls identities to a false sense of acceptance without addressing the demands for recognition and justice. Conversely, the essentialist and alternative regimes lead to an internal reflection, as it were, which foregrounds the community's internal diversity and power politics.

In an often-quoted passage, Benedict Anderson (1983/1991: 15) argues that communities are not distinguished by their falsity or genuineness but by the style in which they are imagined. This is a profound insight that provides another entry point to the relationship between representation and reception: reception of mediated representations of cultural diversity constitutes, in these terms, an encounter between different imaginings of the community: some of these may become hegemonic, dominating alternative imaginings; others possibly lead to a synthesis and a creation of new imaginings; yet others might become obsolete.

To illustrate such arguments we may turn to recent work in media consumption, which shows these varied articulations. In her study of Turkish minority audiences in the Athenian neighborhood of Gazi, Mirca Madianou (2005) found that such community members were content with using the national Greek media, and occasionally watch Turkish satellite television. Madianou argues that, in general, their media consumption is ordinary. This finding is shared by Aksoy and Robbins (2000) and Bennett *et al.* (2006), who also found that general media consumption does not differ significantly between communities, but rather differences emerge on the basis of other factors, such as generation, gender, and class. On the other hand, however, Madianou found that in certain instances the national media produced racist and stereotypical representations of Turkishness – in these instances, her respondents' ordinary consumption was disrupted, foregrounding their identity as members of a particular ethno-cultural minority. Essentialism begets essentialism, argues Madianou.Similarly, Dina Matar (2006) found that her Palestinian respondents living in London "became" Palestinian only when confronted by media representations of Palestinian struggles that they found problematic.

The issue here is not only to reject such representations as racist, but also to note that, through these, minority members "become" in a sense different, they experience exclusion and marginalization from the broader public domain. In these instances, the dominant imagining of the nation excludes some communities. The political ramifications of this are potentially dangerous, especially if there are no means by which to redress such exclusion. Marginalized, disenfranchised, and alienated groups may well become radicalized, turning to violent politics or criminal activities. However, minority audiences can and do respond to this exclusion through directly challenging these representations and through actively constructing alternative ones that allow for an articulation of the multiple parts that constitute a community and an identity.

11.5 Right to Reply: How Can Audiences Respond?

Attempts by audiences to respond to negative and often outright racist representations have a long history. This alone reveals that audiences are far from being passive victims. The first kind of response is to seek a ban on the circulation of media representations deemed racist, often following political and legal routes. More recently, audiences have developed a wider arsenal of responses. These include lobbying media organizations for wider participation and fairer treatment; complaining; boycotting; developing media and PR campaigns; and producing alternative media. These responses have occasionally led to significant victories for cultural diversity. Yet they also reveal a set of ever-present tensions: they raise the issue of who has the right to speak on behalf of others, the issue of what precisely would constitute a more appropriate representation of the community, and of course the issue of freedom of speech. While not necessarily resolving these tensions, it is of crucial importance to keep open the channels of communication between media audiences (in all their diversity) and media producers, and between audiences as citizens and publics and the political institutions and actors that are meant to represent them.

As early as in 1915, black audiences were vocally resisting attempts to racialize them through racist representations. The D. W. Griffith racist film *Birth of a Nation* (1915) led the US-based National Association for the Advancement of Colored People (NAACP) to go to the courts requesting an injunction to stop the film on the basis that it invoked racial tensions which could result in violent confrontations (Stokes, 2007). Melvyn Stokes' recent book on the film offers a compelling account of the fight against it in American cities. The struggle against *Birth of a Nation* illustrates to a large extent the issues, tensions, and dilemmas involved in answering back and seeking redress from the media.

The story began in Los Angeles, with the local branch of NAAPC formulating a series of objections to the film, including its portrayals of black men as having "repulsive habits and depraved passions" (in Stokes, 2007: 130). This film, argued NAACP, had to be either altogether banned or else heavily censored. However, the National Board of Censorship, reflecting the racist attitudes of the time, refused to accept NAACP's arguments – in fact they even refused to allow its representatives to speak for more than a few minutes – and decided against any major changes to the film. The fight moved then to New York, where the NAACP moved towards lobbying political institutions at a local level, such as the mayor of New York, again on the basis that the film produced racial tensions. Other branches of the NAACP protested at local cities and towns, with mixed results: some cities banned the film, while others heavily censored itand yet others showed most of the controversial scenes. Including notable black leaders, such as W. E. B. Du Bois who was at the time the editor of the NAACP journal, *The Crisis*, the struggle against the film revealed tensions and divisions within the black community. Such tensions concerned the objectives of the struggle and what would constitute a satisfactory outcome, while the mobilization against the film failed to involve the whole community. To an extent, this shows the class and educational divisions within the African-American community, as it was mostly the intellectual and well-educated members of the community who were more involved. It also reveals the different context within which the struggle took place: in the American South, where the disenfranchisement of the black community was almost complete, and the community had hardly any means by which to fight the film. In general, the political clout of the black community was at the time too insignificant to lead to any important changes, and any political lobbying was likely to prove unsuccessful.

Melvyn Stokes further describes the attempts of the black community and its friends to produce another film, in which the historical inaccuracies and overt racism of *Birth of a Nation* would be addressed in the language of cinema. This attempt points to another means used by ethno-culturally diverse communities in order to begin a dialogue with the media. But the difficulties involved in conceptualizing, producing, and completing such a film show once again the lack of access to money and power by minority communities. More broadly, to start a dialogue with the media necessitates that the two parties are on an equal footing: more often than not, this is an illusion.

In other instances, such equality is the much-sought-after goal of minority communities, the outcome of the dialogue they want to start.

Moreover, the mixed results of the struggle against *Birth of a Nation* revealed another tension: between racist film representations and freedom of speech. Indeed, freedom of speech is constitutionally enshrined in the US as the First Amendment, denoting its great significance and importance. D. W. Griffith managed to successfully frame his film's potential ban as an issue of freedom of speech, thereby skewing the fight even more in his favor. More broadly, however, this tension, alongside the former two issues, tensions within the community's leadership and divisions among the community, are emblematic of the dilemmas involved in answering back to the media.

More recent media controversies include the infamous Mohammed cartoon controversy in 2005, discussed in Chapter 9. Of particular interest here is the inability of the Muslim community in Denmark to seek redress for what they understood as an insult and an offensive representation of Islam. The success of the Danish political and media establishment in framing this as a matter of freedom of speech was partly a result of the broader negative climate against Islam in the Danish media (Hussain, 2000; 2007). At the same, the Danish Muslim communities' protests were deemed to be offensive to freedom of speech, and characteristic of the "backwardness" and "fanaticism" of the community (Hussain, 2007). More broadly, however, the lack of any channels of communication between the Danish media and the Danish Muslim communities might have fed the controversy. With no one from the media side accountable to the local Muslim communities, the Danish media proceeded to publish of the offensive cartoons. While the cartoons were reprinted in newspapers across Europe, the British press refrained from printing them; this was seen by some as evidence of the improved community relations within the context of the UK (Modood, 2006).

In more general terms, the Danish cartoon controversy shows once more the tensions involved in seeking redress. The Muslim community in the UK and elsewhere – in contexts where it is a minority – was in itself divided, not over whether the cartoons were racist or offensive, but over what should be done about them. Some demanded an outright ban, while others thought that a censure was more appropriate; yet others demanded severe punishments for the "perpetrators of the offense," as evidenced in some of the placards held by protesters in a London march. Furthermore, it is not clear to what extent a ban or even a censure of such material would compromise freedom of speech (Modood *et al.*, 2006). The issue here is that speaking or requesting redress on behalf of the Muslim community as a whole overlooks the diverse elements that make up this community. This is an ever-present tension in all such attempts to instigate a dialogue with the media.

Other means of protest face similar problems. Lobbying media institutions in order to provide more or fairer coverage requires a degree of organization that is in itself considerably problematic. This is because minority associations are largely of a voluntary character and do not have elected leaders representing the whole community. Boycotting media channels or products requires not only a united community, but also one that has considerable buying clout, so that the boycott can actually be effective. Similarly, money and other resources are required in order to design and pursue a media and PR campaign, which would also need some sort of a consensus over the representation of the community – such consensus may be difficult to elicit, since communities are both dispersed and internally diverse. The production of community media was discussed in Chapter 7. Readers will remember that issues of representativeness alongside lack of material resources plague minority media, notwithstanding their important contribution to the communities they serve. In short, the effectiveness of responses to the media is questionable. Given such problems, the easy conclusion would be that it is better not to speak at all.

Yet this would be the wrong conclusion. Noting down some of the problems involved in speaking back should illustrate the tensions always present in communities themselves, and in their often fraught relationship with the mainstream media. It shows, furthermore, the dangers involved in trying to set up a dialogue with a party that does not seem interested. Notwithstanding all of these, however, speaking back to the media is a necessary step. Indeed, as ineffective as these efforts may be, and as politically sensitive and ambiguous, they serve as a crucial and necessary reminder to the media that they are addressing and serving a diverse public. It is only through the consistent and persistent attempt to communicate back to the media that they may eventually begin to listen, and hopefully to engage in a fruitful dialogue over representation. It is only because audiences, minority and mainstream, have protested that the media have reflected upon, changed, and diversified their representations of cultural diversity.

An example here may illustrate the point. In January 2007, the UK Channel 4 broadcast a reality TV show, *Celebrity Big Brother*, featuring local, British, celebrities alongside a Bollywood actress, Shilpa Shetty. The relationship between Shetty and some of the other housemates deteriorated, resulting in what can be described as bullying with racist overtones. Shetty was referred to as "the Indian," and "Shilpa Poppadom," while one of the housemates insisted that she should "f*** off home." The show faced a wave of protests, peaking at 44,500, by far the largest numbers of complaints received by Ofcom, the British media regulator (Ofcom, 2007b). Ofcom investigated the case, finding a number of faults by Channel 4, and imposing a statutory sanction. In addition, one of the show's sponsors, Carphone Warehouse, pulled its sponsorship, considering that its continuation would damage the company.

Ofcom further discussed another Channel 4 program, an episode of the investigative documentary *Dispatches* titled "Undercover Mosque," which showed extreme preaching in British mosques and concluded that "…an ideology of bigotry and intolerance [is]spreading through Britain with its roots in Saudi Arabia" (Ofcom, 2007a). Ofcom received about 364 complaints from individuals, as well as a complaint by the West Midlands police, that the program "incited violence" and that it was heavily edited and took statements out of context. Ofcom eventually found in favor of the program makers, finding no unfairness in the documentary and stating that the program makers had acted responsibly and with sensitivity. These instances reveal the power of complaining but also the limits to such complaints. They show that, if a critical mass of complaints can be generated, then the results are immediate and impressive. But they also reveal the complexities of more equivocal cases in which things are not so clear cut: in such cases the adjudication of an independent body such as Ofcom is necessary.

The broader point involved here concerns the issue of opening up channels of communication between the media and their audiences. Although audiences' behaviors eventually reach the media, these are mainly through commissioned research or the infamous people meters: they are selective and mostly quantitative, while their objective is to increase a broadcaster's audience share rather than ensure fair reporting. Minority communities have relatively small numbers, thereby diminishing their "worth" for mainstream media. What may be necessary therefore is the institution of formal and open channels through which such audiences may communicate their concerns over media products in a direct, qualitative, and transparent manner. But to ensure fairness and representativeness, communities must establish the means by which the community can discuss within itself, where it can open up an internal dialogue over issues of representation, fairness, and appropriate responses. And here once more we come across the important contribution of minority media: they may be seen as enabling such a dialogue to take place.

To conclude this section, we may note several issues: firstly, the dangers inherent in the right to reply, which influence its effectiveness; secondly, the internal divisions and tensions within the community; thirdly, the lack of material and symbolic resources which may enable communities to speak back to the media; and finally, the crucial importance of establishing and maintaining open channels of communication between the media and minority communities.

Box 11.1   Summary of main points

Key terms

- Reception: emphasis on empirically investigating people's engagement with the media
- Consumption: emphasis on the interpretation of media representations and texts
- Use: emphasis on the actual media habits and uses of the media as objects in the context of everyday life
- Cultural capital: the idea of one's background, education, knowledge and experiences as an asset one brings to any encounter with the media
- Right to reply: the institution and maintenance of channels of communication between media and audiences

Key findings and arguments

- Mainstream audiences can and do engage critically with media representations of cultural diversity
- Minority audiences in general have a preference for their "own" media and a "hunger for news"
- Media use by ethnic minority audiences is not uniform, leading to the conclusion that use of the media may be shaped by cultural capital, rather than by group membership as such (Bennett *et al.*, 2006)
- Similarly, interpretation of media representations differs, denoting the diversity within minority communities
- Encounters between media and audiences may be characterized as productive, in the sense that they articulate diverse elements together, often giving rise to new imaginings and new identities
- Talking back to the media is fraught with dangers; it is nevertheless a crucial requirement for change

11.6 Conclusions

This chapter concludes the cycle of mediation. The mediation of cultural difference goes through production processes, representational processes, and politics, as well as through a complex process of reception. This complex process does not merely involve the reception and endorsement of the actual media representations as discrete entities; rather, these representations are interpreted and understood through the audiences' social and cultural capital, their personal trajectories but also their socialized views and opinions. At the same time, however, the encounter between media and audiences is a productive one: it produces identities though bringing together representations and their interpretations and through connecting and changing imaginings of belongingness and difference. The process of reception further involves an investigation of the context of media consumption, of the actual media habits and use of media by different communities and community members. Finally, opening up a dialogue between media and audiences should be considered a right, safeguarded and institutionalized alongside the protected right of freedom of speech. All these factors, alongside the actual diversity of the representational regimes, complicate the issue of audience reception.

12

Cultural Diversity Online

12.1 The Difference the Internet Makes

In previous chapters, the cycle of mediation was located across processes of production, representation, and reception, implying that the boundaries between these processes were clear and distinct. However, the relatively recent arrival of the internet and the world wide web have introduced a new state of affairs that effectively disrupts the cycle of mediation and imposes a different logic on the mediation of cultural diversity. The main reason for this is that the internet blurs the lines between production, representation, and usage. While in the offline mass media, the process of production involves certain professional norms and had a relatively high threshold for participation, the only barrier to content production on the internet is an internet connection. Similarly, while media representations in the mass media followed a certain representational logic specific to the medium they were found in, the multi-media logic of the internet imposes its own norms for representation. Finally, the issue of the consumption of the internet involves not only interpretation of internet representations, but requires an active presence and participation which in turn takes the form of content production. Yet it is also clear that processes of production, representation, and consumption or use also apply to the internet, even if they differ from those of the mass media. To a certain extent, then, the internet disrupts the mass-media cycle of mediation; but to another extent, it reproduces a mediation cycle but with its own rules and norms.

If, therefore, the mass media prioritize questions of representation, the internet foregrounds issues of participation. Available to everyone with the relevant connections, the internet has lowered the threshold and costs involved in producing contents, resulting in widening participation. People can go online and publish their own thoughts and ideas, alongside their videos and photos; they can access and read the thoughts of others; and they can also, crucially, comment on the ideas and images of others. There are no qualms regarding the passivity of users, since their activities are there for everyone to see. This widening of participation has led some to argue that the internet is inherently democratic (e.g. Taubman, 1998) – such views seem to be proliferating once more with the advent of Web 2.0, based on participatory designs

(O'Reilly, 2005). At the same time, the technology of the internet is one linking people across geographical borders – indeed, in Manuel Castells' terms (1997/2000), the internet reinvents geography as a "space of flows." From this point of view, the relevance of the nation-state diminishes as people connect across borders. For diasporic communities this is greatly significant, as it implies that they are, for the first time in their history, able to be connected and brought together in a space out-side their real or imaginary homeland. These two elements, the new internet-specific logic of mediation and the internet-related suspension of geographical borders, sig-nal important changes for the position of cultural diversity. Will the internet bring about a much needed symbolic and material justice for culturally diverse groups? If so, how? In addressing these questions, this chapter will firstly contextualize the rela-tionship between the internet and cultural diversity in terms of related shifts in the social, cultural, and political world, collectively known as the rise of the network society. Secondly, it will examine the cycle of mediation on the internet: the blurring of the lines between production and consumption of content; the online representa-tions of cultural diversity; and the issue of internet use by diasporas or culturally diverse groups.

12.2 Network Society and Cultural Diversity

The main idea here is that technological innovation, linked to shifts in economics, politics, and society, has given rise to a new kind of society and perhaps an altogether new era. There are many names for this – such as knowledge society (Lyotard, 1984), post-industrial society (Bell, 1973), and information society (see Webster, 2006) – but Manuel Castells' concept of the network society seems to provide the most devel-oped account so far. The main proposition put forward by Castells is that electronic media have given rise to new concepts of space and time, which in turn have led to profound changes in society. In 2001, Castells published *The Internet Galaxy*, an echo of McLuhan's *Gutenberg Galaxy* and its associated culture of print. Following a long line of social theorists who foregrounded the importance of technology and media of communication (see also Chapter 5), Castells argues that these media are involved in fundamental shifts in society that are giving rise to new ways of organizing society, politics, and the economy. As Castells puts it, the rise of the network society must be understood as the interaction of two relatively autonomous trends: the development of new information technologies and society's attempts to acquire and use these new technologies (1996/2000: 61). Centre stage in Castells' (1996/2000, 1997/2000, 1998/2004) theory is the concept of the network. This section will therefore begin with a discussion of the network, and the associated shifts in economics, politics, and society, before finally exploring the position of ethnicity and cultural diversity within the network society.

Castells defines a network as "a set of interconnected nodes," whereby a "node is the point at which a curve intersects itself" (1996/2000: 501). More specifically, networks constitute a structure, comprised of numerous points related to each other through connections, referred to as ties, and which are "multiple, intersecting and often redundant" (Barney, 2004: 2). For Castells, the importance of networks lies in their replacement of the individual and the nation as the two main forms of social organization in modernity. The rise of the network as the central organizing principle in current, technologically advanced societies is the outcome of the new electronic technologies and their introduction of new forms of space and time. For Castells, such new technologies have transformed space from a space of places to a space of flows. But space is intricately linked to time: people can only share the same time if they share the same space. While in earlier times, space and time were linked through physical proximity, modernity is characterized by an increasing distance between space and time (Giddens, 1990). Now Castells takes this idea further by suggesting that new technologies have introduced a totally new conception of space, which is based not on physical proximity but on the exchange of flows. Flows are defined as purposeful interactions and exchanges between physically disjointed places occupied by social actors (Castells, 1996/2000: 442). Castells then argues that space in the network society is a space of flows; within this space of flows, time becomes timeless. Within this context, what is the relevance of concepts such as race and ethnicity?

Neither ethnicity nor race cease to exist in the network society. However, Castells (1997/2000) argues that they can no longer provide the basis for a common identity, because they have lost their historical significance due to the delinking between identities and spaces. In other words, because ethnic identities are no longer bound to specific territories, and because also space itself becomes delinked from geography, ethnicity cannot provide meaning for individuals living in the network society. For Castells, two possibilities are open for ethnicity/race: firstly, to become part of a wider "cultural commune," such as religion or nationalism functioning "as statements of cultural autonomy in a world of symbols" (Castells, 1997/2000: 63). Secondly, ethnicity may become the basis for building a defensive trench within certain territories, such as the city, the neighborhood, or even the turf. Between these two, argues Castells, "ethnic roots are twisted, divided, reprocessed, mixed, differentially stigmatized, or rewarded, according to a new logic of informationalization and globalization of cultures and economies that makes symbolic composites out of blurred identities. Race matters, but it hardly constructs meaning any longer" (1997/2000: 63).

To a large extent, Castells considers the redeployment of ethnicity (and other forms of reactionary identities stemming from religious fundamentalism and cultural nationalism) in the network society as a form of defensive reaction against three kinds of threat: globalization, which undermines the autonomy of institutions and organizations within all localities; networks and flexibility, which blur boundaries of belonging and introduce instability in all areas; and the end of the patriarchal family, which provided fundamental mechanisms of socialization, sexuality, and ultimately personality systems. When the world becomes too large to be controlled, people introduce ways of shrinking it to their size, by focusing on localities; when networks dissolve time and space, people react with the development of an attachment to place and recalling (or reinventing) their historical memory; when faced with the end of the patriarchal family, people react by affirming the value of community, family, and God. This is why Castells understands these identities as primarily resistance identities, as opposed to legitimizing identities, that is, identities that gave rise to the civil society structuring the nation-state. A third type of identity may be possible, constructed by people on the basis of whatever cultural materials are new to them and which redefines their position in society; this identity may create new subjects that will bring about social transformations in a proactive and not defensive manner: this is called project identity and characterizes many of the new social movements, such as the Zapatistas.

Ethnicity is therefore seen to belong to a different era, one characterized by territorial nation-states; its position and significance in the network society is primarily a reactionary one, at least in the sense that it its deployed in order to defend its members from the threats of a changing world. On the other hand, the concept of a project identity is significant here. Ethnic difference may be used as the raw cultural material for the creation of project identities aiming at social justice. Indeed, the case of the Zapatistas is instructive here (see Castells, 1997/2000, chapter 2). The movement is drawn primarily from the native populations of the region of Chiapas in Mexico – especially the Lacandon community – and it therefore has a minoritarian ethnic identity. On the one hand it is fighting against 500 years of colonization and oppression, explicitly therefore mobilizing its ethnic basis. On the other hand, it seeks to build solidarity with other inhabitants of the region; in order to do this it mobilizes a more inclusive identity based on the land: a peasant identity. Both these identities are articulated with socialist values of justice and equality for all. In this instance, therefore, ethnic identity became articulated with two more identities – the peasant and socialist one – giving rise to a new, project identity, ready to become one of the subjects of the new social formation of the network society. But the movement only became a network because it managed to successfully harness the potential of the internet. The Zapatistas used the internet in order to communicate autonomously and directly with the world and with Mexican society. Through the internet they managed to both diffuse their message and build a network of support groups, which then managed to protect the movement and its territory from the encroachment of the Mexican army, and the worst excesses of the Mexican government. As Castells put it, the Zapatista movement constitutes "a distinctive expression of the old search for social justice under new historical conditions" (1997/2000: 86).

Network identities are not, however, necessarily progressive. They can become caught up in reactionary and fundamentalist politics and terrorism, as another well-known network, that of Al Qaeda, shows. In Castells' analysis, Al Qaeda articulates a religious (Islamic) with a territorial identity (the territory including the Holy Sites of Mecca, Medina, and Jerusalem). However, Al Qaeda does not construct a new project, but advocates a "return" of the holy lands to Muslim hands, offering therefore a defensive, "resistant" identity to its members. The network that constitutes Al Qaeda has managed, on the one hand, to include an extraordinary plurality of ethnic and national identities and to operate beyond borders in a truly transnational manner. On the other hand, it does not represent a truly popular uprising seeking social justice; rather, as Castells put it, "it is a self-righteous affirmation of the religious values of a segment of the Muslim intelligentsia" (1997/2000: 124). Yet this terrorist network whose values hark back to a pre-modern era of absolute religious rule, made successful use of twenty-first-century technology, including the internet and emails, using advanced encryption systems, as well as satellite-based mobile phones. However, as Castells observes, the network mostly relies on personal networks built through personal contact, as this is the most efficient and safe way of recruitment. At the same time, Al Qaeda has made successful use of the broadcast media, providing spectacular images guaranteed to play over and over in the world's media. Beyond its tactics, however, the rise of Al Qaeda must be understood as a reaction to the social, economic, and symbolic injustice suffered by Muslims in the context of the hegemony of Western modernity. Its success, beyond its reliance on technology, is due to its ability to give voice to the humiliation felt by some Muslims, and to co-articulate religious and territorial identities in a manner that aims to appeal to and unite previously fragmented Muslim communities across lines of ethnicity, locality, and race.

Zapatismo and Al Qaeda constitute two examples of ethno-culturally based networks which lend support to Castells' arguments that ethnicity and more broadly ethno-cultural diversity is not capable on its own of generating new meaning and identity in the network society. Rather it needs to be co-articulated with other identities, to annex itself to larger projects and value systems (that of socialism and Islamic fundamentalism respectively) if it is to create a network of support beyond its immediate geographic location. On the other hand, both these movements operate at the two poles of an imagined continuum: at one end we find the project identity and progressive values of Zapatismo, seeking justice for all; at the other end, we have the reactionary values of religious fundamentalism, effecting a strict division between "true" Muslims and all others. In the middle of this continuum, we find other ethnic identities, which exist in between universal and particular values, in between proposing new projects and defending their values and existence. Their identity, and – if we follow Castells – their very survival depends on how they articulate their ethno-cultural identities with/in the new technological environment. In empirically addressing this question we can now examine the form that the mediation of cultural diversity takes on the internet.

12.3 Mediation of Cultural Diversity Internet Style

If the network society, with its space of flows and its timeless time, sets the new context for ethno-cultural diversity, then we need to examine the internal dynamics within this context. Since the network society's enabling technology or medium is the internet, we will turn to this and examine the ways in which the internet mediates ethno-cultural diversity. As with the "older" or "mature" media, we may see the process of mediation in this context as moving through the processes of production of content, representation or identities, and use of the internet by ethno-cultural communities. As we shall see, although these processes are not as distinct as in the offline media, they still have considerable analytical value, as they allow us to trace the differences and changes between the "mature" and "new" media. The main question here concerns the role of the internet in safeguarding plurality and diversity, as well as in promoting social justice in both material and symbolic forms. With this in mind we can go through each of the subprocesses making up the process of internet-based mediation of ethno-cultural diversity.

12.3.1 Production of online content

As we saw in earlier chapters, when it comes to "mature" media, analyses of the production process are primarily concerned with ownership, organizational values that circumscribe content, and the constitution of the body of media producers. The primary objective of such analyses is to examine the extent to which (mature) media allow for the free, open, plural, and diverse production of content. On the internet, some of these concerns are no longer relevant. For instance, the question of media ownership no longer applies in the same manner, as the internet belongs to no one; similarly, organizational ethos and values do not play a significant role, as the internet is not ruled by media organizations. More broadly, it is very difficult to control or regulate the internet, thereby implementing rules or values for producing content. Internet content regulation is not only notoriously difficult but also very contentious, given the links between the internet and cultures of free speech. On the other hand, there are still questions concerning the context of online content production: these primarily concern the complicated issue of access to the internet.

To begin with, in structural terms, participation in the process of (online) media production has never been easier. The development of new technologies has made media producers of many of us. The use of digital cameras and 3G mobile phones allow people to produce and publish their own content. The low costs involved and the immediacy of the transmission make the expensive and time-consuming process of production in mature media appear a relic of the past. There is no doubt that digital and online technology has widened participation in the production of communicative contents. This proliferation of producers – all of us now can become producers of content – has had the result of blurring the boundaries between production and use of online content. But what exactly does this mean?

The cycle of mediation as discussed in Chapter 5 assumes a constant interaction and even a dialectic between processes of production, representation, and reception and/ in their socio-historical context. A theory of mediation understands these as distinct processes: production is still production even if it is informed by reception and representation. Indeed, when it comes to the "mature," "mass" media, and notwithstanding theories of active audiences, the cycle begins with production, while audiences respond or react to the representational contents developed by media producers. But the internet dissolves the distinction between production and use, because it is actually internet use that produces more content: people write text, post pictures or videos, and comment on other people's contents. From this point of view, online contents are the result not of a single process of production, but of an ongoing collaboration between producer-users. This has led Axel Bruns (2005) to suggest the term "produsage" to refer to this new process that is at once production and use. One of the most well-known examples is Wikipedia, where content is collaboratively produced by its users. In these terms, usage of online content does not merely refer to reading or watching, but to actively producing new content, through posting contents, direct edits of existing content or through commenting on other people's contents. Although the dissolution of boundaries implies that we no longer need to refer to production, representation, and reception or use as distinct processes in online environments, the distinctions between these are helpful for analytical purposes, allowing us to track the changes and differences between on-air and online media and to understand and map different aspects and phases of engagement with the internet.

There is no doubt that the opening of the process of production has had profound "democratizing" effects on the creation of media content. The fact that everybody can write, post, and comment on the internet appears to contribute to an almost dizzying plurality and diversity of contents. But in fact does "everybody" produce online contents? Are ethno-cultural communities actively involved in the production of online content? In other words we need to identify the barriers to content production in online environments in order to see whether indeed such production is in effect available to all.

The first kind of barrier that has concerned theorists is identified as access to internet services. Indeed, internet services require access to the relevant hardware, as well as subscription to internet service providers. The costs involved may be decreasing but they are still considerable for those on low incomes. If we then consider the fact that some ethno-cultural groups are found among the poorer parts of the population, then their internet access is expected to be lower than that of the population as a whole. However, findings from statistical surveys in fact paint a more complex picture. Indeed, the Pew Internet and American Life Project reports that in 2008 Latinos comprised 14 percent of the total US population; of these, 58 percent go online, compared to 77 percent of non-Hispanic whites and 64 percent of non-Hispanic blacks. This, however, is not the case in the UK, where ethnic minority groups in fact have greater access to the internet, with 80 percent of them having broadband internet compared with 74 percent of the general population. Indeed, the Ofcom 2008 report on digital media shows that take-up, interest, volume of use, as well as confidence is higher among ethnic minority households compared with households in the UK generally. Statistics from Germany indicate that more than half of the immigrant population has online access compared to 63 percent of Germany as a whole (Initiative D-21, 2008).

Overall, these are not bad indicators for access to the internet, as they show that online participation is widening. However, caution should be inserted here, as findings suggest that access is primarily reserved for the younger, richer, and more educated members of ethnic minorities, while the older, poorer, and less-educated members tend to be excluded. On the whole, though, it seems that the democratic picture of the internet holds in terms of access as well. This may be attributed to the increase of internet penetration across the board, helped by lower prices for hardware as well as broadband subscription. Such optimistic observations, however, need to be tempered with some more sobering ones. Specifically, although access to the internet is increasing, thus lowering the threshold for participation, other divisions emerge. These are divisions in terms of knowledge, skills, and motivations. Thus, while it takes few skills to watch television and listen to the radio, the internet requires some familiarity with computers, the web, and the overall interactive spirit of the internet. It can therefore be said that the internet requires a different kind of media literacy, aimed specifically towards making users confident and literate in their use of electronic media.

If these are lines dividing minority (and other groups) in terms of being electronically literate or not, there are other divisions, which tend to be more significant in political terms: these concern the question of who is actually representing the community in online environments. Although in principle higher numbers of people from ethnic minority backgrounds are using the internet, in practice not all of them set up relevant websites, or indeed seek to represent their group when online. Rather, as we shall see later on, most internet use tends to be personal. To set up and maintain a website committed to the community requires not only skills, resources, and motivation, but also a level of commitment that is not shared by all. Thus, when it comes to the production of sites that concern the community as a whole, political and other divisions are expected to emerge. These divisions, however, can only be made clear through looking at the actual online contents. These will be discussed in the next section. For now, we can conclude, on the one hand, that production of offline content is more accessible to ethno-culturally distinct groups, and, on the other, that it (re)creates divisions within groups, in terms of age, education, skills, and resources, as well as in terms of politics and motivations.

12.3.2 Online content

The diversity of the internet makes it difficult to exhaust the contents and representations in a few paragraphs. What is perhaps more reasonable in this context is to identify the dimensions that are specific to online cultural diversity. Firstly, as with the offline media, content can be divided into representations concerning ethnicity/race by others and those by the community itself. To this extent, the regimes of representation encountered in offline media are expected to operate online as well. On the other hand, identity/otherness on the internet is obscured by the lack of self-disclosure and the practice of "passing." Users often do not refer to their ethnic identity, either purposely ("passing") or because they do not consider it relevant. In this sense, representations by self and other are blurred. But does this imply the absence of racist representations in online contexts? Probably not: rather, it involves the reconfiguration of racist representations along lines dictated by the new social landscape.

Following our earlier discussion, we can note three relevant aspects, differentiating online representations of cultural diversity. These include the relationship between cultural diversity and the new division of labor in technologically advanced societies; the relationship of ethno-cultural identities to their past traditions and territories; and their projections and imaginings of their future. The domain of the internet is part of the information economy, which divides labor across lines that differ from those of the peak period of industrial modernity; thus, as Lisa Nakamura argues (2002), race in cyberspace is "cybertyped" differently, because of the differentiated needs of the information economy. Moreover, as we noted earlier, ethnicity/race and more broadly cultural diversity are positioned differently in the network society: they either become defensive identities, seeking to protect their past histories and territories, leading to reactionary and conservative contents and representations, or they become project identities, positively contributing to the development of new subject positions that seek to redress injustice and inequality. Thus, the picture of online contents vis-à-vis ethnicity and race is a mixed and equivocal one, betraying some of the tensions within the network society, as well as the burdens of the heritage of early modernity and colonialism.

The racist regime of representation coded race and ethnicity in terms of attributes which allocated certain roles to racialized bodies. Thus, black bodies were mainly for physical work, while Arab bodies were fanatical and primitive, and Asian bodies devious and dangerous. To an extent cyberspace rewrites these representations and replicates them. This is because it serves another master: it is in the service no longer of industrial capitalism but of informational capitalism and consumer culture. Nevertheless it still operates with the codes, symbols, and divisions that it inherited from colonialism and industrialization. In writing on these topics, Lisa Nakamura (2002) uses the term cybertyping in order to describe the ways in which the internet (re)codes race and ethnicity. Nakamura's work shows that the divisions and stereotyping this time concern the highly technological Asians as opposed to blacks, who are either ignored or "cybertyped" as techno-primitive, among the "normal" whites. Nakamura describes the techno-Orientalism of cyberspace, especially as found in cyberpunk stories: here, just as in Said's Orientalism, the Orient is seen as exotic, mysterious, and ultimately ungovernable, but this time it is also projected in the future (Morley and Robins, 1995). This future is bizarre and anarchic, because of the appropriation of high-tech materials and the ways in which humans and machines have become enmeshed. Humanity is still understood as white, with black and Asian characters merely serving to define more sharply what this white humanity is about.

However, the lack of physical bodily presence in cyberspace allows for another relationship between race, body, and the (new) media. The main argument here, as Sherry Turkle (1995) has noted, is that people can experiment and play with other identities as they can assume any kind of identity they choose. This might appear to render the concept of race irrelevant for the internet, where a practice of "passing" for another identity may be common. Nakamura describes this phenomenon as "identity-tourism": people pick and choose different ethnic and racial identities as and when they like, taking pleasure in this shifting between identities. While on the one hand this kind of identity tourism may engage people with other identities and thus promote understanding, on the other it is not as innocuous as it seems. This is because it understands all identities as more or less aesthetic prostheses rather than involved in power differentials and suffering from material and symbolic inequalities. This identity swapping does not engage with the political projects of subverting identities, but rather it often replicates existing representations of techno-Orientalism and techno-primitivism. It further involves a naive understanding of multiculturalism as the colorful existence of multiple identities – often stripped from their embodiments, as in cyberspace we are all meant to be just "minds," but, as Nakamura puts is, "all singing the same corporate anthem" (2002: 99). In this respect, cyberspace engages both the racist regime of representation and the commodification of difference one.

But the internet is not exhausted in these. It further involves the construction of representations from the "inside" of the communities themselves by members who set up relevant sites to redress some of the material and symbolic inequalities they have been subjected to, as well as to speak with their own voices. While on the one hand these community-based websites articulate the concerns of minority communities, on the other they institute new divisions within communities. More specifically, research has documented the many positive aspects of community-related content on the internet. These include: the forging of links between transnational and dispersed communities; the articulation of political goals and an increased public visibility; and an overall empowerment of marginalized groups and communities (Franklin, 2001; Georgiou, 2002; Mehra *et al.*, 2004; Siapera, 2005, 2006a, 2006b, 2007).

Diasporic communities tend to be marginalized and disempowered because they are geographically dispersed and lack a common frame of reference with mainstream communities. The internet, as we saw earlier, operates beyond geographical borders and mobilizes a spatial logic that follows flows rather than proximity. It can therefore link such dispersed communities, which can create online a space that connects them, and allows them to communicate beyond the limitations imposed by geography. This linking between transnational communities can result in a kind of bottom-up experience of transnationalism (Georgiou, 2002), acting as a useful corrective to top-down, corporation-driven globalization. Sites such as Kurdish Media and New Vision, analyzed by Georgiou, show the possibilities of a unity without a centre and the creation of a new public space for members of these communities to find each other and communicate. Through the forging of such links and connections, dispersed and disenfranchised communities may find a new and louder voice. In addition, these communities can articulate and pursue political goals, which can include justice for their homeland, as in the case of Kurds and Palestinians (see, for instance, the Palestinian Solidarity site www.palestinecampaign.org), recognition for injustices (see the Armenian genocide site www.genocide1915.info) or a quest for more political participation by the community (see the controversial MPACUK site, www.mpacuk.org).

There is no doubt that such initiatives enhance the visibility and public presence of the community – this is especially significant given the marginalization and misrepresentation of cultural diversity in mainstream media. Thus, Parker and Song (2007), in their analysis of British Chinese websites, have found that they bring together a marginalized and almost invisible minority, and enable it to articulate its political demands. In this sense, such sites help community members to become more articulate and familiarize themselves with participation in the public domain – they are in this sense pre-political, as they prepare members for political participation (Siapera, 2004, 2005). At the same time, insofar as these sites address not only communities themselves but a general public, they set up links between different communities, thus promoting understanding and exchange and potentially contributing to a kind of conviviality (Siapera, 2007). From this point of view, posting online content supports and empowers community members as well as contributing to the forging of alliances with the general public.

There is, however, another side to the community-oriented posting of online contents, and it is not necessarily a positive one. This side concerns the actual representations of the community and related matters in online spaces which may end up creating new divisions and exclusions. The identity of the community is, as we have repeatedly argued, not a fixed and essential one, but rather a fluid and dynamic identity, changing and mutating across time and places. On the whole, internet participation supports and even enhances this kind of identity exploration (Georgiou, 2002; Nakamura, 2002). People can and do experiment with their identities in online spaces, trying on other identities, but also allowing themselves to express forbidden identities, such as sexual and gender identities. But community websites sometimes take it upon themselves to define and "police" the borders of the community, to accept and recognize certain identities, while marginalizing and excluding others. For example, some Muslim sites publish articles on the history and tradition of Islam and offer lifestyle advice from a Muslim point of view: however, such contents may be problematic because interpretations of history can be controversial and exclusionary, while such lifestyle advice, typically addressing women, tends to be patronizing and to infantilize women (Siapera, 2007). From this point of view, the community becomes divided into dependent members who need advice and those who give it – the dividing lines here tend to map onto gender ones. Another division effected here is between those deemed custodians of history and tradition and those who must "return" back to the ideals of this (imaginary) perfect community of the past.

Similarly, websites such as the US-based Hot Ghetto Mess site (www.hotghettomess.com) appear to "police" the community through sanctioning and promoting certain behaviors. The site is meant to pursue the political project of helping eradicate ghettos and some kinds of anti-social and otherwise problematic behaviors encountered in ghettos, through the public shaming of individuals, whose compromising photos are posted, rated, and commented upon. Notwithstanding the good intentions of the site, it inevitably ends up "policing" the black community, dictating what is acceptable and unacceptable behavior and images. Usually, those behaviors deemed acceptable ("not ghetto mess") seem to coincide with typical bourgeois success measured in money and prestige. In this manner such sites end up setting up a class and taste division within the community.

The broader problem here is that the political goals and the voice(s) of the community are in fact contentious and controversial. Political goals may not be shared by the community as a whole, while it also contains many voices, not all of which can reach online spaces. Insofar as this problem is not addressed, the potential for empowerment entailed in online communication will remain a promise rather than an actuality. On the other hand, internet use is spreading across the board, implying that, eventually, all the voices and political approaches may find an online outlet. Indeed, this is what Castells has argued: if certain issues do not find expression in already existing internet outlets, people will eventually set up their own sites for advocacy and representation of their goals. Although this may indeed appear as a solution to this problem, a word of caution should be inserted here: such developments may end up fragmenting the community and rendering it powerless rather than truly pluralizing it. This argument has been formulated more clearly by Cass Sunstein (2001), who describes a process of cyber-balkanization where people only meet online with those who are similar to them, never becoming exposed to oppositional or dissenting voices.

So far, therefore, the internet's contribution appears to be a replication of the offline media and to encounter the same typologies and dilemmas: a kind of a smorgasbord of identity (Nakamura, 2002) that harks to the domesticated and commodified difference regimes of representation; an oscillation between an essentialized version of identity and a fragmentation of the community; and a reproduction of the tenacious racist regime that subjects online ethnic identities to the same or similarly vicious stereotyping as in offline media. At best, therefore, the internet's contribution so far is similar to that of minority media, including some of the same pitfalls, such as the contentious intra-community politics. But, once more, the internet is not exhausted in these. The internet's uniqueness can be located in its interactivity, its ability to allow for discussing and exchanging communicative contents rather than merely publishing them (see Kiousis, 2002). This interactivity means that community websites and their contentious contents can be challenged directly, both from within the community and by others, who may question the claims put forward. Thus, an altogether better outcome may be reached through ensuring that all parts of the community are represented in the most popular and visible community sites. This will mean that all kinds of political and identity claims are subjected to internal (and external) debate and deliberation. Indeed, this may be a necessary step in order to ensure that the internet does not act as yet another medium for misrepresenting cultural diversity (Siapera, 2005).

The transformative potential of the internet can be therefore understood in part as its ability to democratize the community from within: to allow for contentious issues and understandings of identity to be discussed, rejected, or accepted by different community members. Again, however, this must be seen more as potential than actual: although the technology may provide the means by which it is accomplished, the actual contents that people post may in fact fall short of this deliberative process. But how do people actually use the internet? This will be discussed next.

12.3.3 Uses of the internet

If the production of online contents concerned – in this context – the issue of who is online and who has the capacity to produce online content, this section is concerned with the question of how the internet is used. Through identifying these uses, we can then empirically locate and test the contribution of the internet to cultural diversity. Research suggests that users from a cultural minority background employ the internet for personal and instrumental purposes (Georgiou, 2002; Siapera, 2004); and for public and political purposes (Franklin, 2004, 2007; Parker and Song, 2006a, 2006b, 2007; Siapera, 2005, 2007). In doing so, they politicize personal and identity aspects, while they also re-enact the political dilemmas of multiculturalism. But these uses, alongside the interactive aspects of the internet, end up renewing multicultural politics by allowing for a continuous rearticulation and struggle between contentious points.

It is a well-established fact that most internet use is personal – it is not an accident that email is one of the most successful and popular internet applications. Personal use of the internet includes using the internet to connect with and communicate with friends or in order to discuss personal issues and share personal experiences. Similarly, members of ethno-cultural minorities use the internet to connect and communicate with others either within the same country or transnationally. While relating personal information to one's friends does not have any obvious political benefits for one's community, sharing personal experiences connected to one's cultural identity may be politically significant in two ways: firstly, because it enables others to put themselves in one's place and empathize, thereby promoting understanding; and secondly, because it blurs the boundaries between the public and private domains with wider political implications.

Thus, in their research on Chinese and South Asian UK-based websites, Parker and Song (2006a, 2006b) found that users engage in the description, sharing, and discussion of racist incidents or insults as well as in the sharing of less noxious experiences. Similarly, expressing and sharing personal experiences is common in asylum seekers'/refugee websites (Siapera, 2004, 2005). This sharing of personal experiences and information marks an important departure from the type of communication encountered in both mainstream and minority offline media. It allows for an informal and personalized exchange that resembles interpersonal rather than (mass-) mediated communication. Yet, by being found in a public domain, it acquires a political significance: it lets people share in events and experiences, often shocking and offensive, other times less serious and even funny, thereby allowing people to empathize with others, and to form a kind of virtual relationship. Furthermore, it familiarizes non-community members with the kind of experiences encountered by culturally diverse communities in their everyday lives. Through this informality and sharing, personal information and communication promote intra- and intercultural understanding and familiarity.

At the same time, this personal usage of the internet has important ramifications for the construction of the identity of the community. Sharing experiences and posting content relating to one's position as a member of a culturally diverse community points to the ongoing construction of identity. Especially for those caught up between identities, personal internet use allows the exploration of experiences more closely linked to their own identity. For instance, Parker and Song (2006a) discuss the references in British Chinese websites to the "characteristically British Chinese childhood of working in the family takeaway business" (p. 185) as one of the ways in which this recounting of personal experiences helps shape and define the British Chinese identity. Parker and Song (2006a, 2006b) refer to this as "reflexive racialization": through exchanging personal information, opinions, and experiences people are able to reflect on the issues they face in a multicultural environment. Moreover, this online sharing of these personal experiences of multicultural life provide a bridge between the personal, private domain of experience and the public domain, where demands for social justice and equality can be articulated. It is in this manner that the lines separating the private and personal from the public and political are redrawn in online environments.

More broadly speaking, blurring of the boundaries between the public and private has important political consequences. In her work on the Samoan and Tongan diasporas, Marianne Franklin locates these in the rearticulation of the division by groups that it formerly excluded: women and non-Western others (2001, 2004). More specifically, the division between parts of life that are meant to be public and those delegated to the domestic sphere has been at the centre of European/Western modern understandings of politics and the role of the public sphere (see Habermas, 1989). Feminist critics have argued that this distinction has had the result of excluding important issues from the public domain – such as, for instance, the gendered role of motherhood and other issues concerning women (see Fraser, 1992). Post-colonial critics have similarly outlined the way in which colonial subjects have been seen as part of the private, domestic sphere, unable to articulate political or public speech. The distinction had become, in other words, a means for silencing certain groups. By publishing personal experiences and information online, such groups reclaim their voice, actively challenging not only their position as part of the private domain, but also the very distinction between the public and private (Franklin, 2001).

Political usage of the internet includes these uses that are aimed towards the distribution of power and resources, both symbolic and material ones. This political use has directly political consequences, often very beneficial for minorities. It includes the challenging of representations in mainstream media through coordinating and organizing responses. It further entails proper activism, in the sense of lobbying, protesting, and advocating a fairer deal for cultural minorities. Challenging offensive or stereotypical representations encountered in the mass media is becoming increasingly common, and it contributes to the completion of the circuit of mediation, in allowing for audiences to respond directly to the media. For instance, the MPACUK website has a "Media-Jihad" page, in which it publishes the emails and other contact details for most of the mainstream media in the UK, so that British Muslim audiences can address to them any concerns they have over their representation in particular programs. Parker and Song (2006a) describe how the British Born Chinese site challenged what they considered an offensive representation of the film *Crouching Tiger, Hidden Dragon* in the *Guardian* newspaper, eventually eliciting an apology. This kind of activity enables audiences to directly engage the media in rethinking their portrayals of cultural minorities. More direct activism and advocacy is aimed towards the community itself as well as the broader society: for instance, the UK-based website Imaan seeks recognition for Muslim gays and lesbians, while other sites allow for the direct lobbying of politicians, through emails or faxes.

The political use of the internet is, not surprisingly, contentious. This is in part because the political process itself entails struggle and contestation. But it also involves contentious politics within the community as to what is acceptable and as to which particular goals should be pursued. It further involves contention between the community and society as a whole, concerning the demands articulated by the former, which may well be seen as contentious by the latter. But the contribution of the internet does not lie in its ability to smooth out contentious issues and impose harmony. Quite the contrary, we can locate its contribution in allowing for such struggles to find an outlet, to be articulated and played out. In this manner, the internet contributes to multicultural politics not by providing any kind of solution to the dilemmas it involves, but because it allows for struggles between different positions, identities and ideologies to take place (Siapera, 2006a). In the end, multicultural politics is an arena of struggle between and within difference, and as such the internet appears to be its medium of choice. This is because the internet's open and interactive technology allows for this struggle to be ongoing and to resist closure. It is, finally, important to note that the technology of the internet is not enough; for this type of multicultural politics to be conducted, the personal/private and the public/political uses of the internet must assume a dual orientation: one aimed towards the inside of the community, allowing for the continuous deliberation over identities and goals, and one towards the "outside" or the broader society aimed at social justice and a fairer distribution of symbolic and material resources and power (Siapera, 2005; see Fraser, 1992).

12.4 Conclusions

What is, in the end, the difference that the internet makes for cultural diversity? Firstly, we have seen that new technologies are linked to broader societal changes, which render ethno-cultural diversity the norm rather than the exception. Manuel Castells argues that this is not necessarily a positive outcome, as ethnicity tends to graft on larger systems of signification and ideologies such as nationalism or religion, leading to polarization and conflict. On the other hand, however, new technologies entail a promise for social justice because of the ways in which they have contributed to the openness and democratization of production, representation and consumption. However, issues of digital divides and the persistence of racist and other negative regimes of representation point to problematic continuities between off- and online media.

But the specificity of the internet can be located in its interactivity, which provides the technologically supported possibility for the exchange of information, contestation of

Box 12.1 Summary of main points

- Network society: a society which is characterized by the coexistence of multiple and intersecting networks operating within and across geographical boundaries.
- Space of flows and timeless time (Manuel Castells), the two main parameters of the network society:
  - space of flows refers to the new principle of organizing space not according to proximity but according to flows or exchanges between the nodes that make up networks;
  - timeless time refers to the continuous, always on, undifferentiated time that characterizes networks.
- Internet and cultural diversity:
  - boundaries between production and consumption/use blurred;
  - production open and accessible to everyone with an internet connection and relevant skills; digital divides operate between and within communities;
  - online representations to some extent follow the regimes of representation encountered in offline media; but the internet allows for the multiplication and direct contestation of representations;
  - internet use can be personal/private and public/political, with the result that the distinction private/public is politicized and suspended; through these types of use, the internet becomes the medium of choice for multicultural politics, because it allows for the ongoing negotiation of identities, contestation of claims, and for the creation of new commonalities and connections within and between communities.

viewpoints and claims, and for the deliberation and discussion of issues of multicultural life. In this sense, the difference the internet makes can be summarized as follows: firstly, it allows for the proliferation and amplification of voices in the public domain; secondly, it links these voices and makes connections with others across geographical and cultural borders; thirdly, it provides a platform or a medium for multicultural politics and struggles within and between communities to take place. The internet and the associated societal changes hold a unique promise for multicultural politics; but the extent to which this promise is fulfilled ultimately depends on the ways in which people shape and subsequently employ this technology. Will the internet enable the tipping of the scale in favor of a cultural diversity that exists beyond limits and controls? Will it contribute to a shift in the central tension in mediated cultural diversity between control/containment and responses to these? Time eventually will tell. Until then, we can hope that people's struggles will seek to effect such a change.

Bibliography

Printed and Online Sources

Abu-Lughold, L. (2002), Do Muslim Women Really Need Saving? Anthropological Reflections on Cultural Relativism and Its Others, *American Anthropologist*, 104 (3): 783–90.

ACPI-EMI (2008), Estudio de Medios para Immigrantes: Resumen General 2008, Madrid: Spain, available at: www.acpi-emi.com/resumen_emi2008ok.pdf.

Adorno, T. (1990) *Negative Dialectics*, trans. E. B. Ashton, London and New York: Routledge.

Adorno, T., and Horkheimer, M. (1947/1997), *The Dialectic of the Enlightenment*, trans. J. Cumming, London: Verso.

Ahmed, L. (1992), *Women and Gender in Islam*, New Haven, CT: Yale University Press.

Aksoy, A., and Robins, K. (2000), Thinking across Spaces: Transnational Television from Turkey, *European Journal of Cultural Studies*, 3(3): 345–67.

Aksoy, A., and Robins, K. (2003), Banal Transnationalism: The Difference that Television Makes, in K. Karim (ed.), *The Media of Diaspora*, pp. 89–104, London and New York: Routledge.

Alibhai-Brown, Y. (2000), *After Multiculturalism*, London: Foreign Policy Centre.

Alibhai-Brown, Y. (2004). The Multicultural Excuse, *Connections*, Winter 2004–2005, Commission for Racial Equality, available at: www.cre.gov.uk/publs/connections/articles/04wi_excuse.html.

Allport, G. W. (1954). *The Nature of Prejudice*, Cambridge, MA: Addison-Wesley.

Altheide, D. (2004), Media Logic and Political Communication, *Political Communication*, 21: 293–6.

Altheide, D., and Snow, R. (1979), *Media Logic*, London: Sage.

Altheide, D., and Snow, R. (1988), Toward a Theory of Mediation, in J. A. Anderson (ed.), *Communication Yearbook*, 11, pp. 194–223, Thousand Oaks, CA: Sage.

Althusser, L. (1971), *Lenin and Philosophy and Other Essays*, trans. B. Brewster, New York and London: Monthly Review Press.

Anderson, B. (1983/1991), *Imagined Communities: Reflections on the Origin and Spread of Nationalism*, London: Verso.

Anderson, B. (2001), Western Nationalism and Eastern Nationalism: Is There a Difference That Matters?, *New Left Review*, May–June: 31–42.

Ang, I. (1991), *Desperately Seeking the Audience*, London and New York: Routledge.

Anon. (2004), Zoning is Undemocratic, *Nigerian Newsday*, August 11, 2004, available at: www.nasarawastate.org/newsday/news/nasarawa/10811181607.html.

Anthias, F. (1998), Evaluating Diaspora: Beyond Ethnicity, *Sociology*, 32(3): 557–80.

Aparicio, F. R. (1999), Reading the "Latino" in Latino Studies: Toward Re-imagining Our Academic Location, *Discourse*, 21(3): 3–18.

Appadurai, A. (1990), Disjuncture and Difference in the Global Cultural Economy, *Public Culture*, 2(2): 1–24.

Arendt, H. (1958/1998), *The Human Condition*, Chicago: University of Chicago Press.

Arendt, H. (1970), *Men in Hard Times*, New York: Harcourt.

Atton, C. (2002), *Alternative Media*, London: Sage.

Austin, J. L. (1962), *How to Do Things with Words*, Oxford: Clarendon Press.

Barker, M. (1981), *The New Racism*, London: Junction.

Barney, D. (2004), *The Network Society*, Cambridge: Polity Press.

Barthes, R. (1964), *Elements of Semiology*, trans. Annette Lavers and Colin Smith, New York: Hill and Wang.

Barthes, R. (1973), *Mythologies*, trans. Annette Lavers, London: Jonathan Cape.

Barthes, R. (1977), *Image, Music, Text*, trans. Stephen Heath, New York: Hill and Wang.

Baubock, R. (1999), Liberal Justifications for Ethnic Group Rights, in C. Joppke and S. Lukes (eds.), *Multicultural Questions*, pp. 133–57, Oxford: Oxford University Press.

BBC (2005), Sharia Law Move Quashed in Canada, September 12, 2005, available at: http://news.bbc.co.uk/2/hi/americas/4236762.stm.

Beck, U. (1992) *Risk Society: Towards a New Modernity*, London: Sage.

Beck, U. (2000), *What is Globalization?* Oxford: Blackwell.

Beecher Stowe, H. (1854/1999) *Uncle Tom's Cabin*, Ware: Wordsworth.

Bell, D. (1973), *The Coming of Post-Industrial Society*, New York: Basic Books.

Benhabib, S. (2002), *The Claims of Culture: Equality and Diversity in the Global Era*, Princeton, NJ: Princeton University Press.

Bennett, T., Savage, M., Silva, E., Warde, A., Gayo-Cal, M., and Wright, D. (2006), *Media Culture: The Social Organisation of Media Practices in Contemporary Britain*, London: BFI, available at: www3.open.ac.uk/events/2/2006116_42382_o1.doc.

Benson, R., and Neveu, E. (2005), *Bourdieu and the Journalistic Field*, Cambridge: Polity Press.

Bhabha, H. (1995), *The Location of Culture*, London and New York: Routledge.

Bhattacharyya, G., and Gabriel, J. (1994), Gurinder Chadha and The Apna Generation, *Third Text*, Summer 1994, pp. 55–63.

Bhattacharyya, H. (2003), Multiculturalism in Contemporary India, *International Journal on Multicultural Societies*, 5(2): 148–61, available at: www.unesco.org/shs/ijms/vol5/issue2/art4.

Billig, M. (1995), *Banal Nationalism*, London: Sage.

Billig, M. (2001), Humour and Hatred: The Racist Jokes of the Ku Klux Klan, *Discourse Society*, 12(3): 267–89.

Bissoondath, N. (1994) *Selling Illusions: The Cult of Multiculturalism in Canada*, London: Penguin.

Blumler, J. G., and Katz., E. (eds.) (1974), *The Uses of Mass Communications: Current Perspectives on Gratifications Research*, Thousand Oaks, CA: Sage.

Bogle, D. (1973/2006), *Toms, Coons, Mulattoes, Mammies and Bucks: An Interpretative History of Blacks in American Films*, New York: Continuum.

Bourdieu, P. (1984), *Distinction: A Social Critique of the Judgement of Taste*, trans. R. Nice, Cambridge, MA: Harvard University Press.

Bourdieu, P. (1986), The Forms of Capital, in J. G. Richardson (ed.), *Handbook for Theory and Research for the Sociology of Education*, pp. 241–58, New York: Greenwood Press.

Bourdieu, P. (1991), *Sociology in Question*, trans. R. Nice, London: Sage.

Bourdieu, P. (1993a) *Language and Symbolic Power*, trans. G. Raymond and M. Adamson, ed. J. Thompson, Cambridge, MA: Harvard University Press.

Bourdieu, P. (1993b) *The Field of Cultural Production*, trans. R. Johnson, New York: Columbia University Press.

Bourdieu, P. (1996), *The Rules of Art*, trans. S. Emmanuel, Palo Alto, CA: Stanford University Press.

Bourdieu, P. (1999), *On Television and Journalism*, trans. P. P. Ferguson, New York: New Press.

Bourdieu, P., and Wacquant, L. (1992), *An Invitation to Reflexive Sociology*, Chicago: University of Chicago Press.

Bruns, A. (2005), *Gatewatching: Collaborative Online News Production*, New York: Peter Lang.

Buffington, D., and Fraley, T. (2008), Skill in Black and White Negotiating: Media Images of Race in a Sporting Context, *Journal of Communication Inquiry*, 32(3): 292–310.

Butler, J. (1997), *Excitable Speech: A Politics of the Performative*, London: Routledge.

Cantle, T. (2001), *Community Cohesion: A Report of the Independent Review Team*, London: Home Office, available at: www.homeoffice.gov.uk/docs/community_cohesion.pdf.

Carey, J. (1989), *Communication as Culture*, Boston, MA: Unwin Hyman.

Carstens, S. (2003), Constructing Transnational Identities? Mass Media and the Malaysian Chinese Audience, *Ethnic and Racial Studies*, 26(2): 321–44.

Castells, M. (1996/2000), *The Rise of the Network Society*, Oxford: Blackwell.

Castells, M. (1997/2000), *End of Millennium*, Oxford: Blackwell.

Castells, M. (1998/2004), *The Power of Identity*, Oxford: Blackwell.

Castells, M. (2001), *The Internet Galaxy*, Oxford: Oxford University Press.

Castles, S., and Miller, A. (1993/2003), *The Age of Migration*, Basingstoke: Palgrave Macmillan.

CBC (2005), *Shariah Law: FAQs*, May 26, 2005, available at: www.cbc.ca/news/background/islam/shariah-law.html.

Chakrabarti, D. (2007), *Provincializing Europe: Postcolonial Thought and Historical Difference*, Princeton, NJ: Princeton University Press.

Christiansen, C. C. (2004), News Media Consumption among Immigrants in Europe, *Ethnicities*, 4(2): 185–207.

Clegg, J. (1994), *Fu Manchu and the Yellow Peril*, Oakhill: Trentham Books.

Collett, C. (2007), French Republican Ideas and Immigration, *Logos: A Journal of Modern Society and Culture*, 6(1–2), available at: www.logosjournal.com/issue_6.1-2/collet.htm.

Conversi, D. (2006), Mapping the Field: Theories of Nationalism and Ethnosymbolism, in S. E. Grosby and A. Leoussi (eds.), *Nationalism and Ethnosymbolism: History, Culture and Ethnicity in the Formation of Nations*, pp. 15–30, Edinburgh: Edinburgh University Press.

Cooper, B. (1998), "The White-Black Fault Line": Relevancy of Race and Racism in Spectators' Experiences of Spike Lee's *Do the Right Thing*, *Howard Journal of Communications*, 9(3): 205–28.

Cooper, E., and Jahoda, M. (1947), The Evasion of Propaganda: How Prejudiced People Respond to Anti-Prejudice Propaganda, *Journal of Psychology*, 23: 15–25.

Cottle, S. (2000), A Rock and a Hard Place: Making Ethnic Minority Television, in S. Cottle (ed.), *Ethnic Minorities and the Media: Changing Cultural Boundaries*, pp. 100–17, Maidenhead: Open University Press.

Couldry, N. (2003), Media, Symbolic Power and the Limits of Bourdieu's Field Theory, *Media@lse Electronic Working Papers*, 2, available at: www.lse.ac.uk/collections/media@lse/pdf/EWP2.pdf.

Couldry, N. (2008), Mediatization or Mediation? Alternative Understandings of the Emergent Space of Digital Storytelling, in *New Media and Society*, 10(3): 373–91.

Couldry, N., and Curran, J. (eds.) (2003), *Contesting Media Power: Alternative Media in a Networked World*, Lanham, MD: Rowman and Littlefield.

Croteau, D., and Hoynes, W. (2003), *Media Society: Industries, Images, and Audiences*, Thousand Oakes, CA: Pine Forge Press.

Cunningham, S. (2001), Popular Media as Public "Sphericules" for Diasporic Communities, *International Journal of Cultural Studies*, 4(2), 131–47.

Cunningham, S., and Sinclair, J. (eds.) (2001), *Floating Lives: Asian Diasporas and the Media*, Lanham, MD: Rowman and Littlefield.

Curran, J. (1991), Rethinking the Media as a Public Sphere, in P. Dahlgren, and C. Sparks (eds.), *Communication and Citizenship*, pp. 27–57, London: Routledge.

Curran, J. (1998), Crisis of Public Communication: A Reappraisal, in T. Liebes, J. Curran, and E. Katz (eds.), *Media, Ritual and Identity*, pp. 175–202, London and New York: Routledge.

D'Angelo, P. (2002), News Framing as a Multiparadigmatic Research Program: A Response to Entman, *Journal of Communication*, 52(4): 870–88.

Dahlgren, P. (1995), *Television and the Public Sphere: Citizenship, Democracy, and the Media*, London: Sage.

Dayan, D. (1998), Particularistic Media and Diasporic Identities, in T. Liebes, J. Curran, and E. Katz (eds.), *Media, Ritual and Identity*, pp. 103–13, London and New York: Routledge.

Dayan, D., and Katz, E. (1992), Media Events: *The Live Broadcasting of History*, Cambridge, MA: Harvard University Press.

de Certeau, M. (1984), *The Practice of Everyday Life*, trans. S. Rendall, Berkeley, CA: California University Press.

de Saussure, F. (1916/2006), *Course in General Linguistics*, trans. C. Sanders and M. Pires, Oxford: Oxford University Press.

Derrida, J. (1972/1988), Signature, Event, Context, in J. Derrida and S. Weber (eds.) *Limited Inc: Supplement to Glyph 2*, pp. 1–24, Evanston, IL: Northwestern University Press.

Derrida, J. (1988), Limited, Inc. abc …, in J. Derrida and S. Weber (eds.), *Limited Inc: Supplement to Glyph 2*, pp. 20–110, Evanston, IL: Northwestern University Press.

Diawara, M. (1993), Black Spectatorship: Problems of Identification and Resistance, in M. Diawara (ed.), *Black American Cinema*, pp. 211–20, London and New York: Routledge.

Downing, J. D. (2000) Radical Media: Rebellious Communication and Social Movements, London: Sage.

Downing, J., and Husband, C. (2005), *Representing Race*, London: Sage.

Doyle, G. (2002) *Media Ownership: The Economics and Politics of Convergence and Concentration in the UK and European Media*. London: Sage.

Dubois, L. (2004), *Avengers of the New World: The Story of the Haitian Revolution*, Cambridge, MA: Harvard University Press.

Ducille, A. (1994) Dyes and Dolls, Multicultural Barbie and the Merchandizing of Difference, *Differences*, 6(1): 46–67.

Embree, A. T. (1990), *Utopias in Conflict: Religion and Nationalism in Modern India*, Berkeley: University of California Press.

Entman, R. M. (1993), Framing: Toward Clarification of a Fractured Paradigm, *Journal of Communication* 43(4): 51–8.

Entman, R. M., and Rojecki, A. (2001), *The Black Image in the White Mind: Media and Race in America*, Chicago: University of Chicago Press.

European Broadcasting Union (2007), *A Toolkit*, available at: www.ebu.ch/CMSimages/en/toolkit%20low_tcm6-56142.pdf.

Fairclough, N. (1995), *Critical Discourse Analysis*, Harlow: Pearson Education.

Fanon, F. (1967), *The Wretched of the Earth*, New York: Grove.

Favell, A. (1998), *Philosophies of Integration*, Basingstoke: Palgrave Macmillan.

Fish, S. (1980), *Is There a Text in This Class?*, Cambridge, MA: Harvard University Press.

Fiske, J. (1987), *Television Culture: Popular Pleasures and Politics*, London: Methuen.

Ford, S., and Singh Chanda, G. (2002), Portrayals of Gender and Generation, East and West: Suzie Wong in the Noble House, *New Asia Academic Bulletin*, 18: 1–17, available at: http://sunzi1.lib.hku.hk/hkjo/view/35/3500494.pdf.

Foucault, M. (1966/2002), *The Order of Things: An Archaeology of the Human Sciences*, trans. A. Sheridan, London: Routledge.

Foucault, M. (1969/2002), *The Archaeology of Knowledge*, trans. A. M. Sheridan Smith, London: Routledge.

Foucault, M. (1977), *Discipline and Punish: The Birth of the Prison*, trans. A. Sheridan. New York: Vintage Books.

Foucault, M. (1978), *History of Sexuality*, trans. R. Hurley, vol. 1, London: Penguin.

Foucault, M. (1980), Truth and Power, in C. Gordon (ed.) *Power/Knowledge: Selected Interviews and Other Writings 1972–1977*, pp, 109–33, New York: Pantheon Books.

Foucault, M. (1982), The Subject and Power, in H. Dreyfus and P. Rabinow (eds.), Michel Foucault: *Beyond Structuralism and Hermeneutics*, pp. 208–36, Chicago: University of Chicago Press.

Franklin, M. I. (2001). Inside Out: Postcolonial Subjectivities and Everyday Life Online, *International Feminist Journal of Politics*, 3(3), 387–422.

Franklin, M. I. (2004), *Postcolonial Politics, the Internet, and Everyday Life: Pacific Traversals Online*, London and New York: Routledge.

Franklin, M. I. (2007), Democracy, Postcolonialism, and Everyday Life: Contesting the "Royal We" Online, in L. Dahlberg and E. Siapera (eds.), *The Internet and Radical Democracy: Exploring Theory and Practice*, pp. 168–90, New York and London: Palgrave Macmillan.

Fraser, N. (1992), Rethinking the Public Sphere: A Contribution to the Critique of Actually Existing Democracy, in C. Calhoun (ed.), *Habermas and the Public Sphere*, pp. 109–42, Cambridge, MA: MIT Press.

Fraser, N. (1997), *Justice Interruptus: Critical Reflections on the "Post-Socialist" Condition*, London and New York: Routledge.

Fraser, N. (1999), Social Justice in the Age of Identity Politics: Redistribution, Recognition, and Participation, in L. Ray and A. Sayer (eds.), *Culture and Economy after the Cultural Turn*, pp. 25–52, London: Sage.

Fraser, N. (2000) *Adding Insult to Injury: Social Justice and the Politics of Recognition*, ed. Kevin Olson, London: Verso.

Fraser, N. (2003), Social Justice in the Age of Identity Politics: Redistribution, Recognition and Participation, in N. Fraser and A. Honneth, *Redistribution or Recognition? A Political-Philosophical Exchange*, pp. 7–109, London: Verso.

Fraser, N., and Honneth, A. (2003), *Redistribution or Recognition? A Political-Philosophical Exchange*, trans J. Golb, J. Ingram, and C. Wilke, London: Verso.

Freud, S. (1991), *Jokes and Their Relation to the Unconscious*, Harmondsworth: Penguin.

Galtung, J., and Ruge, M. H. (1965), The Structure of Foreign News, *Journal of Peace Research*, 2(1): 64–90.

Gamson, W. (1992), *Talking Politics*, Cambridge: Cambridge University Press.

Gans, H. (1979), *Deciding What's News*, New York: Pantheon.

Geddes, A. (2003), *The Politics of Migration and Immigration in Europe*, London: Sage.

Geertz, C. (1973), *The Interpretation of Cultures*, New York: Basic Books.

Gellner, E. (1983), *Nations and Nationalism*, New York: Cornell University Press.

Georgiou, M. (2002), Les diasporas en ligne: une expérience concrète de transnationalisme, *Hommes et Migrations*, 1240: 10–18.

Georgiou, M. (2005a), Mapping Diasporic Media Cultures: A Transnational Cultural Approach to Exclusion, in R. Silverstone (ed.), *From Information to Communication: Media, Technology and Everyday Life in Europe*, pp. 33–52, London: Ashgate.

Georgiou, M. (2005b), Diasporic Media across Europe: Multicultural Societies and the Universalism-Particularism Continuum, *Journal of Ethnic and Migration Studies*, 31(3): 481–98.

Georgiou, M., and Siapera, E. (2006), Editorial, *Journal of International Cultural and Media Politics*, 2(3), special issue: *From Culture to Politics and Back: Revisiting Multiculturalism*: 243–7.

Georgiou, M., and Silverstone, R. (2005), Editorial, *Journal of Ethnic and Migration Studies*, 31(3), special issue: *Media and Minorities in Multicultural Europe*: 433–41.

Ghanem, S. I., and Wanta, W. (2001), Agenda-Setting and Spanish Cable News, *Journal of Broadcasting and Electronic Media*, 45(2): 277–89.

Giddens, A. (1990), *The Consequences of Modernity*, Cambridge: Polity Press.

Giddens, A. (1991), *Modernity and Self Identity*, Cambridge: Polity Press.

Gillespie, M. (1995), *Television, Ethnicity, and Cultural Change*, London: Routledge.

Gillespie, M. (2000), Transnational Communications and Diaspora Communities, in S. Cottle (ed.), *Ethnic Minorities and the Media: Changing Cultural Boundaries*, pp. 164–78, Maidenhead: Open University Press.

Gilliam, A. (1991), Women's Equality and National Liberation, in C. Mohanty, A. Russo, and L. Torres (eds.), *Third World Women and the Politics of Feminism*, pp. 215–36, Bloomington: Indiana University Press.

Gilroy, P. (1987), *There Ain't No Black in the Union Jack: The Cultural Politics of Race and Nation*, London: Hutchinson.

Gilroy, P. (1993), *The Black Atlantic: Modernity and Double Consciousness*, Cambridge, MA: Harvard University Press.

Gilroy, P. (1997), Diaspora and the Detours of Identity, in K. Woodward (ed.), *Identity and Difference*, pp. 299–343, London: Sage.

Gilroy, P. (2006), *Postcolonial Melancholia*, New York: Columbia University Press.

Girardelli, D. (2004), Commodified Identities: The Myth of Italian Food in the United States, *Journal of Communication Inquiry*, 28(4): 307–24.

Gitlin, T. (1998), Public Sphere or Public Sphericules, in T. Liebes, J. Curran, and E. Katz (eds.), *Media, Ritual and Identity*, pp. 168–74, London and New York: Routledge.

Glazer, N. (1975), *Affirmative Discrimination*, New York: Basic Books.

Glazer, N. (1997), *We are All Multiculturalists Now*, Cambridge, MA: Harvard University Press.

Goffman, E. (1974), *Frame Analysis: An Essay on the Organization of Experience*, New York: Harper and Row.

Golding, P., and Murdock, G. (1997), *The Political Economy of the Media*, London: Edward Elgar.

Gramsci, A. (1971), *Selection from the Prison Notebooks*, trans. Q. Hoare and G. Nowell, New York: International Publishers.

Gray, J. (1997), *Enlightenment's Wake: Politics and Culture at the Close of the Modern Age*, London and New York: Routledge.

Habermas, J. (1974), The Public Sphere: An Encyclopaedia Article, trans. S. Lennox and F. Lennox, *New German Critique*, 3: 49–55.

Habermas, J. (1989), *The Structural Transformation of the Public Sphere: An Inquiry into a Category of Bourgeois Society*, trans. T. Burger, Cambridge: Polity Press.

Habermas, J. (1992), Further Reflections on the Public Sphere, in C. Calhoun (ed.), *Habermas and the Public Sphere*, Cambridge, MA: MIT Press.

Habermas, J. (1994), Struggles for Recognition in the Democratic Constitutional State, in C. Taylor and A. Gutman (eds.), *Multiculturalism: Examining the Politics of Recognition*, pp. 107–48, Princeton, NJ, Princeton University Press.

Habermas, J. (1996), *Between Facts and Norms: Contributions to a Discourse Theory of Law and Democracy*, trans. William Rehg, Cambridge, MA: MIT Press.

Habermas, J. (1998), *The Inclusion of the Other*, ed. and trans. C. Cronin and P. de Greiff, Cambridge, MA, MIT Press.

Hall, S. (1980), Encoding/Decoding, in S. Hall, D. Hobson, A. Lowe, and P. Willis (eds.), *Culture, Media, Language*, pp. 128–38, London: Hutchinson.

Hall, S. (1990), Cultural Identity and Diaspora, in J. Rutherford (ed.), Identi*ty: Community, Culture, Difference*, pp. 222–37, London: Lawrence and Wishart.

Hall, S. (1992). What Is This "Black" in Black Popular Culture? in G. Dent (ed.), *Black Popular Culture*, pp. 21–33, Seattle, WA: Bay Press.

Hall, S. (1996), New Ethnicities, in S. Hall, D. Morley, and K.-H. Chen (eds.), *Stuart Hall: Critical Dialogues in Cultural Studies*, London: Routledge.

Hall, S. (1997), The Work of Representation, in S. Hall (ed.), *Representation: Cultural Representations and Signifying Practices*, pp. 1–74, London and Thousand Oaks, CA: Sage.

Hallin, D., and Mancini, P. (2004), *Comparing Media Systems: Three Models of Media and Politics*, Cambridge: Cambridge University Press.

Hamelink, C. J. (1993), Europe and the Democratic Deficit, *Media Development*, 140(4): 8–11.

Harindranath, R. (2000), Ethnicity, National Culture(s), and the Interpretation of Television, in S. Cottle (ed.), *Ethnic Minorities and the Media: Changing Cultural Boundaries*, pp.149–163, Maidenhead: The Open University Press.

Hartley, J. (1999), *Uses of Television*, London and New York: Routledge.

Hastings, A. (1997), *The Construction of Nationhood: Ethnicity, Religion and Nationalism*, Cambridge: Cambridge University Press.

Held, D. (1999), The Transformation of Political Community: Rethinking Democracy in the Context of Globalization, in I. Shapiro and C. Hacker-Cordón (eds.), *Democracy's Edges*, pp. 84–111, Cambridge: Cambridge University Press.

Herman, E. S., and Chomsky, N. (1988) *Manufacturing Consent: The Political Economy of the Mass Media*, New York: Pantheon.

Hervik, P., and Berg, C. (2007) Denmark: A Political Struggle in Danish Journalism, in A. Kunelius, R. Eide, E. Hahn, and O. Schroeder (eds.), *Reading the Mohammed Cartoons Controversy. An International Analysis of Press Discourses on Free Speech and Political Spin*. pp. 25–40, Bochum and Freiburg: Projektverlag.

Hesmondhalgh, D. (2006), Bourdieu, the Media and Cultural Production, *Media, Culture and Society*, 28(2), 211–31.

Hobsbawm, E., and T. Ranger (eds.) (1983), *The Invention of Tradition*, Cambridge: Cambridge University Press.

Hodge, R., and Kress, G. (1988), *Social Semiotics*, Cambridge: Polity Press.

Honneth, A. (1995), *The Struggle for Recognition: The Moral Grammar of Social Conflicts*, trans. J. Anderson, Cambridge, MA: MIT Press.

Honneth, A. (2001), Recognition or Redistribution? Changing Perspectives on the Moral Order of Society, *Theory, Culture and Society*, 18(2–3): 43–55.

hooks, b. (1992), *Black Looks: Race and Representation*, Boston, MA: South End Press.

hooks, b. (1994), Sexism and Misogyny: Who Takes the Rap? Misogyny, Gangsta Rap, and the Piano, *Z Magazine*, February: 26–9.

Hovland, C. I., Lumsdaine, A., and Sheffield, F. D. (1949), *Experiments on Mass Communication*, Princeton, NJ: Princeton University Press.

Hudabiunigg, I. (2004), The Otherness of Eastern Europe, in *Journal of Multilingual and Multicultural Development*, 25(5): 369–88.

Huntington, S. (2004), *Who Are We? The Challenges to America's National Identity*, New York: Simon and Schuster.

Husband, C. (1994) (ed.), *A Richer Vision: The Development of Ethnic Minority Media in Western Democracies*, London: Unesco/John Libbey

Husband, C. (2000), Media and the Public Sphere in Multi-Ethnic Societies, in S. Cottle (ed.), *Ethnic Minorities and the Media*, pp.199–215, Maidenhead: Open University Press.

Hussain, M. (2000), Islam, Media and Minorities in Denmark, *Current Sociology*, 48(4): 95–116.

Hussain, M. (2007), The Cartoons Controversy and the Danish Press, *Quaderns del CAC*, 27: 47–58.

Hyman, H. H., and Sheatsley, P. B. (1947), Some Reasons Why Information Campaigns Fail, *Public Opinion Quarterly*, 11: 413–23.

Initiative D-21 (2008) *(N)Onliner Atlas: Deutschlands größte Studie zur Nutzung und Nicht-Nutzung des Internets*, available at: www.initiatived21.de/category/nonliner-atlas

Innis, H. A. (1950), *Empire and Communications*, Victoria, BC: Press Porcepic.

Innis, H. A. (1951), *The Bias of Communication*, Toronto: University of Toronto Press.

Iordanova, D. (2001), *Cinema of Flames: Balkan Film, Culture and the Media*, London: BFI Publishing.

Irizarry, J. G. (2007), Ethnic and Urban Intersections in the Classroom: Latino Students, Hybrid Identities, and Culturally Responsive Pedagogy, *Multicultural Perspectives*, 9(3): 21–8.

Jankowski, N. W. (2002), The Conceptual Contours of Community Media, in N. Jankowski and O. Prehn (eds.), *Community Media in the Information Age: Perspectives and Prospects*, pp. 3–18, Cresskill, NJ: Hampton Press.

Jay, M. (1996), *The Dialectical Imagination: A History of the Frankfurt School and the Institute of Social Research, 1923–1950*, Berkeley: University of California Press.

Jega, A. (2007), *Democracy, Good Governance and Development in Nigeria*, Ibidan: Spectrum Books.

Jenkins, H. (1992), *Textual Poachers: Television Fans and Participatory Culture*, New York: Routledge.

Jhally, S., and Lewis, J. (1992), *Enlightened Racism: "Cosby Show," Audiences and the Myth of the American Dream, Boulder*, CO: Westview Press.

Joppke, C. (1996), Multiculturalism and Immigration: A Comparison of the United States, Germany, and Great Britain, *Theory and Society*, 25(4): 449–500.

Joppke, C. (2007), Beyond National Models: Civic Integration Policies for Immigrants in Western Europe, *West European Politics*, 30(1): 1–22.

Jowett, G., Jarvie, I. C., Fuller, K. H., Fuller-Seeley, K. (1996), *Children and the Movies: Media Influence and the Payne Fund Controversy*, Cambridge: Cambridge University Press.

Katz, D., and Braly, K. W. (1933). Racial Stereotypes of One-Hundred College Students, *Journal of Abnormal and Social Psychology*, 28: 280–90.

Katz, E., and Lazarsfeld, P. (1955/2006), *Personal Influence: The Part Played by People in the Flow of Mass Communication*. New Brunswick, NJ: Transaction Publishers.

Keane, J. (1991), *The Media and Democracy*, Cambridge: Polity Press.

Keane, J. (1998), *Civil Society: Old Images, New Visions*, Cambridge: Polity Press.

Kiousis, S. (2002), Interactivity: A Concept Explication, *New Media Society*, 4(3): 355–83.

Kitzinger, J., and Miller, D. (1992), "African Aids": The Media and Audience Beliefs, in P. Aggleton, P. M. Davies, and G. Hart (eds.), *AIDS: Rights, Risk, and Reason*, pp. 28–52, London: Taylor and Francis.

Kivisto, P. (2002), *Multiculturalism in a Global Society*, Malden, MA: Blackwell.

Klapper, J. (1960), *The Effects of Mass Communication*, Glencoe, IL: Free Press.

Klaus, E., and Kassel, S. (2005), The veil as a means of legitimization: An analysis of the inter-connectedness of gender, media and war, *Journalism*, 6(3): 335–55.

Kristensen, L. (2007), Divergent Accounts of Equivalent Narratives: Russian-Swedish *Interdevochka* Meets Swedish-Russian *Lilya 4-ever*, *Journal of Multidisciplinary International Studies*, 4(2): 1–22.

Kymlicka, W. (1995), *Multicultural Citizenship: A Liberal Theory of Minority Rights*, Oxford: Oxford University Press.

Lévi-Strauss, C. (1963), *The Structural Study of Myth*, trans. C. Jacobson and B. Grundfest Schoepf, New York: Basic Books.

Lévi-Strauss, C. (1970), *The Raw and the Cooked*, trans. J. and D. Weightman, New York: Harper and Row.

Lewis, B. (1982), The Question of Orientalism, *New York Review of Books*, June 24, 1982.

Liebes, T., and Katz, E. (1993), *The Export of Meaning*, Oxford: Blackwell.

Lippmann, W. (1922/2004), *Public Opinion*, New York: Courier Dover Publications.

Livingstone, S. (1998a) Audience Research at the Crossroads, *European Journal of Cultural Studies*, 1(2): 193–217.

Livingstone, S. (1998b) Relationships Between Media and Audiences: Prospects for Audience Reception Studies, in T. Liebes, and J. Curran (eds.), *Media, Ritual and Identity*, pp. 237–55. London: Routledge.

Livingstone, S. (2000) Television and the Active Audience, in D. Fleming, H. A. Giroux, and L. Grossberg (eds.), *Formations: A 21st Century Media Studies Textbook*, pp. 175–95, Manchester: Manchester University Press.

Livingstone, S., and Lunt, P. (1994) *Talk on Television: Audience Participation and Public Debate*. London: Routledge.

Lohmeier, C. (2007), Contesting the Press: Miami Cubans, *The Miami Herald* and *El Nuevo Herald*, paper presented at *Mediations of Cultural Difference: Debating Media and Diversity*, ECREA Diasporas, Media and Migrations Section Workshop, Leeds, September 2007.

Lubiano, W. (1997), But Compared to What? Reading Realism, Representation, and Essentialism in *School Daze*, *Do the Right Thing* and the Spike Lee Discourse, in V. Smith (ed.) *Representing Blackness: Issues in Film and Video*, pp. 97–122, New Brunswick, NJ: Rutgers University Press.

Lyotard, J.-F. (1984), *The Postmodern Condition: A Report on Knowledge*, Minneapolis: University of Minnesota Press.

MacDonald, M. (2006), Muslim Women and the Veil: Problems of Image and Voice in Media Representations, *Feminist Media Studies*, 6(1): 7–23.

McGreal, C. (2007), Ruling Party Candidate Wins "Flawed" Nigerian Election, *The Guardian*, April 23, available at: www.guardian.co.uk/world/2007/apr/23/chrismcgreal.

McLeod, K. (1999), Authenticity within Hip-Hop and Other Cultures Threatened with Assimilation, *Journal of Communication*, 49(4): 134–50.

McLuhan, M. (1964), *Understanding Media: The Extensions of Man*, London: McGraw-Hill.

McLuhan, M., and Fiore, Q. (1967), *The Medium is the Massage*, New York: Bantam Books.

McQuail, D. (2005), *McQuail's Mass Communication Theory* (5th edition), London: Sage.

McRoberts, K. (1997), *Misconceiving Canada: The Struggle for National Unity*, Oxford: Oxford University Press.

Madianou, M. (2005), *Mediating the Nation*, London: UCL Press.

Malik, K. (2005), Making a Difference: Culture, Race and Social Policy, *Patterns of Prejudice*, 39(4): 361–78.

Malik, S. (2002), *Representing Black Britain*, London: Sage.

Mamdani, M. (2004), *Good Muslim Bad Muslim: America, the Cold War, and the Roots of Terror*, New York: Pantheon Books.

Mann, M. (1997), Has Globalization Ended the Rise and Rise of the Nation-State? *Review of International Political Economy*, 4(3): 472–96.

Marchetti, G. (1993), *Romance and the "Yellow Peril": Race, Sex and Discursive Strategies in Hollywood Fiction*. Berkeley: University of California Press.

Martín Barbero, J. (1993), *Communication, Culture and Hegemony: From the Media to Mediations*, trans. E. Fox, London: Sage.

Marx, K., and Engels, F. (2001), *The German Ideology Part One, with Selections from Parts Two and Three, together with Marx's "Introduction to a Critique of Political Economy,"* New York: International Publishers.

Matar, D. (2006), The Palestinians in Britain, News and the Politics of Recognition, *International Journal of Media and Cultural Politics*, 3(2): 317–30.

Meadows, M., and Molnar, H. (2002) Bridging the Gaps: Towards a History of Indigenous Media in Australia, *Media History* 8(1): 9–20.

Means Coleman, R. (2002). Black Sitcom Portrayals: The Good, the Bad, and the Worse, in G. Dines and J. Humez (eds.), *Gender, Race, and Class in the Media*, pp. 79–88, London and Thousand Oaks, CA: Sage.

Mehra, B., Merkel, C., and Peterson Bishop, A. (2004), The Internet for Empowerment of Minority and Marginalized Users, *New Media and Society* 6(6): 781–802.

Mercer, K. (1994), *Welcome to the Jungle: New Positions in Black Cultural Studies*, London and New York: Routledge.

Merton, R. K. (1948), The Self-Fulfilling Prophecy, *The Antioch Review*, 8: 193–210.

Mitra, S. (2001), Constitutional Design, Democratic Vote Counting, and India's Fortuitous Multiculturalism, *Heidelberg Papers in South Asian and Comparative Politics*, Working Paper No. 4, available at: http://archiv.ub.uni-heidelberg.de/volltextserver/volltexte/2003/4009/pdf/hpsacp4.pdf.

Modood, T. (2006), The Liberal Dilemma: Integration or Vilification? *International Migration*, 44(5): 5–7.

Modood, T., Hansen, R., Bleick, E., O'Leary, B., and Carens, J. (2006), The Danish Cartoon Affair: Free Speech, Racism, Islamism, and Integration, *International Migration*, special issue, 44(5): 4–62.

Molina Guzman, I. (2006), Mediating *Frida*: Negotiating Discourses of Latina/o Authenticity in Global Media Representations of Ethnic Identity, *Critical Studies in Media Communication*, 23(3): 232–51.

Molnar, H., and Meadows, M. (2001), *Songlines to Satellites: Indigenous Communication in Australia, the South Pacific and Canada*, Sydney: Pluto Press.

Morawska, E. (2008), The Recognition Politics of Polish Radio MultiKulti in Berlin, *Journal of Ethnic and Migration Studies*, 34(8): 1323–35.

Morley, D. (1980), *The Nationwide Audience: Structure and Decoding*, London: BFI.

Morley, D., and Robins, K. (1995), *Spaces of Identity: Global Media, Electronic Landscapes and Cultural Boundaries*, London and New York: Routledge.

Mosco, V. (1996), *The Political Economy of Communication: Rethinking and Renewal*, London and New York: Sage

Murdock, G., and Golding, P. (1974) For a Political Economy of Mass Communications, in R. Miliband and J. Saville (eds.), *Socialist Register*, pp. 205–34, London: Merlin Press.

Naficy, H. (1993), *The Making of Exile Cultures: Iranian Television in Los Angeles*, Minneapolis: University of Minnesota Press.

Naficy, H. (2003), Narrowcasting in Diaspora: Middle Eastern Television in Los Angeles, in K. Karim (ed.), *The Media of Diaspora*, pp. 51–62, London and New York: Routledge.

Nairn, T. (1977) *The Break-up of Britain: Crisis and Neonationalism*, London: NLB.

Nakamura, L. (2002), *Cybertypes: Race, Ethnicity, and Identity on the Internet*, London and New York: Routledge.

Nederveen Pieterse, J. (2004), *Globalization and Culture: Global Mélange*, Lanham, MD: Rowman and Littlefield.

Nmehielle, V. O. O. (2004), Sharia Law in the Northern States of Nigeria: To Implement or not to Implement, the Constitutionality Is the Question, *Human Rights Quarterly*, 26(3): 730–59.

Oakes, P. J., Haslam, S. A., and Turner, J. C. (1994), *Stereotyping and Social Reality*. Oxford and Cambridge, MA: Blackwell.

Obi, C. I. (2001), *The Changing Forms of Identity Politics in Nigeria under Economic Adjustment: The Case of the Oil Minorities Movement of the Niger Delta*, Uppsala: Nordic Africa Institute.

Ofcom, 2007a, *Ofcom Annual Report, 2007–2008*, available at: www.ofcom.org.uk/about/accoun/reports_plans/annrep0708/public/.

Ofcom, 2007b, *Communications Market Special Report: Ethnic Minority Groups and Communications Services*, available at: www.ofcom.org.uk/research/cm/ethnic_minority/ethnic_grps.pdf.

Ofcom (2008), *The Communications Market 2008*, available at: www.ofcom.org.uk/research/cm/cmr08/.

Ogan, C. (2001), *Communication and Identity in the Diaspora: Turkish Migrants in Amsterdam and the Impact of Satellite Television*, Lanham, MD: Lexington Books.

O'Leary, B. (1998) Ernest Gellner's Diagnoses of Nationalism: A Critical Overview, or, What Is Living and What Is Dead in Ernest Gellner's Philosophy of Nationalism?, in John A. Hall (ed.), *The State of the Nation: Ernest Gellner and the Theory of Nationalism*, pp. 40–88. Cambridge: Cambridge University Press.

Ong., W. (1982), *Orality and Literacy: The Technologizing of the Word*, London and New York: Routledge.

O'Reilly, T. (2005) *What Is Web 2.0? Design Patterns and Business Models for the Next Generation of Software*, Sebastopol, CA: O'Reilly Media, available at: http://oreilly.com/web2/archive/what-is-web-20.html.

Paden, J. (2008), *Faith and Politics in Nigeria: Nigeria as a Pivotal State in the Muslim World*, Washington, DC: US Institute of Peace Press.

Papastergiadis, N. (2005), Hybridity and Ambivalence: Places and Flows in Contemporary Art and Culture, *Theory, Culture and Society*, 22 (4): 39–64.

Parekh, B. (2000), *The Future of Multi-Ethnic Britain*, London: Runnymede Trust.

Parker, D., and Song, M. (2006a), Ethnicity, Social Capital and the Internet: British Chinese Websites, *Ethnicities*, 6: 178–202.

Parker, D., and Song, M. (2006b), New Ethnicities Online: Reflexive Racialization and the Internet, *Sociological Review*, 54(3): 575–94.

Parker, D., and Song, M. (2007), Inclusion, Participation and the Emergence of British Chinese Websites, *Journal of Ethnic and Migration Studies*, 33(7): 1043–61.

Peterson, R. C., and Thurstone, L. L. (1933), *The Effects of Motion Pictures on the Social Attitudes of High School Children*, Chicago: University of Chicago Press.

Pew Internet and American Life Project (2008), *Tracking Survey: Who's Online?*, table available at: www.pewinternet.org/Data-Tools/Download-Data/~/media/Infographics/Trend%20Data/January%202009%20updates/Demographics%20of%20Internet%20Users%201%206%2009.jpg.

Phillips, T. (2005), Civil Service Race Equality Network Annual Lecture, transcript available at: www.cre.gov.uk/Default.aspx?LocID=0hgnew03z#top.

Polanyi, K. (1944/2001), *The Great Transformation: The Political and Economic Origins of Our Time*, Boston, MA: Beacon Press.

Poole, E. (2001), Interpreting Islam: British Muslims and the British Press, in K. Ross and P. Playdon (eds.), *Black Marks: Minority Ethnic Audiences and Media*, pp. 67–86, Aldershot: Ashgate.

Putnam, R. (1995), Bowling Alone: America's Declining Social Capital, *Journal of Democracy*, 6(1), 65–78.

Radway, J. (1984), *Reading the Romance, Women, Patriarchy and Pop Literature*, Chapel Hill: University of North Carolina Press.

Radway, J. (1987) Reading *Reading the Romance*, in J. Radway, *Reading the Romance*, pp. 1–18, London: Verso.

Retis, J. (2007), Non European Immigrants and Spanish Media: From the Construction of Social Representation to the Production of Ethnic Media, paper presented at *Mediations of Cultural Difference: Debating Media and Diversity*, ECREA Diasporas, Media and Migrations Section Workshop, Leeds, September 2007.

Riggins, H. (ed.) (1992), *Ethnic Minority Media: An International Perspective*, Thousand Oakes, CA: Sage.

Rigoni, I. (2002), *Turkish and Kurdish Media Production in Europe: A Comprehensive Overview*, EMTEL project report, available at: www.lse.ac.uk/collections/EMTEL/Minorities/papers/turkishkurdimedia.pdf.

Rigoni, I. (2005), Challenging Notions and Practices: The Muslim Media in Britain and France, *Journal of Ethnic and Migration Studies*, 31(3): 563–80.

Robertson, R. (1992), *Globalization: Social Theory and Global Culture*, London: Sage.

Rockler, N. (2002), Race, Whiteness, "Lightness," and Relevance: African American and European American Interpretations of *Jump Start* and *The Boondocks, Critical Studies in Media Communication*, 19(4): 398–418.

Ross, K. (2000), In Whose Image? TV Criticism and Black Minority Viewers, in S. Cottle (ed.), *Ethnic Minorities and the Media: Changing Cultural Boundaries*, pp. 133–49, Maidenhead: Open University Press.

Rougheri, C. (1998), *Positive and Negative Stereotypes of Internal Minorities and Neighboring Peoples in the Greek Press*, Greek Helsinki Monitor Report, available at: www.greekhelsinki.gr/english/media/sum-oct97-mar98.html.

Rushdie, S. (1982), *Midnight's Children*, London: Picador.

Said, E. (1979), *Orientalism*, New York: Vintage Books.

Said, E. (1982), Orientalism: An Exchange, *New York Review of Books*, August 12.

Said, E. (1994), *Culture and Imperialism*, New York: 1st Vintage Books.

Scannel, P. (1989), Public Service Broadcasting and Modern Public Life, *Media, Culture and Society*, 11(2): 135–66.

Schlesinger, A. (1992), *The Disuniting of America*, Knoxville, TN: Whittle Direct Books.

Schroder, K. C. (1994), Audience Semiotics, Interpretive Communities and the "Ethnographic Turn" in Media Research, *Media, Culture and Society*, 16(2): 337–47.

Schudson, M. (2005), Four Approaches to the Sociology of News, in James Curran and Michael Gurevich (eds.), *Mass Media and Society* (4th edition), London: Hodder Arnold.

Schulz, W. (2004) Reconstructing Mediatization as an Analytical Concept, *European Journal of Communication*, 19(1): 87–101.

Shachar, A. (2001), Two Critiques of Multiculturalism, *Cardoso Law Review*, 23: 253–97.

Shim, D. (1998), From Yellow Peril through Model Minority to Renewed Yellow Peril, *Journal of Communication Inquiry*, 22(4): 385–409.

Shohat, E., and Stam, R. (2007), Culture Debates in Translation, in R. Krishnaswamy and J. C. Hawley (eds.), *The Postcolonial and the Global*, pp. 124–33, Minneapolis: University of Minnesota Press, 2007.

Siapera, E. (2004), Asylum Politics, the Internet and the Public Sphere, *Javnost/The Public*, 11(1): 79–100.

Siapera, E. (2005), Minority Activism on the Web: Between Deliberative Democracy and Multiculturalism, *Journal of Ethnic and Migration Studies*, 31(3): 499–519.

Siapera, E. (2006a), Multiculturalism Online: The Internet and the Dilemmas of Multicultural Politics, *European Journal of Cultural Studies*, 9(1): 5–24.

Siapera, E. (2006b), Islam, the Internet and Multicultural Politics, *International Journal of Media and Cultural Politics*, 2(3), pp. 331–46.

Siapera, E. (2007), Radical Democratic Politics and Online Islam, in L. Dahlberg and E. Siapera (eds.), *Radical Democracy and the Internet*, pp. 148–67, Basingstoke: Palgrave Macmillan.

Silverman, M. (1992). *Deconstructing the Nation: Immigration, Racism and Citizenship in Modern France*. London: Routledge.

Silverstone, R. (1994), *Television and Everyday Life*, London: Routledge.

Silverstone, R. (2005), The Sociology of Mediation and Communication, in C. Calhoun, C. Rojek, and B. Turner (eds.), *The Sage Handbook of Sociology*, pp. 188–207, London: Sage.

Silverstone, R. (2006), *Media and Morality: On the Rise of the Mediapolis*, Cambridge: Polity Press.

Smith, A. (1983), Nationalism and Classical Social Theory, *British Journal of Sociology*, 34(1): 19–38.

Smith, A. (1986), *The Ethnic Origins of Nations*, Oxford: Blackwell.

Smith, A. D. (1998), *Nationalism and Modernism: A Critical Survey of Recent Theories of Nations and Nationalism*, London: Routledge.

Smith, A. D. (2000) Theories of Nationalism, in M. Leifer (ed.), *Asian Nationalism*, pp. 1–20, London: Routledge.

Smythe, D. (1981), *Dependency Road: Communications, Capitalism, Consciousness, and Canada*, Norwood, NJ: Ablex.

Snow, D. A., Rochford, B., Jr., Worden, S. K., and Benford, R. D. (1986), Frame Alignment Processes, Micromobilization, and Movement Participation, *American Sociological Review* 51: 464–81.

Spivak, G. C. (1996), *The Spivak Reader: Selected Works of Gayatri Chakravorty Spivak*, ed. D. Landry and G. MacLean. London and New York: Routledge.

Stabile, C., and Kumar, D. (2005), Unveiling Imperialism: Media, Gender and the War on Afghanistan, in *Media, Culture and Society*, 27(5): 765–82.

Stokes, M. (2007), *D. W. Griffith's* The Birth of a Nation: *A History of "the Most Controversial Motion Picture of all Time,"* Oxford: Oxford University Press.

Sunstein, C. (2001), *Republic.Com*, Princeton, NJ: Princeton University Press.

Tajfel, H. (1981), *Human Groups and Social Categories: Studies in Social Psychology*, Cambridge: Cambridge University Press.

Tajfel, H., and Turner, J. C. (1986), The Social Identity Theory of Inter-Group Behavior, in S. Worchel and L. W. Austin (eds.), *Psychology of Intergroup Relations*, pp. 7–24, Chicago: Nelson-Hall.

Taubman, G. (1998), A Not-So World Wide Web: The Internet, China, and the Challenges to Nondemocratic Rule, *Political Communication* 15: 255–72.

Taylor, C. (1994), The Politics of Recognition, in C. Taylor and A. Guttman (eds.), *Multiculturalism: Examining the Politics of Recognition*, pp. 107–45, Princeton, NJ: Princeton University Press.

Tempelman, S. (1999), Constructions of Cultural Identity: Multiculturalism and Exclusion, *Political Studies*, 47(1), 17–31.

Tharoor, S. (2007), India's Unique Multiculturalism, speech to the Asian Society, October 17, New York City, available at: http://www.youtube.com/watch?v=dr519YB6xko.

Thompson, A. (ed.) (2007), *The Media and the Rwanda Genocide*, London and Ann Arbor, MI: Pluto Press.

Thompson, J. B. (1995), *The Media and Modernity*, Cambridge: Cambridge University Press.

Thompson, S. (2006), *The Political Theory of Recognition: A Critical Introduction*, Cambridge: Polity Press.

Tinic, S. A. (1997), United Colors and Untied Meanings: Benetton and the Commodification of Social Issues, *Journal of Communication*, 47(3): 3–25.

Tully, J. (2000), Struggles over Recognition and Distribution, *Constellations* 7(4): 469–81.

Turkle, S. (1995), *Life on the Screen: Identity in the Age of the Internet*, Cambridge, MA: MIT Press.

Turner, J. C. (1984), Social Identification and Psychological Group Formation, in H. Tajfel (ed.), *The Social Dimension: European Studies in Social Psychology*, vol. 2, pp. 518–38, Cambridge: Cambridge University Press.

Turner, J. C. (1985), Social Categorization and the Self-Concept: A Social Cognitive Theory of Group Behaviour, *Advances in Group Processes*, 2: 77–122.

van den Berghe, P. (1967), *Race and Racism: A Comparative Perspective*, New York and Sydney: Wiley.

van Dijk, T. A. (1988), *News as Discourse*, Hillsdale, NJ: Lawrence Erlbaum Associates.

van Dijk, T. A. (1991), *Racism and the Press*, London: Routledge.

van Dijk, T. A. (1993), *Elite Discourse and Racism*. Newbury Park, CA: Sage Publications.

van Zoonen, L. (1991), The Tyranny of Intimacy: Women, Femininity and Television News, in P. Dahlgren and C. Sparks (eds), *Communication and Citizenship*, pp. 217–35, London: Routledge.

Van Zoonen, L. (1994), *Feminist Media Studies*, London: Sage.

Vertovec, S. (2000), Fostering Cosmopolitanisms: A Conceptual Survey and a Media Experiment in Berlin, Working Paper WPTC-2K-06, Transnational Communities Programme, Oxford University, available at: www.transcomm.ox.ac.uk/working%20papers/vertovec.pdf.

Virdi, J. (2003), *The Cinematic Imagination: Indian Popular Films as Social History*, New Brunswick, NJ: Rutgers University Press.

Waldron, J. (1999), *Law and Disagreement*, Oxford: Oxford University Press.

Weber, M. (1919/2004), *The Vocation Lectures: Science as a Vocation, Politics as a Vocation*, trans. R. Livingstone, Indianapolis, IN: Hackett Publishing.

Webster, F. (2006), *Theories of the Information Society*, London and New York: Routledge.

Werbner, P. (2002), *Imagined Diasporas among Manchester Muslims: The Public Performance of Pakistani Transnational Identity Politics*, Oxford: Currey.

White, D. M. (1950), The "Gate Keeper": A Study in the Selection of News, *Journalism Quarterly*, 27, 383–96.

Whitney, C. D., and Ettema, J. S. (2003), Media Production: Individuals, Organizations, Institutions, in A. Valdivia (ed.), *A Companion to Media Studies*, pp. 157–87, Malden, MA: Blackwell.

Wilson, B., and R. Sparks (1999), Impact of Black Athletes Media Portrayals on Canadian Youth, *Canadian Journal of Communication*, 24(4): 1–36.

Wilson, C. (2000), The Paradox of African American Journalists, in S. Cottle (ed.), *Ethnic Minorities and the Media: Changing Cultural Boundaries*, pp. 85–99, Maidenhead: Open University Press.

Younge, G. (2000), Is It Cos I Is Black?, *The Guardian*, January 11, available at: www.guardian.co.uk/world/2000/jan/12/race.

Zappalà, G., and Castles, S. (2000), Citizenship and Immigration in Australia, in T. Alexander Aleinikoff and Douglas Klusmeyer (eds.), *From Migrants to Citizens: Membership in a Changing World*, pp. 32–81, Washington, DC: Carnegie Endowment for International Peace.

Žižek, S. (1997a), Multiculturalism, or, the Cultural Logic of Multinational Capitalism, *New Left Review*, 1(225): 37–40.

Žižek, S. (1997b), Underground, or Ethnic Cleansing as a Continuation of Poetry by Other Means, *InterCommunication*, 18 (1997), available at: www.ntticc.or.jp/pub/ic_mag/ic018/intercity/zizek_E.html.

Films, Popular Books, TV Programs, and Other Cultural Works Cited

ABC (1994–5), *All America Girl*, USA.

ABC (2006–), *Ugly Betty*, USA.

Baron Cohen, S. (2006), *Borat: Cultural Learnings of America for Make Benefit Glorious Nation of Kazakhstan*, UK.

BBC (2001–6), *The Kumars at No. 42*, UK.

BBC (1998–2001), *Goodness Gracious Me*, UK.

BBC (2008), *The Poles Are Coming* (BBC White Season, 11 March).

Broomfield, N. (2007), *Battle for Haditha*, UK.

Butterworth, J. (2001), *Birthday Girl*, Australia.

CBS and Chris Rock Enterprises Ltd. (2005–9), *Everybody Hates Chris*, USA.

Channel 4 (1985–7), *Tandoori Nights*, UK.

Channel 4 and HBO (2000, 2003–4), *Da Ali G Show*, UK, USA.

Chanda, G. (1993), *Bhaji on the Beach*, UK.

Chanda, G. (2002), *Bend It Like Beckham*, UK.

Coppola, S. (2004), *Lost in Translation*, USA.

Cronenberg, D. (1993), *M. Butterfly*, USA.

Eisenstein, S. (1925), *Battleship Potemkin*, USSR.

Elliott, S. (1994), *Adventures of Priscilla, Queen of the Desert*, USA.

Ford, J. (1928), *Four Sons*, USA.

Fox (1989–), *The Simpsons*, USA.

Griffith, D. W. (1915), *Birth of a Nation*, USA.

Kapoor, K., and Kapoor, R. (1991), *Henna*, India.

Kaufman, P. (1993), *Rising Sun*, USA.

Kiarostami, A. (2002), *Ten*, Iran.

Khleifi, M., and Sivan, E. (2004), *Route 181: Fragments of a Journey in Palestine-Israel*, Israel.

Kusturica, E. (1995), *Underground*, Serbia.

Lee, S. (1988), *School Daze*, USA.

Lee, S. (1989), *Do the Right Thing*, USA.

Makhmalbaf, M. (2001), *Kandahar*, Iran.

Mason, R. (1957), *The World of Suzie Wong*, USA.

Meyers, N. (2000), *What Women Want*, Paramount, USA.

Moodysson, L. (2002), *Lilya 4-ever*, Sweden.

Nava, G. (1997), *Selena*, USA.

O'Donnell, D. (1999), *East is East*, UK.

Parks, G. (1971), *Shaft*, USA.

Riefenstahl, L. (1934), *Triumph of the Will*, Germany.

Rohmer, S. (1912), *Fu Manchu*, UK.

Schonberg, C.-M., and Boublil, A. (1989), *Miss Saigon*, UK.

Scott, R. (1989), *Black Rain*, USA.

Taymor, J. (2002), *Frida*, Miramax, USA.

Toscani, O. (1982–2000), Benetton advertising campaigns, Italy.

Trans TV (2007), *Extravaganza*, Indonesia.

Van Pebbles, M. (1971), *Sweet Sweetback's Baadaass Song*, USA.

Vardalos, N, and Zwick, J. (2002), *My Big Fat Greek Wedding*, USA.

Wang, W. (1993), *The Joy Luck Club*, Buena Vista, USA.

Welles, O. (1941), *Citizen Kane*, USA.

Index